Our Pack

Our Pack
Wolves at 150

PAUL BERRY & JOHNNY PHILLIPS

pitch

First published by Pitch Publishing, 2026
1

Pitch Publishing
9 Donnington Park, 85 Birdham Road
Chichester, West Sussex, PO20 7AJ
www.pitchpublishing.co.uk
info@pitchpublishing.co.uk

Set in Adobe Caslon 11.8/16pt

Typeset by Pitch Publishing

Cover design by Olner Design

Printed and bound in Great Britain by TJ Books, Padstow

The authorised representative in the EEA is
Easy Access System Europe OÜ, Mustamäe tee 50, 10621 Tallinn, Estonia gpsr.requests@easproject.com

A CIP catalogue record for this book is available from the British Library

ISBN 978-1-83680-522-9

Papers used by Pitch Publishing are from well-managed forests and other responsible sources

MIX
Paper | Supporting responsible forestry
FSC® C013056

Contents

Introduction

WOLVERHAMPTON WANDERERS, a club marking its 150th anniversary, and a club steeped in so much history.

From starting out in 1877, becoming one of the Football League's founder members in 1888, to winning three league titles and pioneering European football with the floodlit friendlies of the fifties.

Producing some of the game's greatest players and managers from Stan Cullis to Billy Wright, Ron Flowers to Peter Broadbent, and Bill Slater, the last amateur to play in an FA Cup Final, lifting the fourth and most recent of Wolves' cup wins in 1960.

The sensational stars of the seventies, Kenny Hibbitt, John Richards and company, bringing two League Cups masterminded by Bill McGarry and John Barnwell, Wolves' most recent major honours. Followed so quickly by a dramatic fall from grace. Yet even in those darkest hours a new hero emerged. Ooh Bully Bully.

Promotions to the Premier League under Messrs Jones and McCarthy, followed by a double dip and revival under Kenny Jackett.

And then a truly magical spell under Nuno Espirito Santo, the Revolution of Wolves, which took the club back into the top division, two seventh-placed finishes, an FA Cup semi-final and Europa League quarter-final.

All of this littered with so many magical moments at Molineux, or Molineux Grounds as it was originally known, the club's historic and wonderful home for 138 of their 150 years.

This book, however, isn't a chronological journey through that unique and dramatic history. Following a football club is about so much more than facts and figures.

Our Pack – Wolves at 150 is more of a focus on what it is that makes Wolves tick, how it plays its pivotal role in terms of the city and community. As a one-club city, how deeply and emotionally the club is embedded when it comes to the people, the culture, the fans.

Because, as the great Sir Bobby Robson once said: 'What is a club in any case? Not the buildings or the directors or the people who are paid to represent it. It's not the television contracts, get-out clauses, marketing departments or executive boxes. It's the noise, the passion, the feeling of belonging, the pride in your city. It's a young child clambering up stadium steps for the very first time, gripping his/her father's hand, gawping at that hallowed stretch of turf beneath them and, without being able to do a thing about it, falling in love.'

And so, this is a history based more on the memories and the feelings. Not necessarily the stats on the honours boards, although of course, they do get a mention. We've had our moments, after all.

It is a history which not only involves a journey through some of the great and the good from the early years to the present day, but also through the experiences of the co-authors, both lifelong Wolves fans, whose recollections cover almost a third of the club's 150-year existence.

Each and every chapter tells its own standalone story connected with the club's history. And each includes a specific location, either connected to the subject, the place where an interview took place, or a particular event. A rich tapestry from local landmarks to international footballing hotbeds which have played a part in Wolves' illustrious lifespan.

But put all those chapters together, and they are all connected. Connected by what it means to either play for, work at, or support Wolves. What it is actually like to be a club legend. Or the relative of a club legend. Why on earth a fan would be willing to be strapped to the luggage compartment of a plane to avoid missing out on a precious fixture. Why others found a somewhat different release from attending games during the trials and tribulations of the 1980s. And also an assessment of more recent times, and where the club is now, moving into the next phase of its history.

Welcome to *Our Pack – Wolves at 150*. We hope it brings out the pride and the passion of supporting this great club through all the magnificent ups and the disastrous downs.

Unparalleled. Unique. And unstoppable when it comes to the loyalty and devotion of the fanbase.

We are Wolves.

Chapter 1

St Luke's FC – Birth of a Giant

HEAD UP the ramp situated to the right of main reception at Molineux, or up Whitmore Hill if in a vehicle, and you eventually come to the large brick-built Georgian property which houses the City of Wolverhampton Archives.

An absolute gold mine for anyone with an interest in history and nostalgia relating to the city, once a town of course, of Wolverhampton.

The City Archives exist to collect, preserve and make accessible historical records, and to secure significant modern records to be available for future generations.

Documents available include books, maps, plans, over 30,000 photographs, records of institutions such as the city council, churches, schools and many others.

Also available is an extensive array of microfiche containing back copies of the *Express & Star* and *Wolverhampton Chronicle*, all the way back to the late 1800s.

And that, particularly when it comes to researching Wolves, via the newspapers' coverage across the last 150 years, is a hugely valuable resource. Which is also perhaps fitting, as the building itself used to have close links to the club, from its origins of being owned by the Molineux family.

Benjamin Molineux, a wealthy banker and iron founder, built the mansion in the early to mid-1700s. It remained within the Molineux family until 1860 before the whole estate was purchased by O.E. McGregor, who converted the land into a pleasure park open to the public. Converted to become Molineux Hotel, it became the centrepiece to Molineux Grounds, a wide range of facilities including an ice rink, a cycling track, a boating lake, and, most crucially, an area for football.

It was in 1889 that the grounds were sold to Northampton Brewery, who then rented them to Wolves, becoming the launch of Molineux Stadium as we know it, the first game taking place in front of 4,000 spectators on 7 September, a 2-0 win against Notts County.

Wolves purchased the freehold in 1923 which then prompted renewed motivation to improve the facilities, and of course, later become one of the first clubs in Britain to install floodlights.

Through all this, Molineux Hotel remained, until its closure in 1979, after which, left in a state of disrepair, a catastrophic fire in 2003 almost destroyed the building completely.

That led to the City of Wolverhampton Council launching an extensive restoration project, with funds from English Heritage, the Heritage Lottery Fund, Advantage West Midlands and others, leading to the re-opening of the building as the home of Wolverhampton City Archives in 2009.

It's an open and welcoming environment, the silence of people researching, working, broken only by the odd murmur or rewinding or fast-forwarding of the microfiche.

There is a strapline associated with the Archives which reads: 'Explore the rich culture of Wolverhampton and its people.'

In essence, when it comes to the history of Wolves, it is of course the people that define it.

The stadium is part of the history, the club's facilities and infrastructure; nowadays there are plush training grounds, extensive commercial and marketing strategies. But ultimately, as with anything in life, it is the people who create the history. And Wolves, even from its early days, long before the likes of Cullis, Wright, Flowers and co, is no exception.

The stories exist within those people who first launched Wolves as a football club, who took it through its early years, who not only laid the foundations for the incredible successes which followed, but also tasted some success of their own.

Any history has to start from the beginning, so how was it that Wolves, the football club, was born?

Again, it is about the people, those who helped found the club and then those who carried the torch to shape its early history.

Initially, that was all down to Jack Brodie, real name John, and John Baynton. JB at the double.

Both teenagers, and pupils at St Luke's Church School in Blakenhall, they had been given a football by headteacher Harry Barcroft and soon set about forming a new football team.

A poster which was displayed inviting people to the first general meeting of the team, on 10 November 1876, remains proudly on display in Wolves' Museum.

Rather than calling the team Goldthorn FC, the name of a previous club, they went for St Luke's FC, as so many of the players were members both of the school and church choir. Two years later, St Luke's FC became Wolverhampton Wanderers.

Former Wolves club historian Pat Quirke outlined how Wolves was founded when Brodie was inducted into the club's Hall of Fame in 2017.

'Football was evolving at the time into the new team sport in the country but there weren't many teams about, and Jack tried to join a railway workers' team,' said Quirke.

'They were at West Park, and he went down for a trial but he didn't get in. They thought he was just a boy and they were men, and he was only 14.

'He went back up to Goldthorn Hill where he lived, with his friend James Hill, and they were moaning that they couldn't get into this team.

'James' father, an Irishman called Fergal, was listening to this conversation, and said why didn't they start their own team?

'They put that notice on the church door at St Luke's, inviting young gentlemen interested in the game to come to a meeting, and that was the start of the St Luke's team, which evolved into Wolves a few years later.'

Each player paid a shilling to join the club and Jack got permission from his mother to use her land at Lodge Farm, by Goldthorn Hill, for a pitch.

On a bumpy field, with barely a spectator in attendance, and Wolves apparently wearing blue and white stripes – heaven forbid – having got changed in the bushes nearby, they were beaten 8-0 by the well-established Stafford Road reserves.

But they were off and running. On 13 January 1877. Who could ever have known the joy – and pain – that would follow in the century and a half which has followed?

The club's first league fixture, played at Dudley Road in front of 3,000 spectators on 8 September 1888, came against fellow Football League founders and Midlands rivals Aston Villa, and finished in a 1-1 draw.

Gerson Cox was the name of the first goalscorer in Wolves' history, albeit he never ever played for the club. It was an own goal which broke the deadlock before Villa hit back to draw 1-1.

Across the first six decades or so of the club's existence, they didn't win the top-flight title, although they went mighty close with runners-up finishes in the two years before the First World War.

They also went up and down the divisions on several occasions, actually dropping from First Division to Third Division North before winning their first league titles, Division Three North in 1923/24 and Division Two in 1931/32.

They enjoyed a fair few FA Cup runs, winning the trophy in 1893 and 1908 prior to the World Wars, following up again at Wembley in 1949 and 1960 before the double League Cup success not so long after.

As well as finishing as FA Cup runners-up on no fewer than four occasions prior to the Second World War.

Harry Allen's goal secured the first FA Cup success against Everton in 1893; 15 years later it was a huge shock at Crystal Palace as second-tier Wolves overcame top-flight Newcastle United, who had actually won the league the previous season.

An estimated 20,000 Wolves fans were amongst the 75,000 crowd as a match played in driving rain ended in a 3-1 success for Wolves.

The full-back for Wolves that afternoon, Jackery Jones, was a no-nonsense defender who would be among the first batch of inductees into the club's Hall of Fame just over a century later.

Jones, born in the same year in which Wolves were founded, spent over a decade with the club as a player, and was the first to chalk up 300 league appearances.

He would later wear his cup-winners' medal with pride, on his watch chain, when assistant manager at Molineux.

Another whose legacy has endured from that time, perhaps for his off-field story as much as his talent on it, was the Reverend Kenneth Hunt, who scored one of the goals in that 1908 FA Cup Final.

Hunt, who would become known as 'Wolves' Footballing Parson', was born in Oxford before his family moved to Wolverhampton, where his father Robert was vicar of St Mark's in Chapel Ash, when he was still very young.

Kenneth would be educated at Wolverhampton Grammar School, captaining the school football team where he was described as 'a very promising half, playing with more head than some of his seniors. Kicks and tackles well, and sticks to his man.'

His studies suffered from his abilities and motivation to get involved in many different sports, but he would later still progress to study at Queen's College at Oxford University.

Aiming to follow his father into the Anglican ministry, his studies once again suffered as this period between 1904 and 1908 was when he established himself as an outstanding university, club and international footballer.

Having turned out for the Corinthians side made up of undergraduates from Oxford and Cambridge Universities, and Oxford City reserves, Hunt started playing for Wolves on a part-time basis at the start of the 1907/08 season.

Wolves were in the middle of a financial crisis at the time, and were therefore well suited to utilising the services of this fit and motivated undergraduate, who was keen to hang on to his amateur status and therefore only accepted travelling expenses as payment.

Hunt would finish his studies at Oxford on a Friday afternoon, travel by train to Wolverhampton to spend the night at his parents' home in Chapel Ash, before being available for selection for Wolves on the Saturday. Imagine that scenario today!

Against all odds, Wolves reached that 1908 FA Cup Final, including a third round win against Swindon during which Hunt was twice knocked unconscious, but still finished the game.

It was on 40 minutes that Hunt wrote his name into club folklore. Not known as a regular goalscorer, he tried his luck with a shot from distance, which the Newcastle goalkeeper could only palm into his own net.

The giant-killing was very much a team effort, but Hunt drew plenty of praise, with the *Daily Mail* describing his performance as 'classy' and 'stoic', the man himself underplaying his role by simply remarking that, 'We hustled, we only ever intended to hustle.'

Barely six months after this famous win, Hunt had been selected to play for the Great Britain side which won the football competition at the London Olympic Games. In the space of a year, he had become an Oxford blue, scored in a winning FA Cup Final, and won an Olympic gold. Some going.

He later won a couple of England caps, but his legacy and story were perhaps equally cemented by the fact he was ordained as an Anglican priest the week before Christmas of 1909.

'Wolves' Footballing Parson', combining his football and his faith in delivering a unique story which has passed through the generations and remains an integral part of the club's history.

Even if these days are now so long ago that they are consigned more to the history books rather than via supporters who witnessed them, a string of Wolves' club historians have, over the years, endeavoured to keep the stories alive.

John 'Foz' Hendley was one of those, harbouring an encyclopaedic knowledge of the club's history along with a seemingly insatiable appetite to enjoy the present, attending as many first team, reserve and academy games as was humanly possible!

The club historian role now sits in the very capable hands of Peter Crump, another long-term Molineux devotee, who combines his love of all things Wolves past with a rich enjoyment of Wolves in the present.

Crump's love of Wolves, in time-honoured tradition, came from his family, chiefly his dad and his older brother Mike.

It's a love which was launched and nurtured in the 1990s, a decade which featured no change in divisional status, but plenty in terms of stadium redevelopment, play-off pain, and the odd decent cup run.

'It is only my opinion but for me, your football club chooses you,' he says. 'My dad, his dad and his dad supported Wolves. My two older brothers are Wolves supporters.

'My uncle Peter (Redfern) worked here from 1972 to 1985 and served as the secretary. So, Wolves were a huge part of my family before I even came along – it's in my DNA and was the only club I could support.

'For me, supporting Wolves is also about being a proud Wulfrunian. As it was ingrained in me from my family, Wolves are the only club for me. They are the club that represent where I am from.'

Crump had long travelled home and away before starting to volunteer at Wolves in 2012, initially as part of the flag-wavers building the atmosphere pre-match, and then later as a tour guide at Molineux.

This was to support then club historian Quirke, a great friend and mentor to Crump, alongside other Museum aficionados Neil Pennington and Dave Jones.

Quirke sadly passed away at the age of 72 in 2022, and, when the club decided, a year later, to make the club historian role permanent, Crump was both touched and honoured to successfully land the role.

'Pat is my all-time Wolves hero who it was an honour to know,' he says.

And in returning to the history, one of Quirke's two successful Wolves books was about Major Frank Buckley, manager of the club from 1927 to 1944.

Part of the Manchester Regiment, the Major signed up for a 12-year enlistment in the King's Regiment in Liverpool, and was expecting to serve in the Boer War, but instead was sent to Ireland.

He bought himself out of the army in 1902 to become a professional footballer, which included a small number of appearances for both Manchester clubs before more regular action with Birmingham and Derby.

His career was shortened by the arrival of the First World War, during which he commanded the Football Battalion in the 17th Middlesex Regiment, fighting in the Battle of the Somme where he received wounds to his lung and shoulder.

After the hostilities came his move into management, then featuring 17 years at Wolves, which included making Stan Cullis

– the soon to become the club's most successful manager ever – his captain.

'I soon realised that Major Buckley was one out of the top drawer,' said Cullis. 'He did not suffer fools gladly, and his style of management in football was very similar to his attitude in the army.'

On the pitch, he took Wolves close to that elusive top-flight title with successive runners-up finishes just before the Second World War, as well as being beaten FA Cup finalists in 1939.

One story which burst to prominence during his tenure, and has pretty much lingered ever since, was his decision to offer injections to his players of a form of monkey gland treatment to try and improve physical performance.

It was an approach which had been popularised in the 1920s by Serge Voronoff, a French surgeon of Russian origin, who claimed that the injection of testicular implants would rejuvenate a patient.

It was essentially an example of alternative medicine, and players were given a course of treatment over a six-week period.

Whether it worked, whether it was coincidence, or more likely a placebo, it seemed to improve Wolves' performance to the extent that other clubs also tried the treatment, and the 1939 FA Cup Final won by Portsmouth has since been dubbed 'The Monkey Gland Final'.

It certainly caused a major stir in the football world at the time, with some claiming it was immoral and a form of doping, and the media queueing up to – excuse the phrase – have their pound of flesh.

'Instead of their next dose of monkey gland treatment, I suggest that Major Frank Buckley gives Wolves a severe lecture,' was the cutting opening to a match report from Brian Stuart in *Reynolds News* after a 4-1 defeat at Charlton.

'Gland treatment may be okay, but we want no monkey business,' he wrote later.

Irrespective of the merits or otherwise of the treatment, and the Major certainly had an obsession with peak physical fitness, his legacy was about far more than a controversial approach to the squad's refuelling habits. The work he had done on the youth programme at Wolves did so much to shape the all-conquering years of the 1950s, and his work across almost two decades certainly whetted the appetite for fans who would go on to savour the very best of times after the Second World War.

Incredibly, his near-17-year tenure in the Molineux hotseat – including six during those hostilities – a few months longer than Cullis would be in situ as one of his successors, is not, however, the longest in the club's history.

That honour falls to Jack Addenbrooke, who presided over a staggering 859 Wolves games after being appointed as the club's first secretary/manager in 1885. Some 37 years later, in 1922, he only stood down through illness when he was granted six months' leave, only to sadly pass away in his sleep halfway through that spell, at the age of 57.

It's a managerial reign that will surely never be surpassed in length whether at Wolves or anywhere else. It's a reign which sometimes, according to the *Sports Argus*, included delivering his duties from his beautifully presented tobacconist shop on Dudley Street, which is now a Costa Coffee shop. It's a reign which also included leading the club to their first two major trophies, those FA Cups of 1893 and 1908.

And when it comes to the achievements, but also the people behind them, then whilst the Archives can document their existence, Wolves Museum can bring them to life.

The club's impressive Museum, originally set up thanks to the motivation of chairman Steve Morgan to give a greater spotlight to the club's illustrious history, has been improved in recent years under the guidance of another lifelong Wolves fan.

Sam Warrington is Wolves' museum, tours and heritage manager. As with Crump, it's a labour of love, even if sometimes it is also very hard graft.

'Growing up in Shropshire, there were a lot of Manchester United and Liverpool fans, but my dad is a Wolves fan, and so they became my team.

'I have also always had a big connection to Wolverhampton as well, and spent a lot of time here, and started coming to games as soon as my dad would take me.

'I remember my first match, a 2-2 draw with Gillingham when Leon Clarke scored a late equaliser, and the noise was incredible, and I was like, "Is it always like this?"

'I carried on going to games when I could, and it has always been something really important to bond with my dad over, but did I ever think I would be working here? Absolutely not.

'I was working in theatre before coming here, but had reached a point where I wanted to switch things up, and saw the role advertised on the Wolves website.

'I took a punt, and here I am, which still feels pretty surreal! And what a job it is.

'Obviously football has a lot of ups and downs, which is something that can be difficult to tackle, but being able to work at the club I love and get to speak to the players involved in the history – there is always that joy behind everything that I do.

'For me, I want to be the best advocate for the club. I always want to present the Museum in the best way that we can for the club. And I'm a big collector as well, so I'm very particular!

'When I worked in theatre design, it had to be dynamic, and it had to be engaging, and that's the approach I have taken into the Museum, especially in trying to keep it moving forward over the four years I have been here.

'During my first week I went around it all and then sat down and drew an entire groundplan and a route of how I wanted it to work for visitors. And what I also think is important is that it's not just about the highs. You have to document the lows as well.

'We can't just hide under the sofa and pretend certain things didn't happen. All the events and moments are what has made Wolves what it is today.

'It is about giving people that experience of the history of the club and that includes the tough times as well as the great ones.'

'Wolves isn't just about what happens today, it's built on our legacy,' adds Crump.

'We are a humble school team from Blakenhall, one of the oldest clubs in the country and one of the most traditional.

'And we would not be where we are today without our history. That history isn't just important, it's vital to our story and really makes us who we are today.

'It's not just about trophies, it is also about resilience, because Wolves have been up and down throughout our history.'

Indeed so.

From Brodie and Baynton to Addenbrooke and Akinbiyi. Rev. Kenneth Hunt to Stephen Hunt. Major Frank to Big Frank Munro.

So many players and managers have graced this footballing institution, and from the early Wolves days covered in these pages, to the rest of the history in the chapters to follow, the feelings generated among fans running the whole gamut of emotions, will never ever change.

'Even though I'm older and bearded now, I'm still like a big kid when it comes to Wolves,' Warrington concludes.

'I still get the new kit on the day it's released, I still enjoy meeting the players, and the kid inside will always come out.

'Seeing the joy that the Museum can bring to people, when they look back and remember their time supporting Wolves, is something that is very special.

'I remember we were given Jorgen Strand Larsen's shirt from one of the games and as soon as it was donated, I said we had to put it on display immediately because it was so relevant and something that would grab attention.

'I took out the shirt that was there, replaced it with Strand Larsen's, and at that very moment a kid walked through into the Museum with his mum and said, "Look! Look! It's Strand Larsen's shirt!"

'It was the best thing that could have happened in that particular moment, and he was absolutely buzzing so we had a chat and we got him Rui Patricio's boots to have a look at and hold as well.

'It was just one of those moments that makes everything special and reminds us all why Wolves is so special.

'Because it wasn't just that young kid getting such a great surprise walking in at that moment after that shirt had just gone up.

'That kid was me, or any other Wolves fan who has followed the club. Bringing out the inner child and people reliving their memories of years gone by, with that extra spark that it's about Wolves, is a moment that will never grow old.'

Chapter 2

It's in the Blood

A PRE-MATCH pint in the pub has always been a staple part of British footballing culture. Perhaps accompanied by a crusty cheese and onion cob. Or a packet of crisps or scratchings. Followed, a few hours later, by a post-match drink and debrief after the game.

For many years, the only way for fans to vent and share opinions was via a phone-in on local radio or the letters page of the local newspaper.

Nowadays of course, the existence of internet message boards and numerous social media platforms offers a multitude of additional options for those wishing to put their points across, debate or, as is often the case, vehemently argue.

But the pub on a matchday, that social aspect along with the traditional comfort of a beer or two, has never lost its rightful place in footballing culture. Nor indeed its magic.

It is late on a Sunday morning. Yes, another development across the last generation is the changed kick-off times which have destroyed the traditions of 3pm on a Saturday, and Wolves are about to play their final home game of a disappointing 2025/26 season against Fulham.

At the Great Western in Sun Street, a stone's throw from the old lower-level station which stopped welcoming passengers back in 1972, the fairly warm weather for this mid-May morning sees many fans arriving clad in golden Wolves shirts, albeit an unexpected and heavy downpour then sees them scampering swiftly for the entrance with the pace of an Adama Traore or Tony Towner.

The Great Western is one of many similar hostelries across the city and its fringes which have become part of supporters' matchday routines prior to heading to the stadium.

Men, women, families – all have their own favoured pubs or indeed schedules involving different pubs which either precede – or indeed sandwich – the 90 minutes or more of football at Molineux.

For some fans, this has been a trusted and inescapable routine, barely missing a match, for many decades.

And there are so many who boast fairly incredible records of missing very few games over such a long period of time. Four of them are gathered in the Great Western, ready to bring the curtain down on the Molineux season ahead of the trip to Burnley which will bring a low-key but unwelcome end to eight successive years for Wolves in the Premier League.

Steve Bishop, from Cannock, has only missed one Wolves game in half a decade. He loved going to matches so much in his formative years that he launched Cannock Wolves Supporters Club at the age of 18, which is still going strong. Tyrone Newland, originally from Smethwick but now living in Kingswinford, hasn't missed a game since February 1990. His first match was as an 11-year-old during the 1973/74 season and, with his dad working on a Saturday, his uncle – a West Bromwich Albion fan – would take him to home Wolves games.

And while the loyalty and dedication of both of those devoted fans is pretty incredible, even they doff their hats to our other two guests for a pre-match pint in a snug corner of the pub.

Peter Abbott, committee member of the London Wolves Supporters Club, and a member of the equally legendary Daventry Wolves, has missed just two out of the last 2,477 Wolves fixtures – excluding Covid. A run which stretches back to the 1975/76 season, the only games missed being when his train to Blackburn broke down in 1985, and for his stepdaughter's wedding in 2013. All this having been born in Stratford in east London and first going to away games in the capital as his love of the club developed. He now lives in Ipswich, making even a Wolves home game more than a 300-mile round trip.

And then there's Tony Cowley, who lives on the Isle of Man. Actually, across some water. His Wolves-supporting history is a real-life tale of planes, trains and automobiles, and the rest. And delivers a regular logistical conundrum. Even he has barely missed a game in decades, and usually through no fault of his own. Namely the cancellation or delay of one of the aforementioned modes of transport, or indeed when being knocked down by a car whilst en route to a game against Bristol City a decade ago.

Four very different, but equally incredible stories. Four of many Wolves fans – and indeed football fans in general – who defy all thoughts of sense and logic in terms of the loyalty, expense and hour upon hour which they devote to their team. Yet, to a man, they all play this extraordinary level of devotion down.

An opening gambit of, 'Why do you do it?' is met by a look of almost stunned silence. Even bemusement. As in, 'What sort of a stupid question is that?' Following Wolves has inextricably become a part of life. It's normality.

'I would say there are hundreds and hundreds of Wolves fans who go to a lot of games, and probably want to go to them all, but for different reasons they miss some or just can't do it,' replies Abbott. 'That may be due to family, kids, weddings, work, health, all sorts of reasons.

'Maybe we are the fortunate ones who are able to do it, and in the years since I retired, even with all the travelling, it has got a lot easier.

'And people like us, well, we probably don't think about it too much really. Even though I've never lived nearer to Molineux than a 300-mile round trip.

'Sitting here today, another season is about to end, another one completed, and that's it, simple as that.'

'It's got to speak to your psychology a bit, hasn't it?' adds Bishop. 'It's something you do as a kid, then become addicted to it – it becomes part of your personality.'

'It's like the people who collect things, whatever that might be,' Abbott replies. 'Well, whether it's at the games or having a drink like we are now, or the people we meet on a matchday, we're all collecting memories, aren't we?

'Collecting matches and collecting memories – it's just that we can't swap them!'

Addiction is a very good analogy. And there are undoubtedly far worse things to become addicted to. And a love of Wolves, shared with tens of thousands of others who follow the gold and black, is enough to keep all those intrepid fans coming back for more – win, lose or draw, wind, rain or shine.

For Cowley in particular, given the lengths he has to go to make any game from the Isle of Man, that is certainly true.

'I'd never ever been to Wolverhampton, but in the late fifties, my mum used to take me and my brother on family holidays, and we would stay in Blackpool,' he explains. 'From there, I was taken to away games against Blackpool, Preston and Blackburn, and straightaway I had this thing about Wolves, mainly due to the colours.

'By the mid-sixties, I was getting down to Wolverhampton – I remember a 5-0 win against Altrincham in the FA Cup – but it was only from 1974 when I managed to change my work circumstances that I could start to go every week, home and away.

'And the travel has actually got worse over the last few years. In the early days, the boat was always reliable, but as they have turned into more fancy boats, they get cancelled when there's a bit of wind.

'When I needed the plane, I relied on Flybe and, for a 3pm Saturday kick-off, I could get a flight over at 7am and then one back at 8pm so I could do it all in a day.

'Since Flybe went bust, I can't really do it in a day and have missed a few more games as a result.

'Even the recent home one against Sunderland, a flight got cancelled and I got offered a replacement at 5.20pm, when our game was kicking off at 3pm!

'I'll give you another example from this season, West Ham away, on a Friday night. I got up at 5am in the Isle of Man and drove to the sea terminal at Douglas to get the 7.15am boat to Liverpool.

'From there I got a bus to Lime Street station and the train to Wolverhampton to jump on a 3pm coach to get to West Ham.

'I then got back at 2.30am and fortunately there was another fan driving to Telford who dropped me back at my son's in Bridgnorth.

'The next day I then got a train back to Liverpool where I could get a flight back home. So, I'd done plane, train, automobile, boat, coach and taxi for that one!'

It's incredible dedication. But that's what football generates. And once their heart is set on getting to games, and the routine is set, it takes a lot to get in the way.

For Cowley, he was only able to start regularly attending games from '74 because he went freelance in his job with a brewery in the Isle of Man and was able to hand-pick his hours.

Abbott, when head-hunted for a position during his career as an accountant and auditor, had it written into his contract that he could have time off when needed to attend Wolves fixtures. Jorge Mendes would be proud of that level of negotiation.

Whilst Newland was once faced with the ultimatum that, having already been to many midweek matches during the hectic 1987/88 season, attending one in the Sherpa Van Trophy at Swansea would lead to him losing his job. On that occasion, he had to relent.

Health issues have also, understandably, tried to intervene at times. When unfortunately having that argument with a car whilst crossing the road near Molineux, Cowley suffered a broken fibula and tibia that led to an understandable spell on the sidelines.

Abbott once twice rearranged an eye operation to avoid clashing with Wolves fixtures which had been moved for television coverage and was then warned it was his last chance to avoid a cancellation. Effectively three strikes and you're out.

The operation was then scheduled for eight o'clock on a Wednesday morning. Fortunately, Wolves' midweek fixture against Crystal Palace was the night before, so it worked perfectly.

Both Newland and Bishop also have their own medical tales.

'There was a time during the nineties, when I had this stomach complaint all of a sudden, and needed an ambulance to take me to hospital,' Newland recalls. 'This was on the Thursday, and we were playing Blues on the Saturday.

'I was in Sandwell General, and they did some tests but I was okay and was keen to get home on the Friday night.

'But Saturday morning came around, and I was still there, and I had to ask if I could be let out!

'I got the missus to come and pick me up and then drop me off at Garrison Lane by St Andrew's. So that was a close one!'

Bishop interjects. 'The same thing happened to me when I had a bad stomach problem and ended up in hospital for three days.

'I told a doctor I needed to get out because I had some personal things to attend to, and he let me go, provided I signed a form to say it was at my own risk.

'So, then I went off to see us play Stoke in the FA Cup, before going back to hospital afterwards.

'Then there was my vasectomy. I booked it in for 11am ahead of a 3pm kick-off against Birmingham, but then the game got brought forward, I think to 1pm.

'I still went ahead with the vasectomy and then headed off to the match, pretty much fresh off the table!'

A few eyes were watering at nearby tables in the pub on eavesdropping that particular tale.

And then there are the other obstacles and hurdles to overcome, all often completely out of supporters' control.

There is nothing fans could do about the behind-closed-doors games played during the pandemic during the 2019/20 and 2020/21 seasons.

But when Wolves fans were banned following the crowd trouble at Scarborough on the opening day of the 1987/88 campaign, for six games by the Football League and an additional two by the club itself, well, that wasn't so much an instruction, but more of a challenge.

Remember the terrace ditty? 'Away, away, away, away, you'll never ban a Wanderers fan.'

'Oh yes, we managed to get to all of those games,' is the almost synchronised response from all four fans when asked how they responded to the development.

Even if it took a fair amount of ingenuity.

The club took a proactive decision to ban fans from going to Notts County and Hereford. And the external sanction then took in trips to Cardiff, Peterborough, Stockport, Manchester City, Bolton and Carlisle.

With Notts County, Abbott sprang quickly into action and, courtesy of his *Rothman's Yearbook*, called the club and ended up speaking to the second director on the list who agreed to sell ten tickets to London Wolves provided they picked them up by midday on the day of the game.

Being a part of London Wolves, with a London address and not a WV postcode in sight, certainly played its part in garnering tickets for that and other 'banned' fixtures.

Meanwhile at Hereford, 100 or so Wolves fans turned up at the ground, and then club chairman Jack Harris agreed with the hosts that they could be granted admittance.

Newland sent a blank cheque to both Stockport and Carlisle asking them to fill in the figure required in return for a pair of tickets for each. And they duly obliged, thankfully for him, at the normal price.

He also travelled up to Bolton in a van with four fellow fans from Tamworth, and was the only one to eventually gain admittance to the stadium.

'There were loads of Wolves fans being sent away, but I managed to get in,' he says.

'But when I came out, the van was nowhere to be seen, and I couldn't find anyone else, and there were no mobile phones back then to track people down!

'I milled around for an hour or so, and was wondering what to do when I walked back to the ground and the team coach was still there.

'Being a cheeky bugger, I knocked the window and asked Graham Turner if they would let me on, but they couldn't do it.

'So, I ended up heading to Bolton station and getting a train to Manchester and then another one home.

'It turned out the other lads had been discovered by the police, escorted back to the motorway and told to head down the M6 and that if they tried to come back, they would be nicked!'

Bishop was also part of a carload which headed to Bolton, and mistakenly tried to park where the away coaches used to arrive. Not the greatest idea of their Wolves-supporting existence. Rumbled by the police, they, too, were instructed to return back south.

'But we just went down a junction, turned around, and parked in a side street away from the ground,' Bishop adds. 'This time we managed to get in.

'We'd rehearsed our lines for where we lived and came from, and I decided on a place called Whalley, although it turns out I didn't pronounce it properly!

'But the copper must not have known how to say it either, as he just let me through!'

Being able to acquire tickets amid the most challenging circumstances is a prerequisite and basic task for any football supporter with as strong an attendance record as this particular quartet.

Abbott, when working in Chelmsford, also remembers travelling to Colchester's Layer Road ground on a daily basis at a time when they had banned all away fans, buying four tickets at a time for Wolves pals to use. Bishop once missed the deadline for a trip to Oldham to purchase a load of tickets for people who had booked coach travel. He and a pal travelled up and then basically, in rotation, kept going into the ticket office and buying two or three at a time until eventually they were rumbled.

And then, what about the postponements? It feels tough enough if a home game is postponed without much of a journey involved. But for some of these guys, when so many arrangements have been ploughed into sorting travel and logistics, it's clearly much, much worse.

'I remember when all of us with London Wolves had travelled to Newport for a Friday night game which was then called off,' says Abbott. 'We stayed around and Jack Harris invited us for a chat and a drink before we had to trudge all the way back.'

'Luton,' snaps Cowley, quick as a flash. 'Twice that got called off late, in successive seasons.

'The one time was a sunny day so I've no idea why that was postponed.

'Then there was Torquay in the first leg of the Sherpa Van Trophy semi-final which got delayed for 24 hours because of the weather.

'We got as far as Weston-super-Mare and ended up staying the night in Paignton before watching Wolves train on the beach the following morning.

'And there was another one over Christmas when I'd booked to stay over and a game against Blackpool was called off.'

If it's tough enough for those involved to travel up and down the country every few days, scrambling for tickets, praying for no postponements, living every result, what about their nearest and dearest?

Those family members who perhaps don't share that same love of football and of Wolves, but who are well aware, that for nine months of the year, life's routines are very much shaped by the release of that June fixture list, and all the alterations which follow.

'My wife has always been okay with it, apart from when she was worried about me doing the pre-season tour to America when I was nearly 80,' Cowley reveals with a chuckle.

'I often find it's her friends who get on to her because they can't understand why I do it!'

'Remember Bolton in the play-offs in the mid-nineties?' adds Newland. 'Myself and the missus and our two small kids travelled down to Exmouth in Devon for a holiday on the Saturday morning.

'I settled the family into the caravan, had a night on the site, and then left on the Sunday to come and watch the first leg at Molineux.

'I stayed at home on the Sunday night before travelling back to Exmouth on the Monday and having a couple more days with the family.

'Then on the Wednesday morning, I drove all the way from Exmouth to Bolton for the second leg, watched that awful result, and drove straight back to Exmouth, getting back to the site at 4am, absolutely shattered.

'My missus was chuffed that week as you can imagine!'

Talking of family, it was that which meant Abbott missed his only home game of the last 50 years, for his stepdaughter Sarah's wedding.

Wolves were playing Coventry at Molineux, and Sarah was marrying Jonno in Haughley near Stowmarket, and so it was that he put family first, although a part of the Wolves family did ultimately play its part.

Unbeknown to Abbott, it had been arranged for Steve Bull – with consent from the happy couple – to pop along and surprise him, and soften the blow of being so far away from his beloved Molineux on a matchday.

'My family have always known how important Wolves is, and I had asked them to try and avoid a Saturday for the wedding,' he explains.

'They thought they had managed to set the date during an international break, but it was a week out!

'I was waiting and hoping that the game would get moved for television, but it never did.

'I did sit down with them and, trying not to be rude, said that I personally knew two couples who had split within six months so were they absolutely serious about the day, and each other?!

'I am delighted to say they were, it was a great day, and the good news is that they are still together with twin girls now as well!'

Wolves drew 1-1 with Coventry that day. On the following Tuesday night, Abbott was back at Molineux for a 2-0 win against Oldham, during which he was welcomed on to the pitch to the *Superman* theme to receive a special presentation from Bull and Andy Thompson.

Newland's last home game missed was also due to a wedding, that of his cousin, back in February 1990. Although sadly, that particular couple split up some 16 years later.

A relationship with Wolves, however complex and complicated, is one from which few loyal fans become separated. And which, in many cases, they would always fight to save.

Back in 1982, when the club was in danger of going out of business, and the modern day methods of communications were not even a pipe dream, Abbott recalls 'not doing much work' in the build-up to the 5pm deadline when news finally emerged that Wolves had been saved from liquidation.

Newland was abroad, on his first lads' holiday at the time, and didn't even find out until the day after, that he had a club to return to over the following season.

'I remember going around to all the pubs in Cannock with "Save the Wolves" collection boxes to try and raise a few quid,' adds Bishop.

'There was also a charity match at Hednesford featuring some ex-players which raised the princely sum of £360!'

And yet, for all the many highlights, the cup finals, the play-off final, the promotions, the European runs, it is during those darker and tougher moments, the devastating defeats, relegations, the financial issues, that cement that bond between supporter and club.

When reality bites, when things aren't going well, that is when the siege mentality takes hold, and, almost in contrast to what you might expect, an already fierce sense of pride and togetherness becomes even stronger.

'When we went down from the first to the fourth division, and every week we were losing, you would leave a game and think, "Why am I doing this?"' says Abbott.

'But in a few minutes, I would start to be looking ahead and thinking, "Who are we playing next?" 'I often say this with my journey that because I am jumping in a car, for three hours or so, by the time I get home I am no longer thinking anything bad about the game because I have gone on to other things – life moves on very quickly and you are planning for the next one.

'During that drop to the Fourth Division it almost cemented it all for me because it became more close-knit.

'You would get to know people – in fact you probably knew everyone – and Jack Harris and Dick Homden would always come over to us and say hello.'

'I can still pick out certain games, like Exeter away in the Sherpa Van, when there were only about 1,200 there in total – so I don't know how many we took,' adds Newland.

'There was another Sherpa Van one away at Cardiff when I went to the seats and could actually count how many Wolves fans were there,' Bishop recalls.

'I can't quite remember how many it was, less than 100 for sure, and that was actually the game where Bully scored his first Wolves goal!'

Years later, and during the memorable European run under Nuno, a similar level of dedication was required to make the 6,370-mile round trip, with no direct flights, to the fixture against Pyunik in Armenia.

Just 48 fans managed to make it, and were rewarded not just with a 4-0 win in the Europa League first leg, but also a personalised letter of thanks from captain Conor Coady.

It's certainly worth a mention that there is often support from the club and other sources to help fans overcome challenges to make it to fixtures.

Staying on the subject of flying, the incredible efforts of Albert and Muriel Bates, of the Wolves Official Supporters Club, helped bring about the mass aerial assault on Newcastle on New Year's Day of 1990, when almost 1,000 fans travelled to St James' Park by air.

Six planes chartered by the official supporters' club from Birmingham Airport were added to by one organised independently by Hatherton Wolves, and a private jet that transported the owners, the Gallagher brothers, and their friends.

For Cowley, however, plane transport has sometimes proved slightly less salubrious. Although he has often been able to call on the good nature of various pilots to deliver him safely across the water!

On one occasion he was allowed to travel in a jump seat usually reserved for crew, after which the pilot drove him from Liverpool across Runcorn Bridge to the station to get a connection.

And on another occasion, well, let him tell the story.

'The airmail plane came into the Isle of Man and unloaded all the papers at the airport,' says Cowley.

'I was waiting and was struggling to get a flight and the supervisor at the airport decided he wanted to help me!

'It was going back empty, so he tied me to the floor of the plane, where the mail would normally go, with my legs strapped in, and that's how I stayed for the full flight!

'It was an American pilot flying me over, and I was the only passenger, effectively a package being delivered to get to the game!'

Little wonder that a picture of Cowley at an away game against Grimsby was once featured as part of a Year of Sport exhibition in the Isle of Man Museum. Alongside such sporting luminaries and world champions as Manx Missile Mark Cavendish (cycling) and Geoff Duke (motorcycling).

Some incredible stories, and no doubt just a small selection of so many others which exist within the Molineux fanbase of supporters who have been so loyal and dedicated in following Wolves.

Even during our conversation, many other names are mentioned.

John Reynolds, from Ledbury, Tony Brettle from Stourbridge, Dave Slape, Peter Woodifield and Stan Armett from London Wolves, Russ and Nick Evers and 'Big Dave' – also known as Reg – from Hatherton Wolves, their founder members Dave Meads and Dave Quarrell, Jim Titley from Cannock. Brian Meddings, who travelled with Cannock Wolves for 30 years before his passing in 2025.

There will also, of course, be many others.

And others whom, like Meddings, are sadly no longer with us.

At the start of 2026, Charlie Daw, despite suffering with illness, managed to make his first ever trip to Everton's Hill Dickinson Stadium for the 1-1 draw.

That was his 1,986th consecutive Wolves game, a run which had started with the 4-1 defeat against Bolton in Division Three in 1985.

In the preceding ten years he had only missed seven games, mainly for attending the World Speedway Finals, and his total tally, from his first game against Bury in 1967, was 2,576.

Sadly, however, that Everton game was to prove Daw's last. He was admitted to hospital, followed Wolves' next game in the FA Cup against Shrewsbury via Wolves TV whilst also checking in on his beloved racing via an app, and passed away a few days later.

For many years he went to games with his second wife Jo, along with his good mate Eddie Baker, who drove him to that final fixture at Everton.

Daw and Baker first met outside Loftus Road ahead of an away game at QPR on New Year's Eve in 1977. Born just six days apart, they quickly became friends and travelled to over 1,500 matches together.

'Loyal, determined, cheerful, optimistic, glass half-full, Charlie was all of those things,' says Baker.

'Not at all egotistical, and it was never him that talked about this record of successive Wolves games.

'A really decent and humble man – modest, never boasted – and someone who was devoted to his family.

'He was generous and would do anything to help anyone, and no one ever saw him angry.

'Charlie usually wore a mischievous grin and had an encyclopaedic knowledge of pubs and away stadiums.'

Sentiments very much echoed by our four guests in the Great Western, all of whom had become so accustomed, and happy, to bump into Daw on the road with Wolves.

'I used to laugh and joke when I saw him and call him the number one,' says Abbott.

'I think Steve was ahead of all of us for a while but after he missed the one game, Charlie became the number one.'

And returning to the subject of ingenuity to access fixtures, it was in December of 2002, when Wolves fans were stopped by Millwall from going to the New Den, Daw actually became a Lions member to book his ticket, only for his card not to work as he swiped the machine to gain entry at the turnstiles.

Fearing having to speak might give away his lack of 'cockney' dialect, fortunately the lady on the turnstiles wiped the ticket on her top, returned it, and Charlie gained entry.

There are other equally entertaining tales. He flew out to the Anglo-Italian fixture at Lecce on the plane with the players, albeit having to buy his first wife a washing machine to soften the blow of the considerable expense.

'I'd often see Charlie before games, particularly here in the Great Western before home games, and the thing I will always remember about the number one, he was always smiling,' adds Abbott.

'I think everyone would say that about him, always smiling – as soon as he walked in the room, he had a big grin on his face, as if to say: "We're watching the Wolves … we're happy."'

And that's a thought that extends to all of those who follow Wolves so diligently. Of course they want to see the team win, but their love of the club extends well beyond a result or two.

Having experienced around six or seven relegations apiece, even this latest one, from Premier League to Championship, doesn't hold any fears.

As we say our farewells, they head off in different directions, continuing their pre-match rituals, meeting friends and family.

Whatever the result, whatever the team's fortunes, good, bad or indifferent, they will be back. They always come back.

To some it is unexplainable devotion. Even bordering on insanity. To them, and so many others, it is natural. It's in the blood. Gold and black blood.

Chapter 3

Bully and JR – Our Treasured Heroes

BETWEEN THEM, they chalked up 1,048 Wolves appearances. Scored a staggering 500 goals. And were among the early inductees into the club's Hall of Fame.

Both won promotions for Wolves. Wembley cup finals. They both also scored at Wembley. And both played for England.

They both made Wolves their football and spiritual home. Both are now club vice-presidents and honorary patrons of the Wolves Foundation. They have always represented the city of Wolverhampton with pride and distinction. Effectively over a combined timespan of almost 100 years. And Wolverhampton has loved having them. They are both Freemen of the City, and could legally drive their sheep through the centre. One day they should make that happen.

And on a Molineux matchday, you will always find them, motoring around the Billy Wright Stand with the same positional sense and purpose which served them so well out on the pitch. Meeting fans, posing for pictures, signing autographs. Still representing their club in an ambassadorial role, flying the gold and black flag, where nothing is too much trouble.

Never meet your heroes? Nonsense. In John Richards and Steve Bull, Wolves still have two of the very, very best. Both in terms of their football, their personalities and their affiliation to the club to which they gave so much service and brought so much success. Still giving back, and still giving their all.

Over an early morning cuppa at Wolverhampton's Mount Hotel, a regular haunt for both during their football days and since, discussion traverses a wide variety of subjects across an hour and a half.

Befitting the overall theme of this book, it's not all focused on the events or the big games, the promotions and the relegations, although they do get a fair few mentions. The ups and downs are, after all, part of the story, particularly for two of the biggest legends to have graced Wolves during the club's 150-year history.

But it is also about their thoughts and opinions. Richards is 75 at the time of our interview, and Bull 61. Aside from memories of their own footballing expertise and the adulation that still endures amongst an ever-appreciative fanbase, it's fair to say they still know a bit about the game. And a bit about the city. What works, and what doesn't. Whether changes over time have been positive, or not.

In an era where we are now so obviously short of heroes and positive role models, of those who put in so much painstaking work and blood, sweat and tears to get to where they want to be, how refreshing that two of the very finest are still so humble and approachable. We could all learn a lot.

'It's still about the fans though, isn't it?' says Richards, as if to prove the point.

'It's about the memories, and for us it's just a privilege, to still be able to speak to the fans, and to chat about those memories. We shared them all together.

'When we were playing, we were living their lives. Through us, they were getting the joy that we had from football.

'What would those fans have given to go and play on the pitch just once? And that was enough for me, too, when I first came to Wolves as a kid.

'Coming to Molineux with the big oak-panelled entrance and the trophy cabinets with my mouth wide open and looking at that pitch. And thinking I'd be happy to just play on this once and go back to school and back to work.'

Powerful words, and ones which strongly resonate with Bull.

'We're fans as well now,' he adds. 'We're there watching, still kicking every ball, and still wanting Wolves to do well.

'And then on a matchday, people might come up and ask for a signature or a picture, and you're thinking, "What about the players that are here now?"

'But to be honest it's nice. It still gives you a buzz. I love meeting people. I suppose it's a sign of respect for what we have done for the club but, as John says, the fans are always the most important people, and we both always respected them when we played.'

Richards arrived at the club in 1969, and, after finishing playing, returned as a director, managing director and, as mentioned and like Bull, is now a vice-president. That brings his association with the club and city up to almost 60 years. Meanwhile Bull, in November of 2026, celebrated his own 40th anniversary of association with all things Wolves.

Two incredible contributions and examples of longevity. And two uniquely fantastic stories. The meticulous A-level student who arrived from Warrington to make Wolves his home and the proud Tiptonian who emerged from a combination of non-league and full-time jobs away from football, and then, most gloriously, was bought for a relative pittance from that lot 'down the road'.

Very different footballing backgrounds, but also so many similarities. Similarities which probably helped lay the foundations for their success and continue to underpin their humility and longevity.

Football was very different back in their day. Yes, there were youth training schemes but they were very far removed from academies as they are now where a scholarship programme can effectively be mapped out from the age of seven or eight onwards.

For Richards and Bull, breaking through at first team level had nothing to do with being scouted at a young age and coming through the ranks. In many ways, that probably helped them, offering a grounding and a perspective which fired up their motivation.

So, let's go there. How did it all begin?

'Well, I should probably start, as I was probably about 20 years before Steve,' says Richards.

'I was a toddler back in 1969,' Bull replies. They both laugh.

Richards started out, like so many, enjoying football in the school playground before then representing the school team.

Yet the boy who would become a man and score 194 goals in Wolves' colours as a striker, actually began his footballing life – as a goalkeeper!

'No one else wanted to go in goal,' he recalls. 'So, I volunteered. I was nine years old. There was a cross that came over, I went to catch it, and it went through my hands, hit me on the head, knocked me over and went in.

'We lost 6-0, and I think the teacher, sensibly on his part, realised I was never going to be a goalkeeper. When there was a space, I became a right-back, and then, the following year, right-half.'

Richards was soon moved further forward to inside-right, and became captain of Warrington Town juniors, alongside his school team, and by the time he was studying for his A-levels, he was also turning out for a local youth side and in Sunday League.

Warrington was very much a rugby league town, and most of the football scouts would head to games in Liverpool and Manchester instead.

But via schools football, Richards was selected for the Lancashire Grammar Schools team, and, after impressing at a tournament in Bognor Regis, got picked for England Grammar Schools.

Wolverhampton teacher Tony Penman also did some scouting for Wolves, and, as part of his work with the Staffordshire Schools team, had spotted Richards in the tournament and reported back with a glowing recommendation.

From there Joe Gardiner, Wolves' chief scout and previously the team's trainer, visited the family home to make his pitch, and so, despite strong interest from Sheffield Wednesday and Derby County, Molineux became Richards' favoured destination.

'I had given my word to Joe that I would come for a trial so that's what I did, which led to a one-year contract,' says Richards.

'I'll be honest, at that stage I never knew where Wolverhampton was – it could have been at the other end of the country or a million miles away as far as I was aware.

'I hadn't really been a big fan of any club. I remember the first game I watched on television – in black and white of course – was Tottenham.

'I think it was the FA Cup Final of 1962, and Jimmy Greaves scored in the first few minutes, and he was my hero.

'I suppose in a way Spurs were my team, but only really from that final, and from collecting the chewing gum cards that were around back then. Those cards were how we all got to know the different teams and players.'

Bull's hero growing up was another legendary British marksman in Ian Rush. He would describe himself as an armchair Liverpool fan in his teenage years.

But there wasn't too much time for watching football. Bull was way too busy playing.

'My story is probably the same as so many young lads growing up,' he recalls. 'My mum and dad used to give me a clip round the earhole because I'd leg it home from school, drop my bag off, grab a ball and head out to Jubilee Park in Tipton.

'It would be that quick I wouldn't even get changed out of my school gear, and I'd only really have one school shirt, one pair of trousers and one pair of shoes – that's why my mum and dad weren't happy!

'But I just loved football, it was everything. And because it was my ball, I was selfish. Probably why I became a striker.

'I played for as many junior teams as I could, Princes End Colts, Bustleholme Boys, then Newey Goodman, one of the bigger Sunday League teams.

'Sid Day was the scout at Albion who ran Tipton Town's youth team and he spotted me playing for my school – Willingsworth High.

'I started playing for Tipton's youth team and then the reserves, and the first team, in the West Midlands League. I think I was playing against adults in the Sunday League when I was maybe 14 or 15.'

Richards interjects, 'Against adults? At that age? That must have built up your strength!'

'It did,' Bull replies. 'I'd have to be quick. All these adults turning up after a night on the beer or smoking a cigarette, and then there was me, still pretty small and skinny back then.

'It didn't bother me though. I just wanted to score goals, simple as that. Just like in the park, I saw it as my ball, and my chance to hit the back of the net.'

Bull was combining his Saturday and Sunday football with employment, carrying out various jobs including working in a bed factory, builder's yard and a warehouse.

He'd be working 13 hours a day, travelling in and out via his bike down the canal path, training on Tuesday and Thursday nights and playing both days of the weekend.

Day recommended him to England World Cup winner Nobby Stiles, then youth team coach at West Bromwich Albion, and boss Johnny Giles then agreed to take him to the Hawthorns.

Bull soon found himself in a striker department featuring Garth Crooks, Imre Varadi and George Riley, admitting he did feel somewhat overawed and pressured into passing to them rather than playing his natural and single-minded game.

'I came through the intermediate team and the reserves and once I was in the first team with those other top strikers, I just thought I had to make sure I passed it to them,' he admits.

He made one top-flight appearance with Albion, as a substitute at QPR, along with two Second Division appearances, in which he scored twice, and two in the League Cup, in which he scored once.

Three goals in five games was a more than decent start for a young and raw talent. But a change of manager with Giles, and then Stiles moving on, saw Ron Saunders take over, and Bull no longer in favour. The club made the decision that they were going to sell him.

Remember that legendary suggestion that he didn't have a first touch? Well, much to Wolves' subsequent delight, the striker and his pal and also future Molineux legend Andy Thompson, sandwiched between the similar moves up the A41 of Ally Robertson and Robbie Dennison, headed across the Black Country to ultimately spectacular effect.

Surely though, neither Richards and Bull, nor the fans who adore them, could ever have dreamt of the truly extraordinary impact they would deliver when they first checked in. An 18-year-old in Richards fresh out of completing his education in Warrington. And a 21-year-old in Bull with a handful of appearances for the fierce local rivals. Both still relatively unknown.

If ever the phrase 'the rest is history' rings true, then this is it. Richards would plunder 194 goals for Wolves, including the winner in one of two League Cup Final victories which are still the club's most recent major trophies. And for Bull, a club record haul of 306, the unmistakable focal point of the revival which dragged the team back to respectability from the abyss of near-extinction. How fitting that adding those two figures together produces a round 500.

Heading back to those early days, was there a moment in their formative years when they realised their own potential? When they perhaps discovered the belief and confidence that a successful career in the game was within their grasp? It's a pertinent question, especially given neither had followed that traditional route through the youth system.

'I can definitely give you that moment,' says Richards. 'It was a match, a reserve match, I think in the November of my first year, in 1969.

'Wolves had a lot of different teams and when I arrived, I played in the West Midlands League before moving through to the reserves – I think like Stevie, we both had to put in the work and the graft to try and impress the coaches and the managers.

'This was a game against Blackburn at Ewood Park when we won 5-1 or 5-2 – and I scored all five!

'That laid down a marker, and suddenly the hierarchy, including Bill McGarry the manager, started noticing.

'I nearly made my debut a few weeks later when someone got injured and I was picked up from my landlady Mrs Eagle's house to travel to a game against Nottingham Forest.

'But the game was postponed due to a frozen pitch.

'Then I think Doog [Derek Dougan] got a suspension, and I did make my debut, alongside Hughie Curran in a game against West Brom.

'I played a few games after that and also the following season but it was a good couple of years before I became a regular.

'For a moment though, I definitely believe that reserve game against Blackburn was the one where I really made my breakthrough.'

For Bull, the belief started as soon as he signed his first contract with Albion. From the moment he was able to focus solely on football and not have to combine his passion with gruelling days at work.

'As soon as I signed that first deal, I think it was £125 a week, I knew I could jack my job in and concentrate purely on football,' he recalls.

'That was the moment for me, the moment when I thought I could do it, that I was in with a chance of being good enough.

'I'd always been brought up with a big work ethic, and if it hadn't worked out and someone told me I had to go and clean cars, I'd have gone and done that as well.

'Then I played a few games in the Albion's first team, and scored a couple of goals, before they decided to sell me to Wolves. And that didn't start great to be fair.

'The first three games I was there we lost 3-0, I played in two of them and me and Thommo watched from the stands against Chorley as we were cup-tied.

'But gradually, things started to turn, and we started to get better.'

They didn't half. More of that shortly.

But first, in terms of those footballing upbringings, the grounding and the mentality they developed in those early days – how much of that was instinct? Forged on the streets of Tipton or the school fields of Warrington? And how important was coaching?

Two of the very finest exponents of their art are well versed in answering such questions!

Not least in the sense also of how much about scoring goals is almost natural and automatic. And how much is taught.

'It was instinct for me. I just wanted to play football and I just wanted to score goals,' says Bull.

'I was selfish and I was greedy, and if I didn't score, I would have one on me.

'That was my job, and it's why, to be honest, when I left Albion to come to Wolves, when me and Thommo headed up in that bright orange Ford Cortina, I didn't mind if I was top, middle or bottom when it came to the divisions.

'Graham Turner was building a new team, and one which played to my strengths, and while I ended up scoring a lot of goals, it was always very much a team effort.

'Mutchy [Andy Mutch] and myself obviously had a great understanding, and we had so many great lads and great players, and I loved being part of it, and I always stayed grounded.

'I wasn't bothered about all the stuff that sometimes comes with being a footballer – a big house, a big car or whatever – I just wanted to play, and to score goals.'

'Neither Steve or myself had come through any youth system and maybe that gave us a hunger and a perspective,' adds Richards.

'And I think, when you play like we did over the years, on the streets or for the school, you play in a certain position and develop a skill so that you naturally progress to where you feel comfortable.

'The two of us were quite similar with that, we were both up front knocking the goals in, and it soon became really natural.

'You end up just knowing exactly what position to be in and get yourself in the right places.

'Coaches can tell you what to do, but a lot of being a striker is instinct, with the training sessions then working on things like your touch and how you fit into the team.

'Sammy Chung, who was John Barnwell's assistant, was a fantastic coach for me, probably the best I ever worked with, and he used to put on extra sessions for us.

'A couple of afternoons a week he'd take a group of us including myself and Kenny Hibbitt over to West Park and we just worked on specifics, like hitting balls into each other, our first touch, being able to turn.

'Other players helped as well. I remember Mike Bailey telling me I was running away too much, and that he wanted me to come short to receive the ball, and then go and make my run.

'So certain managers and players might change things slightly, but so much of being a striker is about getting into the right positions, whether that's to hold the ball up or have a shooting opportunity.'

Bull and Richards certainly enjoyed plenty of shooting opportunities during their respective careers. Bull's club record of 306 goals included 52 and 50 in winning the Fourth and Third Division titles, and Richards' 194 featured key contributions in cup semi-finals and finals.

Richards was an integral part of the team which last won a major trophy for Wolves, with those League Cup successes of 1974 and 1980, and Bull of the team which dragged the club back from oblivion in the late eighties after twice nearly going out of business.

Being the key men for the majority of their respective careers, shouldering the responsibility of being not just goalscorers but also reflective and representative of the teams they spearheaded, was something which came naturally to both.

It also meant that when they didn't score, there was always that nagging sense of disappointment.

'I loved that responsibility, because as a goalscorer I just loved that feeling of getting a goal and jumping in front of the fans to celebrate,' says Bull.

'I knew people were coming to watch Wolves and the whole team, but also knew they were looking at me to deliver, and if I didn't score, I didn't feel like I had done my job.

'In the Sherpa Van, I scored in every single round up to the final, and then we beat Burnley at Wembley, and I didn't score.

'After that it took me at least five pints before I could even talk to anybody.

'I was fortunate to play for England and score at Wembley a couple of years after but at the time I was thinking that was my only chance. Those are the ones you remember, when it didn't go well.

'I couldn't tell you about my 185th or 187th goal for Wolves but I could tell you about the ones when I didn't score a goal.'

'It sticks with me too, when things didn't go well,' Richards interjects.

'We lost in three FA Cup semi-finals, and that has stuck with me through the years.

'The same as Steve if I didn't score – I was a goalscorer, and if I didn't score in a game, I would question myself as to why not.

'We always got chances, the way Wolves played in those days, so I wouldn't consider I had played well if I didn't score, even if I had actually performed well and helped other people.

'I remember one game in particular when I was really gutted.

'We beat Man City 5-2 and I scored two and Doog [Derek Dougan] got a hat trick.

'Two of the Doog's goals came when Joe Corrigan parried my shots, and he got two tap-ins, and walked off with the match ball.

'I was really upset if I didn't score and you don't need to be told by anyone else that you hadn't played well!

'But when you were flying, like we were at times and Steve was with the revival, you didn't fear anyone, and felt you were going to score every time you went out.'

At this juncture, discussion moves on to the subject of strength and mentality. There are so many substantial positives to life in academies these days. Young players are left to want for nothing when it comes to their development, be it with the best preparation, the best advice in areas of fitness and nutrition, the best training facilities, the best pitches, the best kit!

No more are they cleaning boots, sorting the first team's kit, running errands, or running up the terraces as part of fitness routines.

With all those developments, the challenge for the coaches and the staff is to keep young players grounded, keep them hungry and keep them motivated. The cream will still rise to the top when it comes to talent and character, but, for many, it can sometimes become too comfortable.

Bull and Richards enjoyed no such luxuries. Both believe that did them plenty of good.

'I know times change but I sometimes wonder if what happens now is necessarily the best way,' says Richards.

'Player welfare is obviously very important but a lot of kids in academies can be given false hope, and taking them away from playing with their pals in their local teams growing up – is that for the best?

'Let them carry on playing for their schools, let them carry on playing in local football. It's what we did, and it never did us any harm. That's just natural for their development.

'Because later on, those that get discarded – and remember so very few actually make it – psychologically, that is such a knock-back.

'When I joined Wolves, there was a 16-year-old lad, whose name I won't mention, who was the striker with England schoolboys, and the world was his oyster.

'As it turned out, that was his level, he had peaked at 16, and was released at 18.

'It's a massive difference now to the way I was developed and Steve was developed and you could argue one way or the other as to which is better.

'I would say that I was lucky with the way I was allowed to progress and it was right for me. I don't think today's development programme would have suited me as coming away from home at 14 or 15 – I'd have hated it and it would have destroyed me.'

'We appreciated every single minute and every single thing that happened when we were coming through,' adds Bull.

'I'm not saying they don't appreciate it now, but, as John says, it's very different.

'We'd have one pair of boots and would be very happy with that. Nowadays, I think a lot is thrown at young players and there is absolutely nothing wrong with that at all, but I do wonder if they still have that hardened edge that we had to develop.

'We had to keep our feet on the ground, and had to roll our sleeves up to make the progress that we needed to.

'It's just the way life goes, isn't it? And how it changes. As does football. On that subject, don't get me started on VAR!'

'We'd have lost half of our goals if VAR had been in!' says Richards.

But staying on that subject of development and creating a mentality, that brings the conversation neatly on to addressing and coping with adversity when it arrives.

And even Bull and Richards, two of the greatest ever, the 'new King born today' and 'King John' – even they had their difficulties.

For Bull, there is regret that he never made it into the top flight with Wolves. That would have been the fairy tale, and the fitting end to the story that he deserved. But there is certainly no regret that he stayed at Wolves to try, and rejected potential moves to Coventry, Newcastle, Celtic and Torino.

What still feels like sacrilege however is that he was once booed by the Molineux faithful. In an FA Cup replay against Bolton – why is it always Bolton?! – after missing a series of chances.

It was more frustration with the occasion and the chance of a big tie with Liverpool slipping away that prompted the jeers. But it happened.

'That was the first time I heard it in my life, and the last time I think,' says Bull. 'But it was frustration. I get it, I just had one of those days when nothing would go in.'

For Richards, the brickbats arrived long after he had hung up his boots. There had been the potential to join Brian Clough's Derby before he chose Wolves at the start of his career, and then nearly a player swap with Birmingham City for Joe Gallagher towards the end.

By that stage Barnwell was under pressure to bring in some revenue, or move players around, and with Andy Gray and Mel Eves at the club, moving Richards on to bring in a central defender emerged as an option.

But after speaking to Blues boss Jim Smith, and talking it over with wife Pam, Richards opted to stay at Molineux for that little bit longer, a loan stint with Derby when he had John McAlle as a travelling partner, and a happy time in Portugal with Maritimo bringing the curtain down on a magnificent career.

His dances with Wolves weren't done, however, even though when he retired from playing, he had no intention of getting involved in football.

'Some of my pals in the game like Kenny Hibbitt and Mike Bailey went into management and I had a bit of a go at a basic coaching badge but it wasn't for me,' says Richards.

'I think football can be a nightmare at the best of times, apart from playing, so once I had finished, I was happy to stay away!

'It was in 1994, when Sir Jack [Hayward] was involved, and Billy Wright had sadly passed away, that he approached me about becoming a non-executive director, because Sir Jack always enjoyed having the former players around.

'It was an honorary position which I took on alongside my job with Cannock Chase Council, until 1997 when there was a bit of a fall-out at the club because Sir Jack didn't like the way it was all going.

'He was recruiting for a managing director, and asked me to go on the interview panel, but, as the process went on, he asked me if I would consider the job, and I said I would give it some thought.

'Eventually I agreed, and it was, as those jobs are, absolutely non-stop and 24-7.

'It takes over your whole life, and you are constantly getting calls from so many different people both inside and outside of the club, and there is never a moment to switch off.

'It was also around the time when Sir Jack and his son Jonathan had fallen out, which has been well documented, and that was rumbling along in the background.

'But at the same time, when I reflected on it after I was sacked in 2000, it was such a formative three years.

'I learnt so much during that time, so much about how to operate, and sometimes things that I didn't like, but all of which I could take on into my next role after I moved on.

'It was a great time as well though, something I thoroughly enjoyed, even though it was sometimes difficult with the finances.

'And I did get some criticism as well. Fans would say, "Where's the money?" and "What are you doing, Richards?", but that's just part and parcel of football, isn't it? It's a passionate game.

'I also think you are never too old to learn, but also that if I sat down now and reflected on things from 30 or 40 years ago, I'd still feel comfortable that I did a lot of things right and got the best out of a lot of situations for the club.'

Richards and Bull did overlap in their roles as managing director and star striker respectively. There was, of course, the FA Cup semi-final of 1998, where boss Mark McGhee's decision not to start with either Bull or Robbie Keane continues to cause plenty of discussion, nearly 30 years on!

Richards was on the pre-season tour of Sweden in 1999 when Bull reluctantly decided he had to call time on his own playing career due to a persistent knee injury.

Talking of Keane, another question which seems to have stood the test of time concerns his eventual transfer to Coventry City, and why there was no 'sell on' clause in the £6m fee which was paid by the Sky Blues.

It's a question which Richards is well aware of, and is more than comfortable in answering.

'There were cutbacks and restrictions at the time and we needed to bring in money, and no one else was offering what Coventry were offering in terms of the up-front payment,' he explains.

'When you have a clause in a deal, it only applies to the first move from the new club, and is a percentage of the profit that the club makes.

'We knew how good a player Robbie was, but you always have to remember nothing is guaranteed and he could have got injured after leaving us or seen his value drop.

'So even though Coventry to Inter Milan was a big move, the money Wolves would have received via any clause was unlikely to be as much as the difference that we had been offered by them in terms of the up-front fee.

'So, we took the decision to take Coventry's offer which meant the money was available to the club immediately at a time when it was particularly needed.'

By way of example, Keane moved from Coventry to Inter Milan for £13m, a profit for the Sky Blues of £7m, of which a ten per cent clause would have seen them having to give Wolves £700,000.

But they had bought him from Wolves for £6m, when the nearest other suitor Aston Villa were only offering £5m, thus backing up Richards' argument that taking that 'up front' offer was the best and most lucrative option at the time.

Overseeing recruitment and player 'ins and outs' formed just one of the myriad of tasks and pressures associated with the job of managing director, especially at a club with such a proud history, passionate fanbase and lofty expectations.

It is why, when perhaps suggesting that Wolves sacking one of their most decorated legends was another piece of Molineux sacrilege, Richards is quick – not to mention as professional as always – to issue a rebuttal!

'It was the best thing that happened to me, moving on at that time,' he insists. 'I think it would have finished me off if I had stayed much longer.

'I don't think it's a role that suited me, and in truth I only said yes because it was Sir Jack, and of course there were times when he was criticised by the fans as well.

'People get sacked in football all the time, and the thing that mattered most to me is the people who know me and worked with me, who know the job that I did.

'It is something that happens in business and in life, and the compensation I received meant I had a bit of time to decide what to do next, because at the time I was around 50 and wasn't going to just walk into another job.

'I then went and worked within leisure services with the City of Wolverhampton Council, and as operations director at Pitchcare, roles I really enjoyed, whilst obviously keeping an eye on Wolves and being delighted to be back and more involved again in recent years.'

For Bull, his association with Wolves since finishing his playing days has been largely ambassadorial and being an integral part of supporting community and charitable initiatives. He is still loved and revered by fans, almost three decades after hanging up his boots.

But there was a time when he had coaching and managerial ambitions, including a spell as player-coach under Graham Turner at Hereford, and then as boss himself at Stafford Rangers.

'I did my badges and went out and gave it a go and applied for other jobs as well such as Kidderminster and Telford, but the thing about being a manager is that you can always get the carpet pulled from under your feet at any time,' says Bull.

'I was thinking, "Do I really want to go through this?", and have that instability, so I decided to keep my head down and work on getting my golf handicap down!

'There was a time when I would have loved to have tried to work my way up and be in the frame for a coaching job at Wolves, but eventually I ended up with what I'd say is the next best thing.

'Being a vice-president of the club, being so involved still coming up to 40 years, that is something which makes me very proud and something that I really enjoy.'

And that is life now for Richards as well as Bull. Both club vice-presidents, both in the Wolves Hall of Fame, both honorary patrons of Wolves Foundation, both Freemen of the City.

All are positions and accolades that they take extremely seriously. From calling up supporters to keep their spirits up during Covid lockdowns, to all those matchday duties with fans and visiting dignitaries, to delivering Wolves Wishes to deserving nominees, supporting club marketing and media activity, both are very much ingrained in doing their bit and all things Wolves.

That also extends to the city which has become home from home, where they have delivered so many wonderful moments for eager Wulfrunians across the decades. And also to their families, with Bull's wife Kirsty and daughter Gracie, and Richards' wife Pam, also very much a strong and integral part of their affinity with club and city.

'I love the place, love the club and I love the people, I love everything about it,' says Bull.

'Anybody has a go at us I'll speak up against them and say, "Leave our club alone."

'That's a feeling that's inside me, gold and black, like our own version of Blackpool Rock!

'But we love doing it – the titles are great and a real honour but, for me, it's speaking to the people that's the best thing of all.'

'I think we both represent our city and our club the best way we can, and what comes with that is a massive compliment,' adds Richards.

'It's an honour and a privilege that we can help and try and promote Wolverhampton in a way that it should be promoted.

'Some people have a bad impression of the city, and every city has its ups and downs, but I still see a lot of good in Wolverhampton, and a lot of positive things going on.

'For Steve and myself, we just want to help in any way we can, and then obviously part of that is also in talking to fans, whether at the games, or in the pubs or restaurants.

'It's great to share those memories, although it's funny as time goes on, it moves from "My mum and dad have told me a lot about you," to "My grandma and grandad remember seeing you play."

'When it gets to a great grandma or great grandad, we'll know we're in trouble!'

So many memories and so many experiences. And, as mentioned already, not all of them favourable.

Bull still refers back to the devastation of that play-off semi-final against Bolton, when probably the best chance he ever had of leading Wolves into the Premier League ended with him slumped on the Burnden Park turf in an iconic image which still moistens the eyes of even the most hardened Molineux devotee.

As well as not scoring under the Twin Towers in the Sherpa Van Trophy Final!

He did, obviously, score at Wembley eventually, and this time in England colours, as well as representing himself, and Wolves, so positively at the 1990 World Cup finals in Italy. The fans who idolised him not only followed him around the country and continent but also puffed their chests out to see one of their own representing the Three Lions. Just magical times.

When you do consider the more difficult days, it's not so much a case of having regrets but more the normal footballing disappointments which impact even the greatest of football careers. Neither would change much if they had their time again.

But for Richards, it is England where maybe, just maybe, if he had his time again, he might have behaved slightly differently.

His one cap – it should have been more – came against Northern Ireland at Goodison Park in 1973, when he was played out of position on the left-hand side.

On that occasion, he wishes he'd done more.

'I was called into the squad at the last minute by Alf Ramsey after Allan Clarke got injured, and was playing up front with Martin Chivers,' he recalls.

'You'd still got people like Bobby Moore in the team, Martin Peters, and it was almost like I was in awe of them rather than playing my own game.

'Like Steve said earlier about how he would think first about passing the ball when he broke into the Albion team, I think I was the same, and rather than take control of my own performance, I let the occasion get to me.'

Richards did, of course, score the winning goal in the League Cup Final less than a year later. A moment still talked about, and one he still cherishes, especially from an era when cup finals were so traditional and special.

Aside from his winning goal, the second leg of the 1974 semi-final against Norwich also remains a strong memory, because it booked that place at Wembley, after Wolves had missed out in two semi-finals the previous season.

With those happy memories to finish on, and our chat at an end, the two heroes are up and off, both with various assignments in store to continue their day, both keeping busy, never standing still.

As much as they are happy to talk and relive so many recollections of so many glorious days, so too are the fans that still count them as true heroes, and still worship the ground they walk on.

Fans who saw either of them represent Wolves so magnificently will forever feel proud and privileged to have done so. Fans who saw both of them in their prime? Well, that's a golden ticket of brilliant moments and experiences that will never be cashed in.

And, best of all, their impact, their connection to the city, their contribution to the cause.

That remains as strong and as unbreakable as ever. Two legendary Wolves who will forever be associated with the pack.

Chapter 4

The Golden Age

THE WOLVERHAMPTON trolleybus system was opened in 1923 and served the community until its closure in 1967. With 14 routes covering the town and surrounding areas, it was the means of transport for many of the players, and the manager, who were part of the greatest era of all in the history of Wolverhampton Wanderers: the fifties.

Dwindling in their number as the years march on, there are still supporters who can recall this golden age with clarity. For the rest of us it is left to the imagination. What must Molineux have been like when the team was the leading light in English football? Beating all before them and spearheading the charge into European competition with those memorable floodlit victories in front of a packed stadium which captured the imagination of an entire continent.

What stands out most of all, when listening to those who speak from first-hand experience, is the sheer normality of it all. These heroes on the pitch led by the club's finest manager, Stan Cullis, were local men who were part of the community. There was very little in the way of special treatment. They were doing their job and, in their eyes at least, it was no more important than any other in the town of Wolverhampton.

'My dad would take me down to the ground,' Andrew Cullis, Stan's son, explains. 'We had trolleybuses in those days which took us from Tettenhall into the middle of Wolverhampton. And of course the players would come that way too. They would appear at the bus queue with their football boots. And the fans would send them to the front of the queue, saying, "You must get there quickly."'

Billy Wright, captain of Wolves during this era of unprecedented success, would regularly mingle and chat with supporters on his way to the match.

'I first met Billy on the bus,' revealed Graham Hughes, the club's long-serving historian and dressing room attendant, in an interview he gave before he passed away in 2021. 'He was on the same bus we got to the match. It was the five-past one bus from Codsall. Billy used to get on halfway and it was always packed. He'd walk through with all the supporters who'd be shouting "Have a good game Billy" and he'd reply "And you enjoy it!"'

Wolves' most decorated player even discovered he had been made captain of his country while on the bus, on 28 September 1948. He was heading back to his digs at Mr and Mrs Colley's house in Tettenhall, where he stayed for the entirety of his playing career.

'He was coming back home one day on the bus,' Hughes continued. 'And Alan the conductor said "Congratulations, you've just been made captain of England." It was in the stop press of the *Express & Star* but Billy didn't know as he'd been travelling back from Denmark after playing for England.'

Wright was the nearest thing to a celebrity player of his day – he married Joy Beverley of the Beverley Sisters pop trio in 1958 – but there was not even a hint of ego about him. 'For Billy Wright, it was always about the team and never about him,' Hughes concluded.

The success was masterminded by Cullis, whose overall services to Wolves remain unmatched. He signed as a player in 1934, aged just 17, and was made captain within two years. A commanding centre-half who learnt his trade under the firm management of

Major Frank Buckley, Cullis went on to captain England, winning 12 full caps and making 20 wartime appearances.

'The best centre-half I have met,' was how England centre-forward Tommy Lawton described him. 'He had the resilience of a concrete wall, the speed of a whippet and the footwork of a ballet dancer.' Cullis finished playing in 1947 to assist manager Ted Vizard, but within a year he was handed the managerial reins while he was still younger than some of those he had shared a pitch with.

'When he came back to playing after the war, he got this bad concussion,' Andrew continues. 'Too much heading of the heavy old ball, obviously. The doctors told him to stop. In the final game of the first post-war season Wolves played at home to Liverpool, with both teams going for the title. Before the game, my dad went on the public address system and announced he was retiring that day. Amazing, isn't it? You couldn't imagine a player doing that today before a game. I think the club realised that he was always a leader and that's why they wanted him in management, he just had that in him really.'

It would have been a fairy tale end to a great career had Cullis lifted the league title, but Wolves lost that final day decider and Liverpool became champions. His career was unquestionably hampered by the Second World War, but arguably those experiences whilst on duty during the war effort gave him the grounding for his later work in management.

'He was stationed down in Aldershot for a bit during the war and he played for Aldershot during that period,' Andrew reveals. 'Several top players apparently turned out for them. I remember going to a match with my dad there, and he said, "Oh, over there, that's where I tackled somebody and they landed up in the crowd."

'And later when he was out in Italy, he organised quite a lot of friendlies, mainly to keep the troops happy. He was a big friend of Matt Busby, and he used to get people like Matt and others to come and play representative matches to keep the troops entertained.

There was another game where he was asked by someone in government if he could put a team together against a Yugoslavian side who had been beating everybody.'

As manager of this representative army side, Cullis assembled a top team and the Yugoslav Partisan Army were beaten 7-2.

'Dad later said it was a bit worrying because around the changing room area were some of the Yugoslav allied soldiers and fighters,' Andrew continues. 'This included some ladies with their machine guns. So, I think he felt he didn't want to beat them by too many!'

When Cullis took over from Vizard, who resigned during the pre-season of 1948, he inherited a very good side. He set about building an even better one. The characteristics that had served Cullis so well as an outstanding defender were soon evident, as a strong and courageous squad developed with total devotion to the team ethic ahead of individual aspirations.

The run to the FA Cup Final during his first season in charge epitomised what this new-look Wolves was all about. A Molineux crowd of 54,983 saw Liverpool beaten 3-1 in the fifth round before 55,648 filled the ground for a 1-0 quarter-final win over neighbours West Bromwich Albion.

But the stand-out performance of the whole campaign came in the Hillsborough semi-final against Manchester United. Wolves drew 1-1 after playing much of the game with just nine men. Left-back Roy Pritchard was severely injured after just six minutes before right-back Laurie Kelly was stretchered off later in the match. Neither player was fit for the replay at Goodison Park, which Wolves won 1-0, although Pritchard recovered in time to play in the final, where Wolves beat Leicester City 3-1 in front of 98,920 spectators.

One of the enduring photographs of the Wembley day is of Wright, clutching the FA Cup under his arm, being chaired off the pitch by team-mates Bill Shorthouse and Jesse Pye. Like Cullis, the captain of the team found his own path to the top affected by the war. Aged only 15, Wright was elevated to the first team for a wartime league match against Notts County in October 1939. He signed professional terms two years later, even playing as a forward in those early days, only moving to the half-back line once he established himself in the team after the war.

In 1942, during the second leg of a Wartime League Cup semi-final victory over West Bromwich Albion, Wright broke his ankle. Such injuries were often career-ending during that era but he found a solution with the help of Ernest Freeman, a Wolverhampton surgeon, who suggested putting a pin in the ankle to help bind the fracture. It was a groundbreaking procedure at the time and Wright was able to make a full recovery.

At the age of 18, he joined the army as a physical training instructor. When the Football League resumed for the 1946/47 season, team-mates and manager, who had been away on service duty, noticed a change in the player.

'The most obvious one was his size,' said Cullis, some years later. 'The little shrimp had become a powerfully built young man. He had also grown in confidence as a person, and all his work as a physical training instructor meant he was positively glowing with strength and good health.'

Wright was a role model on the pitch. Cullis had built a physically powerful, fit and ruthless side, but he needed a captain who could lead by example, never shirking a challenge. The football was often direct, with long diagonal balls played out to the wing forwards. In the title-winning seasons – 1953/54, 1957/58 and 1958/59 – Wolves scored 96, 103 and 110 goals respectively.

'We expected goals, we really did,' Andrew recalls. 'One thing that comes to mind is that in those days, and it's extraordinary really, sports journalists would ring our home and speak to my dad. That's incredible, isn't it? Because you wouldn't do that nowadays. I can remember Desmond Hackett from the *Daily Express* ringing our home phone one day and I answered and he spoke to me and asked, "Do you think Wolves will win at the weekend?" And I said, "Oh, they'll score five." He put it in his column: "Young Cullis, confident of big win!" Actually, Wolves scored six in the game.'

The excellence of Wolves in this period can be put into context by the team's year on year league placing during this heyday. Cullis's side never finished outside the top six over nine consecutive seasons between 1952/53 and 1960/61, and prior to that had lost out on the title in the 1949/50 campaign only on goal average to Portsmouth. There was a relentless nature to the way they set about winning matches. There was also a strict methodology behind the strategy Cullis adopted.

'Dad was very strong on fitness, on hard work and, although sometimes the players said they didn't like him, in terms of the team spirit amongst the players, that was very strong,' Andrew continues. 'Many years ago when the Wolves Former Players' Association started, I'd go along with my dad to the meetings. And the sort of camaraderie amongst those old Wolves players was incredibly strong. I think they really had a very strong spirit. They had exceptional players, too, like Billy Wright who was very good positionally. And when you had two wingers like Johnny Hancocks and Jimmy Mullen who could beat any player and cross the ball as they did, that was a huge strength.

'One of the people that my father spent time with was Charles Reep. He was a wing commander in the RAF, who was based at Bridgnorth. He was the first statistician of his kind in football and he used to analyse hundreds of matches. He would come out with terms like "binomial distribution" which didn't mean much to my dad, but he was interested in his statistics. Reep's big thing was winning the ball back in the top third of the pitch. He argued that actually there weren't many passes before you scored a goal. He plotted this with his own analysis and, when he saw my dad, his figures matched up with a lot of what Wolves were doing at that time. Most goals were scored after just two or three passes when possession had been won.'

Before moving to Shropshire, Reep had been brought in as a consultant at struggling Brentford midway through the 1950/51 season and was credited with an astonishing upturn in playing fortunes that helped them avoid relegation from the Second Division. Cullis was keen to meet him. Reep's data analysis was far superior to anything available at the time and Cullis's own beliefs in the way football should be played were now reinforced with new evidence which supplemented his own diligent research.

Hancocks and Mullen initially provided the supply line, with Norman Deeley succeeding Hancocks later. Roy Swinbourne, Dennis Wilshaw and, later, Jimmy Murray were the main goalscoring threats with Peter Broadbent's craft at inside-forward invaluable. Alongside this attacking prowess, there was a half-back line that drew many admirers. In the days of the 2-3-5 formation, it was the combination of three from Wright, Eddie Clamp, Ron Flowers and Bill Slater which made a formidable triumvirate. Wright switched seamlessly to the centre of the defence midway through his career, having been equally at home as a wing-half. Wolves even provided the heart of the England team during the 1958 World Cup finals, with Clamp, Wright and Slater lining up together on three occasions in Sweden.

'We were very fortunate in having a set of players who were not only skilled but were very good fellows off the field,' Cullis later reflected. 'They were men of integrity.'

The manager was supported by a loyal trainer, Joe Gardiner, who was a former team-mate in Buckley's Wolves side. The pair were undoubtedly influenced by the 'Iron Major', who had a reputation as the hardest of disciplinarians during his modernising reign at Molineux between 1927 and 1944, although Gardiner was widely regarded as more approachable as far as the players were concerned.

Scouting for new talent, Cullis regularly took it upon himself to watch as many players as possible, occasionally taking his son along for the ride.

'He would look at reports from scouts, but without television or video he would want to watch players as well,' Andrew explains. 'When I was around ten years old we went to Blackburn to watch a player and I was put in the ladies' tea room while my dad went into the directors' room before and after the game. After the match he completely forgot about me and he drove out to the edge of Blackburn before recalling that he'd brought his son with him. But that was how he was, just so focused.

'There was another occasion where I was with my mother and sister, Susan, at home, sitting down for supper, and we were asking where dad was. Then we switched on the television, and the BBC News was on, showing a picture of the Wolves players getting on a plane to go to Moscow. My dad never told my mum he was going to Moscow. He was so focused on his football. So that was slightly memorable!'

That 1955 tour to Moscow, to play Spartak and Dynamo, followed hot on the heels of the famous floodlit friendlies which put the club at the forefront of the European game. Wolves were not the first club to install floodlighting at their ground, but the £10,000 outlay in 1953 was perhaps the shrewdest decision that the board made. On 30 September, the lights were turned on to welcome a South Africa XI to Molineux and two weeks later Celtic were the visitors as the concept quickly caught the imagination of the paying public. The following year, Wolves welcomed Racing Club of Buenos Aires, First Vienna, Maccabi Tel Aviv and Spartak Moscow to Molineux before the match that broke new ground took place.

The Honved fixture, on 13 December 1954, was witnessed by a crowd of 54,998 packed inside Molineux. Wolves had by now produced a shiny satin shirt, which had first been tested in wintry league conditions three years earlier, but had been developed to stand out under the floodlights for the benefit of spectators and, for the first time, a television audience at home.

'Wolves were the first club to sign a television deal, you know,' Hughes insisted. 'With the BBC when they played Honved, although they only had two cameras at the ground. They agreed on a fee of £600 to televise the second half of the match. We've still got the letter at the club that Sir Stanley Rous had written down.'

'I was only six at the time and we had a babysitter that night,' says Andrew. 'Just the second half was televised, wasn't it? And I was told by my parents, "If you're awake and the babysitter is agreeable, you can go and watch the second half." So, I kept awake and all I can remember is my blue dressing gown. I can't remember the game at all. I can remember going downstairs in my blue dressing gown and asking the babysitter if I could watch the game.'

The match took place a year after England had been stunned by Hungary at Wembley, losing 6-3 to a Ferenc Puskas-inspired side, and just six months after the Hungarians had routed England 7-1 in Budapest. Honved were the champions of Hungary and their side contained five of the 'Mighty Magyars' team who finished runners-up in the 1954 World Cup Final in Switzerland, and six who had played at Wembley. Wolves were champions of England.

The game was billed as a European club final by the international press. When Wolves came back from 2-0 down to win 3-2, the British press was captivated by the achievement. Peter Wilson wrote in the *Daily Mirror*, 'I may never live to see a greater thriller than this. And if I see many more as thrilling I may not live much longer anyway.'

Headlines such as 'Hail Wolves – Champions of the World' and 'Wolves The Great' were plastered across the back pages. This reaction was greeted with scepticism in the European press, though, and it set in motion a chain of events that led to the formation of the European Cup.

In France, *L'Equipe*'s football editor, Gabriel Hanot, a former French international and long-time proponent of a European club competition, wrote, 'Before we declare that Wolverhampton are invincible, let them go to Moscow and Budapest. And there are other internationally renowned clubs, Milan and Real Madrid, to name but two. A club world championship, or at least a European one, should be launched.'

L'Equipe produced a format for a European club competition, to be considered by UEFA. The UEFA congress of March 1955 saw the proposal raised, with approval given in April. The first-ever European Cup competition was held in the 1955/56 season. But Wolves could not retain their league title. Instead, it was Chelsea who won the First Division, only to be barred from entering the tournament by a Football Association concerned that their participation would affect domestic midweek attendances.

Wolves entered the competition for the first time in 1958, after securing their second league title of the decade, but were beaten in the first round by Schalke 04. A year later, after a second successive league title, they made it a round further before losing heavily to Barcelona in both legs.

'I went to those later games, and you realised then how good the other teams were from Europe,' Andrew recalls. 'Wolves played Barcelona and lost 5-2 at home. I can recall the Barcelona player on the right wing flicking it over the head of our left-back then volleying it across for their centre-forward to head it in, and it was just astonishing. All the Wolves fans just stood up and applauded, it was just such a wonderful bit of skill. So, I think one realised that we had a long way to catch up.'

Wolves came within a point of a league and cup double in the 1959/60 season. Slater lifted the FA Cup at Wembley after a 3-0 win over Blackburn Rovers, who had a young Derek Dougan in their ranks. Despite scoring 106 goals, Wolves were pipped to the First Division title by Burnley by a single point. The following season saw a third-place finish and defeat to Rangers in the semi-final of the European Cup Winners' Cup. Of all the successes since Cullis's first trophy win in 1949, there is one season that Andrew believes his dad treasured most of all.

'The season that really pleased him was 1957/58 when Wolves won the First Division, the second team won the reserve league and the youth team won the FA Youth Cup. That was when the youth team lost 5-1 away in the first leg of the final to Chelsea and turned it around in the home match, winning 6-1. There was a huge crowd for that final, and I think the fact that they won at all levels of the club that particular year pleased my dad the most.'

By the mid-1960s Wolves had been pulled back into the pack of also-rans in the First Division. John Ireland took over as chairman on 29 July 1964 and within two months Cullis had lost his job. A dreadful start to the 1964/65 season, where the team clocked up just one point from the opening seven games with the manager absent, heralded the end of Cullis's 30-year service to the club.

'At the beginning of that season he really was not well,' Andrew reflects. 'He was off for several weeks. Quite with what, I don't know. And when he came back the directors had made their decision.'

Cullis returned from his break to oversee a 4-3 home win over West Ham United. Ireland had asked his manager to resign on health grounds, prior to the game, but Cullis refused. The following day, 15 September, the club released a brief statement:

> The Wolves board of directors have informed their manager, Stanley Cullis, they wish to be released from their contractual arrangements with him. This he has consented to do.

'When the sacking happened, we had cameramen and reporters camped outside our house,' Andrew continues. 'And they literally camped outside for about three days, as I recall. And my mother said to me and my sister, "You must not go in the garden." I did actually meet a journalist many years later who told me he climbed up a tree to get a picture of our house. It was very big news. If Stan Cullis can get the sack, then anybody can. So it was difficult. And I think for Dad, having spent so long at Wolves, it was a very difficult time.'

For all the disciplinarian aspects of his management style, there was a side to Cullis that was never revealed to the wider world, and there were those in the game who saw a deeper character whose love for the club was unsurpassed.

'Stan was volatile and outrageous in what he said, he never swore and he could be as soft as mash,' Bill Shankly wrote in his 1976 autobiography. 'He would give you his last penny. Stan was 100 per cent Wolverhampton. His blood must have been of old gold. He would have died for Wolverhampton. Above all, Stan is a very clever man who could have been successful at anything. When he left Wolverhampton, I think his heart was broken and he thought the whole world had come down on top of him. All round, as a player, as a manager, and for general intelligence, it would be difficult to name anyone since the game began who could qualify to be in the same class as Stan Cullis.'

'Yes, he had that soft side,' Andrew adds. 'He enjoyed doing gardening and playing golf. And he loved listening to opera. I think that came from being in Italy during the war, where he went to listen to opera. Coming from his background, which was a very poor working-class background in Ellesmere Port, there's no way that they would have ever listened to any opera. And he had quite a lot of records, old vinyl that he bought of opera. He loved that.

'We went to Tettenhall Church on Sundays, which was just down the road, which was good. And he also loved reading military history and I think he loved it because of the strategy. That really appealed to him, because obviously you've got to try to be strategic in your management.'

Having devoted three decades of his life to Wolves, managing 680 games in 16 years, the separation was tough. Cullis took charge of Birmingham City 15 months after his sacking and remained there until March 1970. On leaving professional football he did not set foot anywhere near Molineux for over 20 years.

'And it was only when Sir Jack Hayward became president at Wolves and said that they ought to do something there, and invited Dad back, that he returned,' Andrew explains. 'They had a benefit match for him [on 9 August 1992 against Aston Villa] because it was Doug Ellis at Villa who had heard that my mum and dad were struggling. Mum was not well and they were struggling financially. So, they had a benefit match, and then of course later on he had the north stand named after him and got a statue as well. Sir Jack really resurrected this, and I think that was a very healing thing for my dad. He was able to go back and enjoy being there again.'

The reunion has been a wider family experience for Andrew, with his own children and grandchildren experiencing being part of the Wolves story.

'It was very restorative for my dad,' he continues. 'And it's interesting because we have been up to Wolves quite a few times now with the family. When we go past my dad's statue we occasionally ask someone if they can take a picture of us on the camera phone, which they always do. And if they ask why we are having a photo we'll explain about my dad, and the reaction we get is extraordinary. Sometimes people will say, "Oh, you used to live in Tettenhall, didn't you?" And some of the older fans even know the house we were at.

'I can remember going along with my dad to Wolves in the years after we were invited back by Sir Jack. He found it amusing when all these youngsters came up to him and asked him to autograph their programme. I remember one girl had broken her arm and said, "Will you autograph my plaster cast?" And dad was quite amazed by all this attention.'

Most supporters may not have been alive, but the legacy ensures they know the story of Wolves in the fifties. The statues of Wright and Cullis at Molineux are just two of the permanent reminders of what was achieved in this golden age. Thanks to their leadership on and off the pitch, and the qualities of a team where each member understood and excelled in their role, the club was able to enjoy sustained and unparalleled success.

The Wolves Museum is perhaps the most tangible reminder of these heady days, fittingly located in the Stan Cullis Stand, where today's supporters can immerse themselves in the artefacts and films of an extraordinary period. A time when the devotees of Wolves travelled with their heroes to Molineux to attend the match and left sure in the knowledge that this was the greatest team in the land.

Chapter 5

The Kids Are Alright

THE SCENE was Old Wulfrunians Football Club in Castlecroft, a well-known part of the city's footballing scene having been formed in 1922, producing a wide range of adult teams in various leagues as well as boasting a thriving junior section still in force to this day.

Not to mention once being privileged to employ Molineux legend Dave Wagstaffe as its main steward, looking after the facilities and the clubhouse.

'Old Wulfs' is just down the road from the more recently formed AFC Wolverhampton City, formerly AFC Wulfrunians, which is housed on the Castlecroft training ground which played host to Wagstaffe and so many other Wolves icons for so many years.

A venue graced by so many Wolves greats of yesteryear. Where fans young and old were able to visit, watch and not only get a glimpse but share time and conversation with their heroes.

One of those long-standing fans, Les Green, became a renowned academy scout after taking retirement from his previous employment which for the most part was working as a telephone engineer.

A meticulous and dedicated scout, one of so many to have worked within the Wolves youth set-up over so many years, almost recreating the incredible successes enjoyed by Mark Crook, who seemingly almost starting the trend for regular recruitment of young talent via the nursery club, Wath Wanderers, in North Yorkshire.

It would have been the mid-1990s when Green headed into Old Wulfrunians to watch an under-13s fixture against Penn Colts.

Green was prolific in the number of matches he went to. Wherever they were played, whoever was playing, it was always worth a watch.

And on this particular occasion, that was to prove pivotal to the eventual recruitment of a schoolboy who went on to hit the heights not just at Wolves, but at Premier League and international level as well.

Green takes up the story.

'I had just started scouting for Wolves, working for a guy called Tony Painter, and he would phone me on a Friday night to tell me which game to go and watch over the weekend.

'No mobiles or internet back then, I was told to check the *Sports Argus* for details on where games might be and had to buy a new recording system for the house phone to make sure I didn't miss any message.

'He called me and said I didn't have to go, but if I was available could I cover a game at Radcliffe Borough between West Midlands County and Manchester County.

'And that if I went, to get the phone number of a guy called Smith, who was the manager of the West Midlands team.

'I'd got the non-league handbook, and felt like I was back to being ten years old trying to find football stadiums again, heading down a terraced high street and finding Radcliffe's ground.

'Anyway, I got there, met Mr Smith and he gave me his number, and I watched the game. I was early on in my scouting career, and I think they were testing me, to see if I would go and do it, and whether I had the initiative.

'A couple of weeks later, I'd been into Wolves on a morning, and went out in the afternoon and saw there was a game at Old

Wulfrunians. I parked the car, and walking up to have a mooch at the game on the lower pitch, a couple came up to me and told me they had seen me at Radcliffe Borough.

'Turns out I'd been watching their older son, who was at Aston Villa, and their younger son was playing in this game. I'd been given the name Les Scott to watch at Radcliffe, but when I'd got there I realised it wasn't Les Scott but actually Lescott – Aaron Lescott, who I'd watched.

'At this game it was Joleon playing, who was a really busy player, getting box to box, so I got talking to his mum afterwards as I said I'd really like another look at him. She was asking who the coaches were at Wolves, and said he was going to train at Villa because Aaron was there, but was a very different player to his brother.

'Long story short, I ended up putting my report in, we signed him, and the rest is history!'

Lescott did actually come away from the academy for a time as he wanted to return to playing schools football back in Birmingham, but he was later spotted turning out for Derby at under-16 level in a fixture played at Wolverhampton Grammar School.

Fortunately for Wolves, academy director Chris Evans had been astute enough to keep Lescott's registration when he decided to step back, and so ensured he was brought back into the Molineux set-up, and was handed a full-time scholarship.

'And that's the story of how I scouted my first scholar,' says Green. 'I was chuffed, as you can imagine. It came very early in the process, when I was learning the trade, and learning about players.

'But I always remember something one of the coaches Rob Kelly said to me. He gave me really good direction, and said if I scouted two players in a season, and both were taken on, then that was a very good return.

'There were sometimes scouts who would recommend eight or nine over a season but for me I think reputations were built on the quality of player, and if you became known for that, if you sent in one or two you knew there was a very good chance they would be signed.'

It was the start of a fantastic career for Lescott at Molineux. He made 235 appearances, scoring 13 goals from the centre of defence, and was one of the key figures in the 2002/03 play-off-winning season, landing the Player of the Year award which he won again two years later, having unfortunately missed the entire Premier League season in between through injury.

Eventually, with a gentlemen's agreement in place which came into force if Wolves didn't return to the Premier League, Lescott was sold for a total fee of £5m, joining Everton in the summer of 2006. Big money, and all profit for the club, given how he had been recruited and emerged through the academy.

He went on to join Manchester City, twice winning the Premier League along with an FA Cup and League Cup, as well as securing 26 senior England caps, scoring against France in the European Championships in 2012.

An incredible journey, and one which began thanks to the hard work and diligence of a scout, who was also in the right place at the right time. As so often needs to be the case.

And which has been the case so often with a plethora of young talent to have progressed through to the first team during Wolves' 150-year history. Or some, such as Ryan Green and Johnny Gorman, who made it to senior international status with Wales and Northern Ireland respectively, even before making their senior Wolves debuts.

At most clubs, supporters love and cherish a young and homegrown player. It feels that much more special to support 'one of our own'. In an era of expectant and hungry fanbases, they are probably allowed more leeway, more time and space to make mistakes.

Lescott is one of the many, indeed one of the most successful, to have made the grade during a period over the last three decades which has, at different times, proved a golden era for the youth and academy programme at Wolves.

Mateus Mané, in the 2025/26 season, remains the most striking example of that, whilst 16-year-old Jerome Abbey, in coming off the bench for the final game of the season at Burnley, became the club's youngest-ever Premier League player, and second-youngest in the club's history.

Going back to the start of that history, many among the club's youngest-ever talents were given their chance long before the development of any sort of structured youth programmes or training schemes and academies which have become the norm today.

The youngest ever, although one not included within the official records as such as he only featured in wartime football, is inside-forward Cameron Buchanan, who was born in Holytown in Scotland.

Of 18 appearances made for Wolves during the Second World War, his first, against West Bromwich Albion in September 1942, came at the tender age of 14 years and 57 days.

Head further back meanwhile, to October 1885, and striker Harry Wood, at 17 years and four months, made his debut in a 7-0 win against Derby St Luke's.

Whilst Alan Steen, who made his debut in March 1939 prior to league football being suspended due to the war seven months later, was a mere 16 years and eight months old, making him the club's third-youngest player at the time of writing.

Abbey, 12 days younger than Steen, is the club's second-youngest as mentioned, but the player still holding the record as the youngest ever is a Wolves legend whose contribution will forever be etched in Molineux folklore.

Outside-left Jimmy Mullen made 486 appearances in Wolves' colours between 1939 and 1959, putting him at tenth in the club's all-time appearance list. Born in Newcastle, he arrived at the club as a trainee, and made his debut, aged 16 years and 43 days old, in a 4-1 win over Leeds United in February of 1939.

Indeed, for Steen's debut, against Manchester United, it was he and Mullen on opposite flanks, both still just sweet 16, as Wolves won 3-0 at Molineux. Incredibly, Steen was among the goalscorers, along with Dicky Dorsett, also then a teenager, and Tom Galley. It was Mullen who laid on Steen's goal.

It was something of a makeshift Wolves team that afternoon as several first team regulars had been rested ahead of the FA Cup semi-final the following weekend.

The Wolves careers of Steen and Mullen certainly moved in very different directions after that Molineux afternoon.

It was to prove Steen's only first team appearance for Wolves, and the arrival of the Second World War saw him serve as a wireless operator with the Bomber Command. Unfortunately, his plane was later shot down over Germany and he spent the last two years of hostilities as a prisoner of war, thankfully being released and later continuing his football career with Luton, Aldershot, Rochdale and Carlisle.

Mullen, however, went on to become one of Wolves' greats. He featured in that FA Cup semi-final the following week, as Wolves beat Grimsby 5-0 in front of what is still a record Old Trafford attendance of 76,962. He wasn't selected for the final, a surprising 4-1 defeat against Portsmouth, but he did pick up a winners' medal a decade later, as Wolves beat Leicester 3-1.

That was the prelude to the magical days of the fifties, when Wolves won their only three top-flight titles to date, and Mullen was involved in all three of them. He also won 12 caps for England, was his country's first ever substitute in replacing Jackie Milburn against Belgium in 1950, and was in the squads for both the 1950 and 1954 World Cups, scoring against Switzerland in the latter. That was one of his six goals he scored for England, on top of the 112 he notched in club colours for Wolves.

Mullen, who represented England at schoolboy level, had arrived at Wolves as a young player at just 14, choosing the club instead of Newcastle back home, to become one of many young players who initially thrived under the management of Major Frank Buckley.

The Major, who hailed from Manchester, was a formidable character, who had fought for his country with the 17th Middlesex Regiment during the First World War, earning the rank of major, a title which then followed him into the management career which followed his playing days prior to the war.

As a boss, he was regarded as one of football's toughest authoritarians, famed for his own particular brand of hairdryer treatment long before Sir Alex Ferguson was dishing out a similar brand of discipline in his hugely successful years in Manchester over half a century later.

Players feared the Major, but that hugely demanding personality was balanced, as with one of his illustrious successors Stan Cullis, by a drive to make young players better, to give them the best chance of forging a successful career.

In the early 1930s, a trio of young players in Joe Gardiner, Cullis and Galley arrived almost unnoticed. But they were to have an enormous impact on the club in the decades to follow.

Buckley took Wolves to the brink of success, finishing runners-up in the league in both 1937/38 and 1938/39, as well as that FA Cup Final defeat in 1939. So, he never quite managed to bring a trophy back to Wolverhampton.

What he did do was help prepare the club for the successes which were to come, in part, by showing what could be achieved by bringing in, and blooding, young players.

Not only did he sign so many who went on to play key roles at the club, he also looked at the infrastructure underpinning that mindset, purchasing a hostel in the town for his team's young players, with recreational and medical facilities. It was almost a forerunner to modern day academies, whilst in another trait later employed by Sir Alex, he employed 'spies' who would keep an eye on youth players in terms of potentially breaking curfews or frequenting the local pubs and clubs.

'Buckley's Babes' never quite received the same adulation as the 'Busby Babes' who flourished under Sir Matt at Manchester United, but he was certainly revered as a manager, talked of in the same breath as the all-conquering multi-league winner at Arsenal and Huddersfield, Herbert Chapman.

In Billy Wright, the Major made one acquisition which would go on to reshape the club and leave a legacy that remained unmatched to the present day. Initially the manager didn't think this young Ironbridge schoolboy would make the grade when he arrived on the groundstaff, effectively for a trial, at 14. He felt that Wright was too small.

Fortunately, he eventually reconsidered, and the young man who helped pack the team's kit as they headed to Wembley for the 1939 FA Cup Final, would end up becoming one of Wolves' and England's most famous footballing names.

Making 541 appearances, leading Wolves to their three league titles and the 1949 FA Cup, and becoming the first international player to win 100 caps for their country – Wright would eventually amass 105 for England of which 90 were as captain – there has never been a youth 'graduate' that has made the same impact since!

But in keeping alive the need for good young players, perhaps almost 'paying it forward' given the opportunity he was given at Molineux, Wright also ensured those following in his footsteps were given as much support as possible.

'I was Billy's boot boy, and he was great with me,' winger Terry Wharton once reflected of the legend who he held in such high esteem.

'He told me later on that when he became Arsenal manager, he put a bid in for me, but Stan [Cullis] wouldn't let me go.

'He also once asked me to go along to Walsall Town Hall and judge a beauty contest with him for which he gave me half a lager and a bunch of flowers to take home – he was a smashing chap, was Bill.'

There were other 'homegrown' players to have an extraordinary impact for club and country around the same time as Wright and then later on.

That's a route that included those who came through at Wath Wanderers under the guidance of Crook.

Wath-on-Dearne is a small town in South Yorkshire, situated about five miles north of Rotherham and almost midway between Barnsley and Doncaster, and it was here, under the guidance of Major Buckley and Cullis, that what must be seen as one of football's earliest YTS equivalent schemes was born.

Crook, an outside-right in his playing days who appeared in the same Wolves team as Cullis, which was managed by Buckley, had decided to set up the nursery club after hanging up his boots, to help Wolves attract talent not just from Yorkshire but further up the country in the North East as well.

In later years the likes of Gerry Taylor, Bob Hatton, Steve Daley and Alan Sunderland were among key personnel whose youth careers saw them develop at Wath and move to Wolves.

But in the early days of the nursery club, the two star names who effectively joined Wolves as young players were Ron Flowers and Roy Swinbourne.

Flowers was a huge influence on all three Wolves league titles of the fifties, whilst Swinbourne notched 24 goals to help Wolves to the first of those titles, and remains one of the Honved heroes after his brace helped down the Hungarian giants in one of the famous floodlit friendlies.

Such was Mark Crook's influence on Wolves that, only very recently, authors Ashley Ball and Chris Brook teamed up to put together an extensive book – *Feeding the Wolves* – chronicling his impact and legacy in terms of the young players he developed for the team.

'I think Mark's achievements had been one of football's great untold stories, and it's clear to me that he was utterly devoted to Wolves,' says Ball. 'His idea to supply Wolves with players from a hotbed of football almost 100 miles away was ahead of its time and incredibly successful.

'A Wolves team without Ron Flowers in it would not have enjoyed the incredible success they did and that was all down to Mark. Even into his 70s, he wanted to ensure the best talent from a football hotbed like South Yorkshire went the way of Wolves.'

There is an incredible stat, that from the 1938/39 season when Crook set up the nursery club, to 1978/79, there was only one season when no one who had emerged from Wath Wanderers appeared in the Wolves first team. A phenomenal achievement.

Moving on from there, and Wolves' last two major trophy successes, Cannock schoolboy Geoff Palmer was a double League Cup winner in 1974 and 1980 having joined the club as an apprentice, and Mel Eves, brought up in the Red Lion in Wednesfield and educated at Wolverhampton Grammar School, joined him in the 1980 line-up.

Even if Wolves haven't repeated those heroics of a major honour in the many years that have elapsed since, there have been many individual stories of players who developed through the youth ranks with substantial success.

Lescott was joined by keeper Matt Murray and defender Lee Naylor in a team otherwise packed with experience which so spectacularly won the 2003 play-off final and took Wolves into the Premier League for the very first time.

Others such as Keith Andrews and Adam Proudlock were also in and around that squad, following on from defender Jamie Smith who had made nearly 100 first team appearances in the 1990s after coming through the system.

Whilst Mick McCarthy's young and hungry brigade won promotion largely through bringing those players in at low cost, goalkeepers Wayne Hennessey and Carl Ikeme also came through the academy route, which also proved pivotal for the League One rebuild under Kenny Jackett, spearheaded by Brierley Hill-born Danny Batth.

But perhaps the biggest trio across the last three decades in terms of overall impact have comprised Robbie Keane in the late nineties, Morgan Gibbs-White more recently, and Mateus Mané in 2025/26.

Three very different stories, and very different journeys in being scouted, but all have gone on to make an impact at the very top, with Mané hoping there is much more to come.

The Keane story is up there with the very best.

Thanks in part to the brilliance of Irish scouts such as Willie Byrne and Eddie Corcoran, Wolves had so much success in bringing across young Irish talent, of which Keane was very much a shining light.

It was Corcoran who first spotted the potential of Keane, who had turned out for local club Fettercairn and then Crumlin United as a youngster, and academy director Chris Evans and coach Robert Kelly went out to visit him at the family home on a council estate in Tallaght in Dublin.

Liverpool, Leeds, Nottingham Forest and West Ham were amongst others pursuing the striker's signature. But Evans' pursuit was relentless. He got his man.

'I probably had five or six trials in total, a fair few different clubs, but Wolves is the one where I instantly felt at home,' Keane recalls. 'They were in the Championship, and I didn't know a great deal about them to be honest.

'For some reason I had just assumed the stadium wouldn't be great, maybe because they weren't in the Premier League, but as soon as I came over, I was just blown away.

'The colours in the stadium, the training ground, how everyone made me feel like it was home, and they wanted me to come over and start as soon as I could.

'Chris was a massive part of it, him and Rob Kelly, they both came over to meet the family and that little attention to detail made such a difference.

'How good they were with my family, coming over to sit and talk to them – nobody else did that.'

And so, four days before his 16th birthday, Keane was on a plane heading across the Irish Sea in the first chapter of the pursuit of his dream.

Little over a year later, after a goal-laden season at youth level, and impressing whilst training with the first team during pre-season, Keane started the season in the Championship at Norwich, promptly helping himself to two excellent goals in a 2-0 win.

His parents Anne and Robert had been flown over by Evans to enjoy the game, making for an emotional afternoon at Carrow Road.

'The number 8 jersey, wearing Adidas Copa boots, a sunny day, roasting actually, like it always should be on opening day,' Keane recalls. 'I kind of had a feeling I would score, genuinely.

'I had been on pre-season in Scotland with the first team and felt comfortable in that environment and had been progressing every day in training.

'I'd had a year in the youth team where every time I scored a goal – and I scored a lot – I was given £20 to spend at McDonald's because I needed to build myself up.

'I got broader and I really filled out, and while I was still a kid, and still quite skinny, I was able to play at a level where people bigger than me couldn't just push me over.

'So, from the day I reported back, I wanted to be in that first team for the opening game.'

Mark McGhee was the manager who first gave Keane his chance in the team, at that still tender age of 17.

But he brushes aside any praise and plays down any suggestion of it being a brilliant tactical decision, insisting that there was literally no alternative.

'As soon as I saw him training, it wasn't even a question if he should play or not, he was ready,' says McGhee. 'I had gone over to watch the youth team train and was chatting to Chris Turner about him – straightaway I wanted him to train with us and the first team.

'I couldn't quite believe his ability – he was already one of our best players – because when people tried to tackle him, he just moved the ball away and was gone.

'Very quickly we made sure he was on a proper contract, I think that ended up being improved fairly regularly, and I had no doubt about putting him in the team at Norwich.

'My son Ben still talks about that day even now. He was sitting behind Robbie's parents, and remembers them crying because of all the emotion as he scored his two goals. It was a very special day.'

It was also a special day, and also a memorable 2-0 away win for Wolves in the FA Cup, which greeted Gibbs-White's arrival in the first team, at Stoke in early 2017.

Just like McGhee, his fellow Scot Paul Lambert had watched Gibbs-White in training and was convinced he had both the game and the temperament to go in early.

Twenty days shy of his 17th birthday, Gibbs-White became the first player born in the 2000s to represent Wolves at first team level, and at the time he was the fifth-youngest in the club's history.

His emergence was very different to that of Keane. Gibbs-White had been at Wolves since the age of eight, having been scouted by Brian Punter, who saw him playing in a tournament for Stafford Town Juniors Under-10s.

Punter, who played reserve team football for Wolves and featured in an FA Youth Cup Final before forging a career with Lincoln City, has long remembered his initial scouting report, which highlighted Gibbs-White's excellent heading ability alongside his other attributes.

He says: 'I've still got my report from that day – 28 September 2008 – where Morgan was playing in a tournament at Penkridge.

'The thing that stood out for me, which is strange given he doesn't need to use it so much now, was his heading.

'Obviously it wasn't 11-a-side football at that age, but Morgan was dominating the games, and I was surprised that no one else had picked him up previously.

'I remember speaking to his dad [Kirk], who was very pleased that Wolves were interested, and he was actually one of the last players I recommended as I finished scouting not long after. I then had to take him on his first day to introduce him to the coaches which is what used to happen when you were a scout.

'It's nice to think I maybe played a little part in helping start him off and it has been great to see his career continues to progress.'

Gibbs-White went on to be part of the England Under-17 team which won the World Cup in 2017, scoring in the 5-2 win in the final against Spain as part of a group including Phil Foden, Marc Guehi, Jadon Sancho and Callum Hudson-Odoi.

Having been given his bow by Lambert, and then utilised by Nuno Espirito Santo, Gibbs-White, like Keane, actually had to leave Wolves to achieve more greatness, with 58 of his 88 appearances coming from the bench.

Since then, he has gone on to flourish both in the Premier League with Nottingham Forest and also with England at senior level, having also been part of the squad who won the European Under-21 Championship in 2023.

The most recent example of young stardust to grace the first team at Wolves is Mateus Mané, who joined the academy from Rochdale as a 16-year-old in February of 2024, making his debut as a 17-year-old just over 12 months later.

And then, in a dismal 2025/26 campaign for Wolves as a club, Mané's progress as an individual in chalking up 27 further

Premier League appearances, and scoring three goals, was a rare shining light.

Mané actually spent the first eight years of his life growing up in Barreiro, a small city on the opposite side of the River Tagus from Lisbon, with the local team Barreirense the first he ever played for.

The family then moved to Manchester, where the football journey continued with Manchester Cobras and the Bee Inspired Football Academy, before being recruited by Rochdale, and then Wolves.

'When I first came to Wolves I thought, "Yeah, this is the place,"' he reveals. 'I spoke to my mum and dad about it, and it just felt like home, with the players and the staff.

'The first day I came in, the players welcomed me and were talking to me like I'd been here all my life. The staff welcomed me too, and have always made sure I have everything I need.'

So many different academy graduates, so many different routes into football, and to Molineux.

But one thing that has always endured is the skill, the persistence, the determination of those who have represented the club's scouting team down the years, in trying to spot those diamonds in the rough, those players who will go on to help the team, perhaps bring in a lucrative transfer fee, or both.

There are so many scouts, both full-time, part-time and even volunteers, to whom that description applies.

Green, who spotted Lescott all those years ago, spent 23 years working full-time for the academy, and his close colleague, Bob Bennett, 21 years.

Just like the players they have identified, their own backgrounds, and support of Wolves, is also very different.

Bennett was brought up in the Rough Hills area of Wolverhampton and counts Hughie McIlmoyle as his early Wolves hero, having himself been a promising striker who was with Walsall as a youngster before going on to play at a high level of non-league.

When he moved to Codsall with wife Lynne in 1986, a chance meeting with then Wolves defender Mark Venus saw the two start running a Sunday League team.

From there he coached the Bilbrook Juniors team in which his son Steven was playing, and later Willenhall Town Youths, before his footballing pedigree and coaching nous attracted the attention of Green and Wolves via another scout in Tony Parkes.

'It was a time when we were getting scouts in, they were learning the trade, and then six months later they were buggering off to other clubs,' says Green.

'I remember saying we needed more scouts who were Wolves fans, people who would be proud to wear the Wolves shirt and tie and do it for the love of Wolves, just like I did.'

That's a sign that Green's journey into following the gold and black has been a very different one.

Born in Ilford in 1938, when his father, a West Ham supporter, returned after serving in the Second World War, he started taking him to games at Upton Park.

Then, in a decision which would ultimately change Green's life, a year after Charlton had won the FA Cup, his dad decided to take in a game between the Addicks and Wolves at The Valley.

'And from there onwards, I was totally in love,' says Green. 'It was a nice warm night, with those wonderful old gold shirts, with players like Billy Wright, Bert Williams and Jimmy Mullen, and I was just blown away – my eyes were sticking out!

'The colours of teams in London at that time were a mix of navy and white, red and white, blue and white, but then you had these old gold shirts, with the black collars and little white buttons.

'I always remember that it had been a warm night and those shirts were heavy so you could tell as they walked off the pitch at half-time who had worked the hardest by the amount of sweat on them. It's probably no surprise that Billy Wright had the biggest sweat patch!

'So, at the age of 11, I decided I was going to be a Wolves supporter, which didn't really help my dad, who said I should be supporting my local team.

'But I was always a precocious devil as a kid – I'd already been to a few West Ham games on my own, on the old trolleybuses, when I'd get there early enough to make sure I could stand at the front and see the game.

'I started getting to Wolves games in London whenever I could, and then when I was old enough, to Molineux.

'I remember it vividly, my first trip to the "Mecca". It was 1955, I was 16, and I came and saw us beat Arsenal 3-1.

'As soon as I came to Wolves, I just felt like I got on with the people, walking through the town, it was about the people as well as the football, and I started getting to as many home games as I could.'

Green had to complete two years of national service in Dortmund, during which he met another Wolves fan, one of the cooks Vic Appleby, who hailed from Heath Town.

Once both were demobbed, Green would sometimes come up and stay with Appleby and his family when attending games, but eventually decided that it wasn't quite enough. And so, in 1967, he managed to engineer – excuse the pun – a transfer up to Wolverhampton, and uprooted with his wife and two children, to Bilbrook.

At one time he went seven years without missing a game home or away, and although being a keen runner meant he often had to miss games to compete, he has never been too far away from Molineux, including having a season ticket for many years with partner Jill.

After retiring in 1991, he was 'minding his own business' watching Paget Rangers when Alan Parsons, a legend with non-league Boldmere St Michaels, started chatting, introduced him to Wolves' chief scout Ron Jukes, who then invited him to come and work for him and his assistant, Painter.

From there, it all started with a trip to Radcliffe Borough to Old Wulfrunians, scouting Lescott, and then so many more.

For both Green and Bennett, it became a labour of love for a combined total not far shy of half a century. So many miles of travelling, ridiculously long hours, standing on the side of open pitches with little to no protection from the elements, for scant monetary recompense, certainly when compared to some of the riches on offer throughout the rest of the sport.

Their job satisfaction? That comes via their colleagues, part of the team at Wolves in which they worked in such a thriving set-up involving the likes of Evans, Tony Lacey, Glyn Harding, Nick Loftus, and other scouts – there is always the danger of missing people out – such as Geoff Blackwell, Colin Eaton, Morris Baker and Jeff Gregory.

It comes through seeing players make the grade to the benefit of Wolves, the club they support, but just as much to do so elsewhere, to build a career in the game even if not at Molineux.

It comes through being able to keep in touch with those players, because so many of them do, recognising the impact and contribution that the likes of Green, Bennett and others played in their lives. Of seeing them grow and develop, start families of their own, move into coaching.

It comes through the little gestures, which ultimately mean so much more. Of Lescott, presenting Green with a match shirt at the end of his first season in professional football, even better being one of the 'old gold' versions from 2000/01. Or of Gibbs-White, even though he hadn't actually been initially spotted by Bennett, recognising the substantial impact he had on his overall development, seeking him out at a Wolves end of season dinner a few years later to say thank you.

Thoughtful gestures from good characters, good personalities, which is probably half the reason they were recruited in the first place.

'Talent is obviously important but you are also looking closely at mentality,' says Bennett.

'When you are watching a young player, mentality is a quality that some of them don't even know that they have.

'You watch them, and you can see it, how they carry themselves, how they respond to adversity, because when it comes to that side of the game some players will sink and some will swim.

'There's one of the sayings that I had – the best ships rise in the ocean – and those are the players who, when they get into the group, go on and progress and get better.'

'Professional football is one of the toughest professions you can have,' adds Green. 'Not just for the pressure but even within your own dressing room – the banter, it might even be called bullying. Mentality is so important.

'I remember watching Matt Murray when he was 14, and in the first half of a game he made a couple of mistakes, and they went in 2-0 down. He came out in the second half, had an absolute blinder, and they won.

'Straightaway I remember thinking he had character, 100 per cent character, to respond like he did at that age, and that was proved over the years.

'If you haven't got that mentality, however much talent you've got, you haven't got a chance. You can be whatever you like off the pitch, but as soon as you step on, you need that mentality, that's part of your job.'

Amid the way football has changed in recent times, and the way Wolves itself has changed, with a more globally focused ownership, many years in the Premier League, and a different outlook on young players, it has become harder and harder for talent from the youth ranks to break through.

Recruitment has also changed in terms of a greater reliance on data and analysis, but as any self-respecting scout will tell you, those tools are best used alongside the 'eye test', what you see in a player, and their character and mentality.

Over 150 years of Wolves' history, the many scouts who have patrolled touchlines, scoured fixtures of all natures and in all weathers, and diligently spent hour upon hour filing reports, have produced so many fantastic players who have gone on to grace the first team.

And for fans, for whom those stories usually land the best, long may that continue.

Chapter 6

Sounds – and Shoes – of the Seventies

THE SMART streets which form the city of Turin, rich in culture and history, are generously stocked with museums, libraries, art galleries, churches, opera houses, piazzas – the list goes on.

For young Wolves hopefuls Steve Daley and Alan Sunderland, nearly 1,000 miles from home, those were the sights which greeted them as they took a stroll around the shops of the Italian hotspot back in March of 1972.

Daley and Sunderland were both just 18, having been scouted by the legendary Mark Crook from Wolves' nursery club Wath Wanderers in Yorkshire, their footballing dreams still fledgling as they set off on the long and winding road towards a career in the game.

In contrast, they were accompanied on their shopping trip by a figure and personality who was very much at the other end of the scale when it came to profile and experience: Leeds United, Juventus and Wales legend John Charles.

In something of a masterstroke, Wolves manager Bill McGarry had asked Charles, then 41, to accompany his squad as they embarked on the first leg of their 'Italian job', the quarter-finals of the first-ever UEFA Cup back in the 1971/72 season.

A fourth-placed finish the previous season had secured a tilt at European football, following on from appearing in the Anglo-Italian Cup, and winning the Texaco Cup.

Knowing the scale of the task ahead against one of the giants of not just Italian football but across the entire continent, McGarry had taken Charles to try and negate that hostile atmosphere. The theory was that the esteem in which the Juventus fans still held the undisputed legend would take up much of their attention, and reduce the level of vitriol they directed at Wolves.

It worked. Not just on the pitch, in training and the game, but off it as well. To the benefit of the club's two young wide-eyed shoppers!

'We were walking around Turin with "Charlo", and everywhere we went, people would just stop and start clapping their hands,' Daley recalls. 'And that certainly wasn't for me and Sunny!

'We were walking past a shoe shop and Alan asked John if we could pop in as he wanted to buy a pair of shoes. I ended up going in for a pair as well, and as we both went up to pay, the shop assistant said, "No, no, if you are with Charlo, you don't pay."

'So, we didn't. And as we left the shop, I turned to Charlo and said, "Eh John, I was thinking of getting a nice new suit as well!"'

Daley at his finest.

Anyway, when the game eventually came around Wolves drew 1-1 with Juventus, and it was Italian midfielder and future England boss Fabio Capello who was the one putting his foot in it. The hosts were sufficiently riled that Capello spat in the direction of goalkeeper Phil Parkes after he had collected a back pass from Gerry Taylor. Charles said many of the Italians wouldn't fancy the second leg after only drawing at home, and he was right. Parkes was particularly keen to welcome Capello back to his home turf and the return at Molineux. But Capello was, perhaps unsurprisingly, among the many absentees. Wolves won the second leg 2-1 in front of over 40,000 on another special Molineux night. The semi-finals beckoned – and much more besides.

That Wolves team of the seventies are still so fondly remembered and revered. They still remember those precious days so regularly between themselves.

Fast-forward some 54 years from Turin to a small enclave of the Fox pub in Shipley on the A449, more commonly known as the Bridgnorth Road, linking Wolves to the much-loved picturesque Shropshire town.

Run by well-known charity fundraiser and general top bloke Neil Taylor, the framed shirts on the wall of the pub are just another indicator of the support for Wolves which permeates the entire establishment.

A group of former Wolves players from that era are meeting for one of their regular social lunches, sharing updates, and memories, over a bite to eat and a tipple of choice.

All former players are welcome. No matter what their contribution, how many appearances, clean sheets or goals they amassed. Whether or not they won any medals. It's driven mainly by those players from the seventies, many of whom have stayed so close and in contact long since hanging up their respective boots.

At this particular gathering, at the end of the 2025/26 season, Gerry Farrell, a Liverpudlian who came through at Wolves as an apprentice but would only ever play youth or reserve team football for the club, is talking about former boss Bill McGarry. Farrell is waxing lyrical about how McGarry made it clear on his first day that he was in charge, not just of the players but also even the directors as well!

Elsewhere there is discussion between the midfield triumvirate of Daley, Willie Carr and Kenny Hibbitt about their days together in the engine room – and who scored the most goals.

When Daley throws one or two gentle brickbats in Hibbitt's direction about his 'mishit' strike in the 1974 FA Cup Final, an answer comes like a shot from elsewhere on the table: 'At least he was on the pitch!'

The banter never stops. And nor should it. Neither does the strong sense of camaraderie and companionship.

The continuing success of former players getting together is due largely to the work of the Wolves Former Players' Association (WFPA), led by chairman John Richards and vice-chairman Daley, with the support of administration manager Richard Green and a committee featuring other former players Geoff Palmer, Phil Parkes and Mel Eves.

It was back in 1988 that the organisation was formed, initially as a result of the passing of one of their own, legendary outside-left Jimmy Mullen, still the youngest ever to have represented Wolves in a competitive first team fixture.

Mullen was just 16 years, one month and 12 days old when making his debut against Leeds in 1939, the first of 486 appearances he would make for the club, during which he plundered 112 goals.

Mullen, who would later run a sports shop in Wolverhampton, passed away in October 1987 at the age of 64, and it was at his funeral that his former team-mates decided that only meeting up in such circumstances was not sufficient given how many experiences they had shared together at Molineux.

They met at the Express & Star Sports Club in Danescourt Road in Tettenhall, and the Wolves Former Players' Association was formed with the aim of meeting far more regularly for social occasions, not just through sad and difficult times at funerals, but in happier circumstances, or for the odd round of golf.

The guest list that night featured a who's who of Wolves legends from the 1950s.

The new president was to be Stan Cullis, the club's greatest-ever manager. The chairman? Billy Wright, the club's most successful player and first man in international football to chalk up 100 caps for his country.

Treasurer was Malcolm Finlayson, double league champion goalkeeper and later chairman of the FPA, whilst others in attendance included the legendary Ron Flowers, stalwart of all three of Wolves' league titles, Dennis Wilshaw, the only man to score four goals in an England/Scotland international, and Bill Slater, another who was a part of all three of Wolves' titles.

An incredible line-up, to reflect an incredible era. One which those legends were keen to continue, via their stories and their memories.

Holding the organisation together for so many years as secretary was Peter Creed, advertisement director at the *Express & Star* and lifelong Wolves fan, who earned the trust of those legends and would both back them and protect them through many post-playing challenges.

Later, Wolves' head of marketing and communications Matt Grayson worked closely with Creed and then also Green, former commercial director at the *Express & Star*, to ease a smooth transition and handover.

'The nature of football is that fans often have special attachments to particular periods of a club's history,' says Grayson. 'More often than not it's the first teams they watched as youngsters, which for Peter, was undoubtedly the title-winning teams of the 1950s.

'Over the years, he did a wonderful job of supporting the WFPA, as well as playing a key role in a number of testimonials for former players. As the balance of the WFPA naturally shifted towards players of the 1970s onwards, Peter knew it was time to hand over the reins.

'Enter Richard Green, former commercial director and ex-colleague of Peter's at the *Express & Star*. I first got to know Richard when we were looking for a printer for our matchday programme and he was running the printing operation for the *Express & Star*.

'A lifelong Wolves fan, he shared Peter's passion for the club, along with a vision of how the WFPA could move on to the next level.

'We both wanted to see the WFPA's independence retained whilst bringing them closer to the club and to integrate the WFPA into the Wolves Foundation as much as possible, especially given the Foundation had secured charitable status for the first time.

'Richard made a point of visiting other former players' associations, such as Everton and Aston Villa, to gather best practice and swap notes. Others from Wolves, including programme editor and club historian John Hendley, were also central in developing the plans.

'Richard and the WFPA subsequently played a key role in supporting the Wolves Museum, the Hall of Fame induction events and many Wolves Foundation activities.

'Notable events included the 1960 cup final anniversary celebration which included players from both Wolves and Blackburn Rovers. And, on a sadder note, the funeral of Sir Jack Hayward.

'I've always felt that a good benchmark of a great club is how they treat and respect former players. It's been great to watch on from afar as the WFPA has gone from strength to strength.'

The gentle reshaping and reorganisation then paved the way for club legend Richards, another who enjoyed a successful career in business after finishing his playing career, to come in and give the FPA fresh impetus and profile.

When another of Wolves' list of inspirational captains, Mike Bailey, had to step down as chairman due to ill health, Richards took on the role, with Daley becoming vice-chair.

One of Daley's main responsibilities is to lead the Annual Golf Day, held every September at the Oxley Park course where the likes of McGarry, Flowers and many more used to enjoy a round back in the day, raising thousands of pounds which are then distributed to specific projects being delivered by local charities.

So, community, supporting good causes, is very much a motivator and a touchpoint for the FPA.

But it is now about so much more than that. The social lunches at the Fox are a key part of keeping players engaged and connected, as well as keeping a caring and watchful eye on anyone suffering with their health or in danger of drifting away from the group. Former Wolves defender Neil Masters, whose career at Wolves was painfully limited due to injuries, and has since gone on record about challenges faced with his mental health since his playing days ended, popped along with Robbie Dennison and Andy Mutch during a visit from his home in Norway and was visibly lifted by the experience.

It's not just about the former players themselves. On the day of this particular lunch at the Fox, a group of wives, partners and widows are enjoying a 'social' of their own, a tour of Molineux and spot of afternoon tea in the Chairman's Suite.

The FPA is also far closer to Wolves as a club now. As owners, Sir Jack Hayward and Steve Morgan were particularly keen to celebrate Wolves' heroes of yesteryear – the latter bringing in the Hall of Fame and Wolves Museum during his tenure – and with Richards also being a club vice-president and attending all home games with wife Pam, current relationships are strong.

One of the key motivations now is the overall health and wellbeing of the former players. With more and more players across the country now being diagnosed with dementia and CTE (chronic traumatic encephalopathy), their welfare and access to care is becoming more and more of an issue as time goes by. Richards, along with Daley and Green, have remained in close contact with all the different groups and organisations who are either seeking help for former players or aiming to provide it, including the Premier League, PFA, and 'Football Families for Justice', set up by John Stiles, son of World Cup winner Nobby, who suffered from advanced dementia before his death in 2020.

The FPA have also set up a link with Nuffield Health, the UK's leading healthcare charity, to provide advice and support to former players, along with other partnerships with key charities including Wolves Foundation, the Grand Theatre and Compton Care.

'Our ethos is to offer support and guidance to former players and their families, and to continue to provide opportunities for social interaction between all of our former players,' says Richards.

'We're fortunate to have a very active and enthusiastic committee of former Wolves players who organise all of our social and fundraising events, and who are totally committed to helping their former colleagues in whatever way they can.

'We want to help these former players and their families, and ensure that they can find the right services which can make their lives just that little bit easier, as well as providing support in other areas for any former Wolves player who might be going through difficult times.'

Sadly, as time goes on, the need for that help increases. Parkes, always such a popular figure amongst his former team-mates and supporters alike, suffered a life-changing accident in the first half of 2025 that has left him needing plenty of support. That support, befitting the man and the esteem in which he is held, has always been there.

Fans love him, just as they do so many from that era, and it is fitting that the group from the seventies remain so close and equally still so popular amongst supporters.

Because they are the group who last won a major trophy with the club, the 1974 and 1980 League Cups, as well as a sixth-place finish in 1979/80 which remains Wolves' best for the last four and a half decades. Only Nuno's team, with successive seventh-place finishes, have come close. Those days out for the cup finals, those experiences at Wembley. As a fan, that's what it's all about.

The crowds back then were also phenomenal. A total of 97,886 as Wolves beat Manchester City 2-1 in 1974, and 96,527 for Nottingham Forest, a 1-0 victory, in 1980.

Wolves, under McGarry in '74 and John Barnwell in '80, were underdogs in both. Palmer is one of four Wolves players who featured in both games and became League Cup double winners, alongside Richards, Hibbitt and Derek Parkin.

He was just 19 for the City game, and can still vividly remember looking across at the opposition in the tunnel before walking out.

'I had a glance across and there was Colin Bell, Mike Summerbee, Franny Lee, Rodney Marsh, Denis Law … it was just another Saturday afternoon game for them,' he says.

'They were just knocking the ball about and talking, they were used to it. I was 19 and there were a few butterflies knocking around. But as soon as I got out there, they disappeared, and I just got on with the match.'

Hibbitt, who with a transfer fee of just £5,000 from Bradford Park Avenue is up there as one of the greatest value-for-money signings Wolves have ever made, opened the scoring just before half-time.

'I can still remember the moment, and how the ball took the three stripes off the side of my boot and kind of lobbed into the net,' he recalls. 'What a feeling – I thought I was going to wake up from my dream!

'I remember my mum telling me she barely watched the second half as she was looking at my name in lights on the scoreboard. My dad was such an influence on both myself and my brother Terry's careers but he sadly passed away before getting the chance to see us play professionally.

'He was very much in our thoughts that day and my mum was just thinking how proud he would be. She had tears in her eyes throughout the second half.'

After Hibbitt's opener, Bell equalised for City in the second half but, on an afternoon when 'stand-in' Wolves goalkeeper Gary Pierce delivered an incredible performance on his 21st birthday,

Richards was perfectly placed to pounce on a deflected cross to fire home an 85th-minute winner.

'I've scored better goals and important goals in semi-finals and league matches but this is still the one everyone wants to talk about, all these years on,' says Richards.

'It was one of those moments you dream about as a school kid when you're playing in the playground, and no one will ever be able to take that moment away from me. It's never forgotten and will never be forgotten for a lot of Wolves supporters from that generation.'

Some six years later, it was Nottingham Forest – reigning European champions managed by the legendary Brian Clough who would retain the trophy at the end of the season – and also going for their third successive League Cup, who stood between Wolves and more history.

Wolves needed to find a repellent to the Forest fire, and they found it, thanks to a tactical masterstroke devised by Barnwell and his assistant Richie Barker. Midfielder Peter Daniel was detailed to take up a position on the right-hand side of midfield, with a particular brief on curtailing the attacking impact of left-wing talisman John Robertson.

That gave added protection for Palmer at right-back, and also allowed him to contribute defensively elsewhere on the pitch.

Modern TV pundits would have had a field day dissecting the tactical masterplan, which ensured Wolves kept things right, and were then able to fully profit from Andy Gray's tap-in midway through the second half following a mix-up between Forest keeper Peter Shilton and defender David Needham.

'We were the underdogs again because of Forest's record in the competition, but we were doing well in the league,' says Richards. 'The build-up to the match was completely different to 1974 and was far more low-key, treated just like another league game.

'Before the 1974 final we went away to London for a few days to prepare. I remember we went to a show on the Thursday night and stayed down for a big banquet after the match.

'Chairman John Ireland had organised a celebration event regardless of the result, at the Hilton Hotel in Park Lane, who displayed a large stunning ice sculpture of a wolf on the top table.

'But [manager] John Barnwell and [assistant manager] Richie Barker just wanted to keep the Forest game exactly the same as a league match, even though it was a cup final.

'As senior players at the time, we had a few discussions and even disagreements with John and Richie because we felt it was being underplayed and undervalued.

'It was a bit of a dour game in the end. I had a goal disallowed for a foul supposedly on Peter Shilton, but we got the win again, and another trophy.

'Obviously another big story that day was with our captain Emlyn Hughes, because the League Cup was the only one he hadn't won during an incredible career with Liverpool.

'I remember as we came out of the tunnel our fans were singing "You'll Never Walk Alone" which was a lovely touch, and he went and played out of his skin after that!'

Two cup successes, and that era could even have been better for the much-loved team of the seventies. During this spell, they also reached three FA Cup semi-finals, losing to Leeds, Arsenal and Tottenham, and another League Cup semi-final, also being beaten by Spurs.

Not to mention that epic European run which, prior to the quarter-final with Juventus, had seen Wolves overcome Academica Coimbra of Portugal, FC Den Haag from the Natherlands and Carl Zeiss Jena behind the Iron Curtain in East Germany.

'Of all our trips, that felt the biggest in terms of the occasion and how different it was to travel to East Germany, a real shock to the system,' adds Richards. 'The whole place was so grey and miserable, frightening almost.

'Every time we went back to the hotel, we had to identify ourselves as well, otherwise they wouldn't let us in.'

'You always felt that someone was watching you over there,' adds Parkes. 'I saw some goalie gloves in the window of a sports shop and went in to try and buy them but they wouldn't sell to me because they knew I was the opposition!'

The progress continued, and after overcoming Juventus, a record-breaking Daley goal after just 17 seconds of the second leg against Ferencvaros helped Wolves to a 2-1 victory following a 2-2 draw away from home.

Parkes saved a penalty in both legs – 'I went the wrong way both times and saved them with my left foot' – to help Wolves through to the final of a European competition against … Tottenham!

'What a letdown,' Parkes recalls. 'To reach the final of the UEFA Cup, and play two legs against another team from England, felt like another two domestic fixtures.'

'After the final we just got on the coach and went straight home,' reflects Richards, after Wolves followed a 2-1 defeat at Molineux with a 1-1 draw – not enough to overhaul the deficit – at White Hart Lane.

'In one respect, and with hindsight looking back, getting to the final was a great achievement, but it didn't feel like that at the time.

'We just knew Spurs so well from playing them so often so it didn't feel like a European final, and even the medal at the end of it was disappointing, like one of those tokens you get from a petrol station!

'Speak to the fans now about that UEFA Cup run and I don't think they talk about their memories of the final, but more about the journeys they went on and the places that they saw.'

Talking of fans in Europe, sometimes it's not a case of Wolves travelling out to the continent, but the continent coming to Wolves!

The club now boasts many different supporter groups across Europe and indeed the globe, but there are a couple in particular whose love of the club is inextricably linked to the seventies' heroes.

Supporters from Scandinavia have developed long and lasting affiliations – and dedication – to Wolves, in part due to the fact they were among one of the first live games shown on television in the region.

In Norway as an example, Wolves' 1-0 win against Sunderland in 1969, Hughie Curran the scorer, was the first ever match shown on live television. And that was a landmark appropriately recognised by the 'Viking Wolves' supporters' club when making one of their regular pilgrimages to Molineux for the corresponding fixture towards the end of the ill-fated 2025/26 Premier League season.

Norwegian Wolves was initially the brainchild of Odin Henrikssen, who lives in Bergen, the second-largest city in the country after Oslo.

Born in 1962, it was Odin's Uncle Atle who first developed an interest in Wolves when travelling to Wolverhampton to study in 1966. He would return home with pictures and autographs of the players, along with experiences of being able to work with the players at Molineux as part of his studies in physiotherapy.

'And that was it,' says Odin. 'When he came home and told me about all this, I really liked his stories, and the colours of the team. I became a fan, and I have been ever since.'

Coming over to watch Wolves as a youngster just wasn't feasible, but in 1984 Odin made his first visit to the city, then a town, during a detour from a family holiday in Wales.

He went across to Castlecroft to watch the team train, met manager Tommy Docherty and the players, and cemented a love of the gold and black which now sees him as a season ticket holder, despite all the distance involved.

It was those players of the seventies, many of whom help drive the FPA and attend the socials at the Fox, who Odin revered, particularly as he spent most of that decade compiling scrapbooks made up of cuttings of coverage of the team.

A large Norwegian newsagent, Narvesen, sold English newspapers at the time, and Odin was a very regular, and meticulous, customer.

'One kiosk wasn't far from my home where I took the school bus,' he adds. 'So, every Monday, I would look at all the papers on the stand. Sometimes I would be told off by the vendor for spending too long there without buying one. But I wanted to make sure I found the one with the best pictures and the largest article about Wolves, and then I'd buy that. I started to write down all the scores and cut out the reports in the papers. They wrote a lot about English football in the sports pages here.'

A dual love of Wolves and memorabilia then came together in what is now an incredible museum, dedicated to the club, which Odin has developed at his home.

It contains photographs, paintings, programmes, books, badges, boots and newspapers not to mention almost 200 shirts, many of them match-worn, including the last one worn in his Wolves career by Richards, which he has signed.

Richards and other legends including Hibbitt, Daley and Colin Brazier had the chance to view the museum at first hand when attending the Viking Wolves' 30th anniversary celebrations with their partners in 2019.

The dedication of Odin, and other Viking Wolves members including close friend Stig Vangsnes, to make it to games is incredible.

Not only that, they also try and take in other big Wolves landmarks such as the 50th anniversary celebration of the League Cup at the Grand Theatre in 2024, as well as many other similar events, not to mention organising their own.

'Many people have asked me how much money I've used on Wolves, but I really don't care,' Odin says. 'It's a passion, it's a lifestyle, it's not so important for me, it's worth it, absolutely.'

Those sentiments are echoed almost word for word by Truls Mansson, founder and chairman of the Swedish Wolves supporters' club.

The group was officially launched in 1998, a year after Truls had first started running a website about Wolves, but also stemming from the seventies when the club toured Sweden almost every summer as part of their pre-season preparations.

'Nearly 30 years later, we're still going strong,' says Truls, who also highlighted the importance of the first *Match of the Day* in Sweden showing that Wolves against Sunderland fixture back in 1969.

'What started as a simple idea has grown into an established supporters' club, bringing together Wolves fans from across Sweden and keeping the gold and black spirit alive far from Molineux.

'Over the years, we have consistently maintained a membership of around 500 supporters. We gather to watch every Wolves match together at our home pub, The Crib in Stockholm, creating a fantastic matchday atmosphere despite being over 1,500 kilometres [930 miles] from Molineux.

'We travel to Wolverhampton several times each season, and every April we organise our flagship members' trip, which attracts more than 50 supporters. The highlight is our annual Molineux Dinner, where we present the Swedish Wolves Player to Watch award to the club's most promising academy player.

'Throughout the years we have welcomed many special guests, including Wolves legends John Richards, Kenny Hibbitt, Geoff Palmer, Willie Carr and Mel Eves. We have even had the pleasure of hosting lifelong Wolves supporter and Led Zeppelin legend Robert Plant.'

Swedish Wolves always aim to attend as many of the big games as possible, including the play-off final of 2003, FA Cup semi-final of 2019, and numerous Europa League away games, as well as heading out on many pre-season tours.

Other trips have included organising conferences at Molineux House to learn more about the club's history and heritage, and regularly attending Wolves Women fixtures, having sponsored the team for more than 20 years.

Those heroes from the seventies, whom they are so privileged to have hosted on so many occasions, will forever be high up on supporters' list of favourites.

'For many of our members, the Wolves teams of the 1970s represent the club's golden era, and those players remain true heroes to this day,' Truls adds. 'We have a large number of long-standing supporters in our club who grew up watching and following that generation, which is why former players from that period are always welcomed with tremendous enthusiasm whenever they visit us.

'And one of the greatest rewards of running Swedish Wolves has been the friendships it has created. Over the years, I have met so many wonderful people, both in Sweden and in England. What started as a supporters' club has become much more than that – it is a real community, a family united by our love for Wolves.

'People I have never met often get in touch just to say thank you, share a memory, or simply have a chat about the club. Those moments mean a lot, because they show that what we have built together goes far beyond football.

'One experience that has always stayed with me was when a member I had never met called me out of the blue. He was going through a difficult divorce and was deeply upset. We talked for a long time, and I did my best to comfort him. It reminded me that Swedish Wolves is not just about matchdays, trips or events. It is about people looking out for one another.

'That is what makes this club so special. We celebrate together, we suffer together, and when life becomes difficult, we support each other. We may come from different backgrounds and live in different places, but we are united by the same colours and the same passion.'

So, memories of Wolves heading into Europe, and so many Europeans heading across to British soil to support Wolves. Just as they did later, with the games against PSV Eindhoven in 1980 and Nuno's team of just before the Covid pandemic.

But so much of the appeal of fans was generated – and remains so – thanks to the heroics, and history, produced by the icons of the seventies.

Will they also be the last collective of former Wolves players to continue meeting in such numbers once they have finished their careers? They are the only current group who meet regularly, and as the game has become more global, and the world itself has become smaller, the cosmopolitan make-up of Wolves squads will make it difficult.

For now, they will continue to be loved and celebrated by fans, and rightly so. Their impact on the pitch is now being matched by their impact in the community. Both in supporting local charities and helping people who need it, as well as helping each other through some tough and testing times. The power of football. The power of a strong dressing room. Where bonds are formed which will never be broken.

No idea, however, what happened to Steve Daley's posh Italian shoes.

Chapter 7

Diogo Jota – Never Forgotten

LONG INTO the small hours of the morning on a bank of the Douro River in Porto, a group of Wolves fans could be heard singing an ode to their hero, to the tune of Abba's 'Voulez-Vous'. It was late November 2019. Those supporters, and many thousands more back home, were living through their greatest days supporting this club.

> Di-o-go, Jota. Running down the wing, Jota. Hear the Wanderers Sing, Jota. We're all going to Gdansk.

The following evening, those fans would head a few miles up the road to Braga for the next instalment of a European adventure. The Europa League would be Diogo Jota's stage that season. Nine goals, including two successive home hat-tricks against Besiktas and Espanyol, helped Wolves into the last 16 of the tournament. And how he would have loved that song reverberating around the streets of his home city.

Less than six years later, on a serene July morning in Gondomar, a district of the city a few miles east along the river, Diogo and his younger brother, Andre Silva, were laid to rest. A funeral service at Gondomar's parish church was attended by family, friends and many more who paid their respects from the football world. Diogo's great friend and former Wolves team-mate, Ruben Neves, was a pall bearer.

It was incomprehensible and raw. Aged 28, Jota and his brother died in a car crash in Spain on 3 July 2025, just ten days after he had celebrated his wedding to his childhood sweetheart, Rute, with whom he was bringing up three young children. It is hard to move past the human tragedy that ended this story but as Neves so poignantly stated at the time, 'They say you only lose people when you forget them. I'll never forget you.'

Wolverhampton Wanderers changed forever when Jota and Neves signed for the club in July 2017. A mid-table Championship team was transformed under the stewardship of Nuno Espirito Santo and his coaching team and the financial might of owners Fosun International. Previous teams built for promotion, or to stay in the Premier League once that aim was achieved, always had a British and Irish core. The serious money was spent on familiar recruits. Dave Jones turned to the likes of Nathan Blake, Mark Kennedy, Kenny Miller and Colin Cameron when the finances were put on the table by Sir Jack Hayward. Mick McCarthy achieved promotion on a shoestring budget but his most expensive Premier League recruits were Kevin Doyle, Steven Fletcher, Jamie O'Hara and Roger Johnson.

The £20m spent on Neves and £10m on Jota caught the eye of a wider audience, particularly as the clubs they came from were hardly European minnows.

'They had the pride to come and play in the Championship,' says Conor Coady. 'A lot of players from Porto or Atletico Madrid would look at the Championship and think, "I'm not going there." Looking at that period, we didn't know what was going to come from it. To look back now, it was amazing, an incredible time for the football club and an incredible period for me as a player. To see those players walk through the door was eye-opening.'

For the first time, Wolves became a club operating at an elite level of recruitment overseas. Of course, it was down to the connections of Jorge Mendes and there was still plenty of scepticism given the negligible impact made by some of the club's European recruits the previous summer.

But it was soon apparent that Neves and Jota were at a different level, not just in terms of their ability. Jota brought an incredible drive to the Compton Park training ground. It was a powerful mix of ambition, professionalism, determination and energy. Perhaps much of this was characterised by what had gone before.

Throughout his entire junior football career, Jota's parents paid subs for him to play in the academy of Gondomar, a lower league club on the outskirts of the city. There were trials and rejections at Porto and Benfica along the way, but the youngster's determination to succeed never dimmed. Not until the age of 17 did Jota's persistence and hard work reap rewards, with a move to Paços de Ferreira and a first professional contract. He never looked back.

By the time a 21-year-old Jota returned to Portugal with Wolves in Europe, he had already played in the Champions League, won promotion to the Premier League and been capped for the first time by his country just two weeks earlier. The academy in Gondomar would soon be renamed the Diogo Jota Academy.

If his youth career suffered knock-backs, his professional journey quickly took on a different life. While Wolves were labouring through the 2016/17 season, Jota was proving himself on his biggest stage yet. Having signed for Atletico Madrid, he was immediately loaned out to Porto, where Nuno was head coach. His first start came against CD Nacional de Madeira in October and within the opening 45 minutes he scored a hat-trick. In December, just three days after his 20th birthday, Jota scored his first Champions League goal in a 5-0 home rout of Leicester City. He played in all of the club's Champions League games that season.

Wolves was not an obvious next step, but with Nuno in no doubt of his talents, Mendes made sure that he became a priority for the Championship club in the summer of 2017.

'Jorge and Valdir [Cardoso] spoke with me,' Jota explained, speaking in December 2022. 'The season before, Jorge had mentioned Wolves but then they almost went down. So then when they came to me the next season with the story of Wolves again – what a great club it was and how they would go up – I said, "Yeah, yeah, you said that last year and they almost went down!" It is always a bit tricky in football, results are never guaranteed but when I saw Ruben signing and Nuno becoming the manager after the season I had with him in Porto, I really felt that could be the start of something good.'

'That was the best part for his growing – to play in the Championship,' Nuno explains. 'It is the real English football and he loved it. The contact, the adrenaline, it was beautiful to see. He was a player who loved the game, loved to work. He went home and tried to understand the game and that is always helpful for a manager.'

Jota carried the ball like nobody else in the Championship during that promotion-winning season. Every stride he took, opponents closed in trying to stop him. Yet still he ran, ball at his feet, twisting, feinting, weaving his magic. He top-scored with 17 league goals as Wolves romped to the title.

'His tenacity was something that I'd never seen before,' Coady continues. 'I was lucky enough to share a football pitch with him every day and I saw it out on the pitch in terms of finding a way to get through people, finding a way to score goals, to force through challenges and end up with the ball. We all saw that when he went to Liverpool, too.'

His bravery in possession – so often the victim of reckless challenges – won him admirers in the stands. Off the pitch, Jota's influence was profound; he improved the players around him through his sheer weight of devotion and commitment.

'I've never seen a stronger person mentally and physically, in terms of what he was doing in the gym and the professionalism he had to make himself better,' Coady adds. 'When he first came into the club he was very serious, but he knew when to have a laugh and how to have a laugh. You knew when he came into the room and wasn't happy about something – he'd tell you about it. Players raised their standards during that time and he was a massive part of taking the club to the next step.'

'When I was growing up it always seemed that England at under 16s, 17s and 18s would be doing unbelievably well,' Ryan Bennett says. 'England Under 21s were always doing really well, and then it would just stop and the foreign teams seemed to take over at senior level. I always struggled to understand that until I went to Wolves and saw these guys like Diogo and Ruben. That was because it wasn't about how good they were or anything like that, it was just the mentality. The will to win, the drive to win.'

Jota showed his adaptability in the front line of Wolves' attack after promotion. Primarily a wide player in the Championship, he formed a productive partnership with Raul Jimenez in attack in the Premier League whenever Nuno went with two up front. Jota made the transition look easy and the pair produced some stunning link-up play during their time together. Perhaps the most memorable goal of all came in the last away game before the Covid-19 pandemic caused the 2019/20 season to be paused. Picking the ball up in his own half, Jota skipped past his markers in the Tottenham Hotspur team as if they were not there before setting up Jimenez for the winning goal in a 3-2 triumph in north London.

A standout Molineux memory came 12 months earlier when the Portuguese forward completed a hat-trick in added time, to secure three points for Wolves in a seven-goal thriller against

Leicester City. The chaotic finale saw Nuno sent to the stands for racing on to the pitch to celebrate the winner with his players, after Jota slammed home a Jimenez cross in front of an ecstatic South Bank.

'Diogo spoke to me and said he felt it would be easier to play in the Premier League than the Championship,' said Rui Pedro Silva, Nuno's assistant at Wolves, speaking in October 2022. 'I asked him why and he said that the way they were pressed in the Championship was crazy. Diogo said, "I didn't have space to play in the Championship and I always had to fight for the ball. In the Premier League I will have space to play."'

It was no surprise to those within the club that Jota would progress further. After his second season in England and two seventh-place finishes with Wolves, Premier League champions Liverpool came calling.

Just as at Wolves, Jota became a key member of a squad that was gradually rebuilt by manager Jurgen Klopp. The pinnacle was his final season, and fifth with Liverpool. Arne Slot had taken over and Liverpool would end the 2024/25 campaign as champions, ten points clear of Arsenal.

'Diogo was always good with everyone, he accepted everyone for the people they were,' Slot says. 'He was a friend of all the players without putting that much effort in, he was always himself and players really liked him because of that. He helped the club so many times in difficult moments. The more difficult it was, the better Diogo was for us.'

Jota had become a crucial member of the Portugal squad during this period too, and on 8 June 2025 he came off the bench, along with his great mate Neves, to help Roberto Martinez's team to victory over Spain in the UEFA Nations League Final at the Allianz Arena, Munich.

'We first met in the under-21s and he was always someone very committed to fulfilling his dream,' Bruno Fernandes recalls. 'He was the perfect example of a player and person you wanted with you; a guy that is very eager to win, to fight, to give everything for the team. There was no ego at all. The time we played together on the pitch, the time we fought against each other when he was at Wolves or Liverpool, we never came off the pitch with anything bad to say about each other. And when we came together in the national team I knew what I could bring out of him and he knew what he could bring out of me in the game.'

During the first week of February, 2026 at the Wolves Museum in the Stan Cullis Stand, Jota was inducted into the Wolves Hall of Fame. It is a coveted list of the club's most significant players. The small ceremony ended with his photograph being mounted on the museum's wall amongst others recognised on the list. He was the last former player to be inducted before the club's 150th anniversary. The Hall of Fame committee includes legendary striker John Richards, the club's vice-chairman.

'We are very proud to have inducted Diogo into the Wolves Hall of Fame on behalf of the club and the supporters,' Richards reflects. 'For us, it was a decision that was heartbreaking, but easy, to make. Following the outpouring of grief and love from the supporters and the club itself after the accident, we acted quickly as a club and a Hall of Fame committee to induct him into the Hall of Fame. We've been very proud to have been able to do this, and hope that in some way, it gives the family and his friends comfort in knowing that all his achievements for Wolverhampton Wanderers and his memory will forever be remembered here at Molineux.'

Then, a few weeks later, as Wolves and Liverpool met twice at Molineux in four days, another ceremony of tribute and remembrance. Former Wolves captain Jody Craddock, now an accomplished artist, had been asked to produce some artwork to commemorate Jota which was officially unveiled in an informal but emotional ceremony in the reception of the Museum.

Using ink compressed from the floral tributes left by fans outside the stadium following his death, Craddock produced two giant paintings – one of Jota celebrating a goal and another highlighting one of the hundreds of poignant messages left in tribute. The unveiling was attended by Wolves head coach Rob Edwards and several of the team's players, including Jota's former club and country team-mates such as Matt Doherty and Jose Sa, just hours before the FA Cup tie with Liverpool.

'This has brought me immense pride, with who it is and what it represents,' says Craddock, who then attended the fixture with wife Shelley and their sons Joseph, Luke and Toby. 'The club turning flowers to paint was a fantastic idea, and for them to ask me was very nice because it meant they trusted me to do a good enough job to produce pieces to hang up there forever. The balance of the two together is perfect and I'm really pleased with them.'

The tifo displays from supporters at the opening home game of 2025/26 and then again during those matches against Liverpool had illustrated just how fondly Jota is remembered. There is no escaping what might have been, for a player who was cut off in his prime. Alongside the human tragedy, first and foremost, there will always be an immense sense of loss amongst his professional peers and coaches. In words that have gained an added poignancy since his death, Rui Pedro Silva once spoke about the potential for Jota and Neves as future coaches.

'They are very intelligent guys,' Rui Pedro Silva said, back in October 2022. 'I think in the future they will be a management team. Neves will be a head coach and Jota will be his assistant. Jota is a very smart guy and Neves, the way he makes his decisions, it's very easy for him. They started working for us at 20 but it was like having 27- or 28-year-olds, they are very mature guys.'

It will never come to pass. But Jota will be remembered for what he did achieve during a life which touched so many.

'We won the league against Tottenham and that evening we were all together, and his young children were there,' Slot recalls. 'One of his sons just wanted to keep on going to the dance floor, keep on going, and every time Diogo joined him. That tells you how good of a father he was. What I take comfort in is this: for the last month of his life he was a champion in everything. A champion for his family, a champion for his country and of course a champion for us by winning the Premier League.'

'Diogo knew how to light up a room,' Coady adds. 'That summed up the character he was because he was an outstanding person and a really good friend to a lot of people.'

'We all loved Diogo,' Nuno concludes. 'He was a very special boy, a fantastic character with his love for the game, his dedication, and his love for his family.'

Chapter 8

The Eighties – Part One

'WE CAME here, to The Mount Hotel, to celebrate,' Doug Hope recalls. 'It had been a long day, so we came here for something to eat and later the local newspaper reporter, Dave Harrison, came and joined us.'

Hope, now in his 70s, is sharing his story in the bar of the same hotel in Tettenhall where he sat down with his business associates to savour a deal that he thought would lead Wolves out of a troubled period. As it happened, 30 July 1982 proved to be the starting point of the most difficult period of ownership in the club's history.

But how had it come to this? On 1 October 1980 striker Mel Eves scored for Wolves in a 1-0 win over PSV Eindhoven at Molineux in the second leg of a first-round UEFA Cup tie. The previous season, Wolves had lifted the League Cup at Wembley, beating European champions Nottingham Forest. They had also finished sixth in the First Division under manager John Barnwell, a single point behind Forest. Just a little over a year and a half after that win against the Dutch in Europe, Wolves had been relegated, gone into receivership, been declared bankrupt and ceased trading. The receivers, appointed in July 1982 to sort out the administration, set a four-week deadline for a buyer to come forward and save the club from going out of existence.

Opened in 1979, the Molineux Stand – later renamed the John Ireland Stand before being changed again to the Steve Bull Stand

– was the source of the club's problems. It was built to replace the ageing Molineux Street Stand and, for its time, was an impressive two-tiered structure with some of the first executive boxes in the country. It was constructed 50 yards from the pitch perimeter, with chairman Harry Marshall's intention being to redevelop the entire ground towards that side of the new stand to create space for a new Waterloo Road Stand, which was hemmed in by the busy road up to the town centre.

But in 1982, three years after the Molineux Stand was opened, the club was struggling to pay off the Lloyds Bank loan secured to build the structure, which became known locally as 'Marshall's Folly'. The financial difficulties sparked off a bitter boardroom battle. An extraordinary general meeting was called on 8 June 1982 to try and oust Marshall and his vice-chairman Wilf Sproson. Wolves' former FA Cup-winning goalkeeper Malcolm Finlayson and former Aston Villa chairman Doug Ellis were presented as boardroom candidates in the event of Marshall's departure. A shareholders' vote saved Marshall, but he had seen enough dissent and resigned from his position on 16 June. Ellis was soon appointed the new chairman, but it proved to be the shortest of boardroom reigns at the club. One of his first acts was to request that Lloyds Bank, the club's major creditor to the tune of £1.85m, call in the receiver.

It was front page news at the *Express & Star*, which ran with the headline 'WOLVES HAVE GONE BUST' alongside a photograph of Ellis reading out his statement. The players appeared stunned at the news. Striker John Richards, who was the club's all-time leading goalscorer at the time, said, 'The players have just got to hope for the best. Wolves are one of the biggest clubs in Britain, and were one of the biggest in Europe. It was a great shock to hear of today's developments. It would be a tragedy if they went out of business. Everyone in Wolverhampton and all those connected with football will be hoping the club pulls through.'

The receiver set a deadline of 30 July for new owners to be found. Throughout that month, several candidates from different backgrounds expressed interest in gaining control of the club, including Wolverhampton Town Council; a consortium led by Ellis and Finlayson; another involving former chairman Marshall and Walsall chairman Ken Wheldon, a scrap metal merchant; and a third consortium led by Ken Hollinshead, an insurance broker from Tettenhall. More unlikely interest came from Essex businessman and nightclub owner Anton Johnson, who had a controlling stake in Rotherham United at the time.

Midway through the month, Sir Jack Hayward flew back from his Bahamas home to meet with interested parties about a rescue deal, but no concrete offer materialised from the future owner of the club. On the Saturday before the receiver's deadline of Friday, 30 July, the players took matters into their own hands.

Despite having been relegated to the Second Division they organised a bus tour of Wolverhampton to sign autographs for fans and raise money for the revival fund. Meanwhile a local nightclub, Eve's, put on a fundraiser with appearances from Bev Bevan, drummer of the Electric Light Orchestra, and Roy Wood, lead singer of Wizzard.

The real rescue act was taking place far from the gaze of the local media. Hope was born and raised in Glasgow. When he was 16 years old, his mother, who was originally from Shrewsbury, died and family life became tough. By the age of 19, Hope was working as a sales representative for a subsidiary of Dunlop Tyres. With those family ties south of the border, he moved to the West Midlands and progressed to work in car dealerships and property.

'I knew a businessman called Mike Cornwell, who I had sold a Rolls-Royce to some time ago,' Hope explains. 'His parting shot was: "If you get any situations that come up then give me a ring." So, 18 months later, I rang him up and said there is a situation here, some scope to develop at Wolves, but the key is that you've got to keep the football club working. To cut a long story short, he introduced me to Mike Rowland, a director of Allied Properties, and his associate John Starkey, who was an architect.'

And that was the start of the Bhatti brothers era, the most notorious owners in the 150-year history of the club. Mahmud Al-Hassan Bhatti and Mohammed Akbar Bhatti owned Allied Properties. What they needed next was a person to front the consortium.

'I knew Derek Dougan, I'd just known him socially for years,' Hope continues. 'Everybody knew Derek. He was on the scene in Wolverhampton. And we were chatting one night, at The Mitre pub in Tettenhall, that's now a block of flats. I said to him that I had people who would be interested in the club, but I'd got no expertise in the football. So, we had the initial meeting with Rowland and Starkey and then the Bhattis themselves.

'We met at a very glamorous Portakabin, if there is such a thing. They had a business called Grosvenor Aviations, which was based on a factory estate at Manchester Airport. That was the only time I saw the Bhattis dressed in traditional Arab dress. They didn't say much but they were quite impressed with what Derek had to say. He stressed all along that if Wolves could be saved there was a property deal there and we were looking at the land on the North Bank car park as a possible supermarket site. Because if they got planning permission for the supermarket, the cash flow from the supermarket would have provided an income to stabilise the club. In those days that would have been a very good income.'

Hope knew that a deal was on almost immediately. But the looming deadline, while ensuring a quick outcome for the future of the club, would bring its own problems and leave a lasting impact that may have been avoided had time been on their side.

'The trouble was that everything had to be done by 30 July, so a lot was taken on trust, handshakes, that sort of thing. Talking to the receiver, confirming that the council would give us some backing and would be supportive, so it was nods and winks, really. With hindsight, that was always going to be problematic if people change their minds.

'The receiver asked for £2m and in order to be sure of getting the club, we bid £2,050,000. That's what we paid for it. Derek and I gave two guarantees of £150,000 each. That was basically as a sort of indemnity towards the Bhattis. But at half past four, on the day of the takeover, the league said that they wanted a director's guarantee that we would fulfil that year's fixtures. So we had to give another £50,000 guarantee for the fixtures, which we did. That was at half past four otherwise the deal was off.'

Dave Harrison was the Wolves correspondent for the *Express & Star* at the time, and recalls a frantic time at his newspaper's Queen Street headquarters.

'I'd written two stories: one that Wolves had gone to the wall and one that it had been saved,' he reveals. 'The paper was waiting to press the button on one of these two stories, with the editor and managing director wondering which one they should go with. It had gone to press earlier in the day, but they were doing a special run at five o'clock because of Wolves, that's how important it was. They were holding the paper until the fate of Wolves was known.

'There were no mobile phones in those days. So, I had to sit in the office with my two stories and monitor the situation. The meetings were happening in Birmingham with Peat Marwick and Mitchell, the accountants who were the receivers. The only way of finding out what was happening was by ringing the Football League. The guy there was a good contact, Andy Williamson. He was the press officer and I had a good relationship with him because there were all sorts of stories going around with Wolves at the time. I was ringing him every 15 minutes. It got to about quarter to five and he said, "Nothing's happening Dave, I think you're probably going to go to the wall."

'I rang again five minutes later and there was no reply. I thought Andy had gone home and Wolves had probably gone to the wall. I frantically started trying to get hold of other people. I tried Peat Marwick and Mitchell, then made one more call to the Football League a minute before five o'clock, and Andy picked up. I said, "Where have you been?" and he replied, "Oh I just went to get my coat because I'm going home now. You're alright, they've been saved." I said, "Who has saved it, is it Dougan's lot?" He said he couldn't tell me as there was a confidentiality agreement, so I said, "If it's Dougan's lot put the phone down," which was an old technique we used. The phone line just clicked and went dead so I knew we'd got the story to press the button on the paper. We printed 30,000 copies after five o'clock and they sold out in the town.'

The official receiver, Alastair Jones, confirmed that talks broke down at 4.30pm, only to restart a few minutes later allowing a deal to be completed at 4.57pm, just three minutes before the deadline. 'WOLVES GO ON PLAYING' announced the headline in the *Express & Star.*

Dougan was named chairman and chief executive of the club, and he stamped his mark on the place early on. 'He sacked Jack Taylor, who was the commercial manager, Phil Shaw, who was the long-serving secretary, and then sacked Ian Greaves, the manager,' Harrison explains. 'I think it was the *Daily Express* who ran this cartoon that said "Dougan sacks himself". He was a strange character, such a contradiction. I had a good working relationship with him when he was chairman and chief executive of Wolves. He appointed Graham Hawkins, who was assistant manager at Shrewsbury Town and who I became very friendly with, and Jim Barron as his assistant.

'The place was in ruins, you'd walk in in the morning, open the dressing room door and a load of cockroaches would come crawling out. Graham did a fantastic job, they finished runners-up in the

Second Division in his first season. When he got the job he was told money would be available but he ended up using a load of kids.'

'Considering where we started that season from, we just built a group together more by accident than design,' Hope adds. 'We had Bill Tweddle, the doctor. He was a supporter who just turned up and offered his services and he became the club doctor. Denis Conyerd was a great physio.'

The pair had responded to a request on local radio from Dougan, who was trying to assemble a backroom team in time for the new season. Conyerd started work immediately, with Hawkins asking him to treat a handful of players when he turned up for the interview at Molineux.

'We took over on 30 July, and this was probably within two or three days,' Hope continues. 'It was almost like a start-up company. There was no infrastructure there at all.'

The team for the first game of the Second Division season, at home to Blackburn Rovers on 28 August 1982, included four teenage debutants: Ian Cartwright, Paul Butler, Billy Livingstone and David Wintersgill, who was a 16-year-old plucked straight from school. But there was still a sprinkling of senior talent on the books, with Geoff Palmer, Kenny Hibbitt, Andy Gray and Mel Eves playing their part guiding the youngsters through.

The opening day side also included a right-back, who would be the only ever-present outfield player of that promotion-winning campaign. London-born John Humphrey played in the same Hertfordshire League junior team as Kenny Jackett, Stuart Pearce, Gary Waddock and Gary O'Reilly. It was a tour match against a Wolves development side that got Humphrey invited back for a trial, which earned him schoolboy terms, before working his way up to a full professional contract. He was 19 when he broke into the first team in April 1980, a month after Wolves' League Cup triumph at Wembley. He played just twice that season, on consecutive days.

'Southampton away, we won 3-0,' Humphrey recalls. 'I remember being told I was playing just around two o'clock. Geoff Palmer had a fitness test before the game and failed it, so I came in. And I just, I don't remember too much of the day, I just remember winning 3-0. We played Southampton on the Easter Monday and stayed down on the south coast and played Brighton the next evening – don't tell me about players now need a week in between games!

'We lost 3-0 at Brighton and I didn't play again after those two games as Geoff got back into the team. I was just substituted at Brighton and I remember Emlyn Hughes coming in afterwards, being critical of the performance. He turned to me and said, "Where were you on the third goal?" I just turned around and said, "I was on the bench," because I'd already been taken off. He lacked a little bit of pace by then but he still had the organisational skills, he'd been England captain. But as a player he had too much clout.

'Him and Andy Gray were dominant in the dressing room. Sometimes that's good when you need people to say things but how do you argue with the England captain? Andy didn't hold back, either. I remember even in training, if we were doing set plays against the youth team he attacked the ball like he would on a matchday. So you had youth team players with cuts over their eyes, but that was Andy, he was just so clear. He always used to lead like this, you wanted him in your team, you didn't want to play against him.

'Another game I remember vividly was the following season, we beat Liverpool 4-1 and Emlyn scored against his old team. We came off the pitch and went straight to the sports hall where Emlyn was to be the guest on *This is Your Life*. So, as soon as we came off the pitch and headed down the tunnel, we went off to film the programme.'

In a surreal scene, Hughes was doorstepped by television presenter Eamonn Andrews on the edge of the pitch with his famous red book. With such a convincing win over the soon-to-be European champions, few could have predicted that Wolves were about to begin such a decline.

'Derek Parkin, John McAlle and John Richards were so good with the young players. I remember when we drew 0-0 away at Manchester United that season and Mick Hollifield and I got into the team. It was only Mick's second game, and we were two young full-backs. That was a big, big game for us.'

Humphrey was making his way with a team that had high hopes for the decade ahead. That said, if the new Molineux Street Stand was causing problems off the pitch, it was met with little love on it.

'When we went out there, we just said the atmosphere changed,' he adds. 'With the old stand, everybody was on top of you. To go from that was strange. We thought, because of the space, that they were going to rotate the pitch around.'

Wolves finished the 1980/81 season with just one win in the last six games and that form continued into the following campaign with only two victories in the opening 12 games.

Manager John Barnwell resigned in January after a dispute with Marshall, to be replaced by Greaves, who became the first sacking of the Bhatti era.

The 1982/83 season brought with it new ownership off the pitch and a memorable new face on it. The only other ever-present was a goalkeeper. This was no ordinary number one. Those who met John Burridge would never forget the experience.

'There were matches, when we were attacking down one end, and you'd turn around, and Budgie was sitting on his crossbar,' Humphrey recalls. 'The crowd loved it. We went to Spain at the end of the season as a thank you from the chairman. There was a Mr Magaluf competition one night, and all of a sudden, from the side of the stage, Budgie comes on naked, doing a handstand. So, you've got all these muscle men on there, and Budgie just walking across the stage on his hands. And that was Budgie all over, just bonkers.

'He bought a massive house up in Tettenhall and I used to go around there and see him a lot. We used to sit and watch television with his wife, who would have an apple or an orange, and every now and then she used to throw it at him, and he'd have to react and make a save. He just loved goalkeeping.'

'Those initial few months were a very exciting time to be involved in the club,' Hope adds. 'Graham bought Alan Dodd from Stoke City, who was a steady influence and things were going really well. Mel Eves got 18 goals that season and that got us promoted. But the masterstroke was signing Burridge, he was just something else in the dressing room. We played Newcastle on the final day and he went out on to the pitch dressed as Superman. I remember the expression on Kevin Keegan's face, he couldn't believe it.'

'We'd already clinched promotion and couldn't win the league so there wasn't really anything at stake in the final game,' Burridge explains. 'I knew I was going to get the player of the season award and I was driving to the ground when I spotted a fancy dress shop. The fans were coming along for a celebration so I thought the crowd would enjoy something different – so I decided to dress up in a Superman uniform.

'My wife Janet told me I'd look like an idiot, but I did it all the same, going out to warm up dressed as Superman and I think I wore the tights under my goalkeeping kit for the game as well. I think I played a part in saving Wolves in that first season. The promotion was so important. When I went to a club, I gave a dressing room life. I was happy at Wolves, I loved it there.'

Burridge was named player of the year in that promotion-winning 1982/83 season. A goalkeeper scooping such an award after a successful campaign is perhaps an indication of how the club needed to strengthen. But despite the promotion, cracks were emerging behind the scenes. The Bhattis did not allow

Hawkins to improve the squad, despite the best efforts of the management.

'Graham came into us in the summer and said he'd like six players,' Hope reveals. 'He gave us a list. He wanted Mick McCarthy, who was the best centre-half outside of the First Division. Gary Lineker, who we'd spoken with Leicester about during the trip to Spain after promotion when Leicester were staying in our hotel, and we agreed on a £110,000 fee. There was David Seaman, Micky Gynn, who worked with Jim Barron at Peterborough, Ashley Grimes, who was a left-back at Manchester United, and Paul Bracewell.

'Derek [Dougan] had a rush of blood and bought Tony Towner, who was a good player, but he wasn't on Graham's list. Graham was on holiday. At that point, we thought there was some more money available, but it didn't materialise. Unfortunately, we didn't support him as well as we would have liked.'

Wolves finished the 1983/84 season rock bottom of the First Division. It was a dismal campaign punctuated only by a bizarre win at champions Liverpool, who would go on to win the League Cup and European Cup as well as retaining their First Division title. The 1-0 win at Anfield in January saw Steve Mardenborough's only goal in nine league appearances for the club. The teenager had not even been scheduled to travel with the Wolves squad to Merseyside, but a late injury to Eves opened the door.

It was during this period that any chance of the Bhattis and the council coming to an agreement on the proposed supermarket plans died a death. Hope believes that the town council changed their approach to the Bhattis' plans when Manders Properties intervened and raised the argument that a supermarket would take trade away from the town centre, specifically the Mander Centre.

'We'd had a meeting with councillors John Bird and Ken Williams and they were very positive that the club was going to get saved [in 1982], and promised that they would support a development,' Hope insists. 'But then, after that, Manders got involved. Their argument was that if the development was outside the ring road, it was outside the local plans. The local establishment regarded us as upstarts.'

Hope has kept a letter from Williams, chief executive of the council, dated 27 March 1984 which ended any hope the owners had of proceeding with a supermarket development:

> The Borough Council have taken the view, however, that they must balance any advantages to the football club of a supermarket development at Molineux, the disadvantages to Wolverhampton town centre of taking trade away from it. This is a perfectly proper planning consideration which the recent public inquiry examined in considerable depth.

Former Manchester United manager Tommy Docherty was appointed for the 1984/85 season. Humphrey points to a clash of personalities leading to further trouble on the pitch as the team slid out of the Second Division. Between mid-December and the beginning of April, Wolves failed to score in 14 of their 17 league matches.

'Tommy had a real falling-out with [forwards] Tony Evans and Tommy Langley,' Humphrey reveals. 'It was something that happened behind the scenes. We just couldn't score that season, goals just dried up. And I always blame Tommy for that because whatever the problems were, the team should have come first.

'Tommy was a real joker but it was the wrong time, wrong place. Whilst players were out warming up, he'd cut the ends off people's socks. He'd give you a right bollocking after we lost and then somebody would put their sock on and it would come up their leg and he'd sit there laughing. So after having a right go at us, within five minutes it was all a laugh and a joke.'

It was clear the Bhattis had lost interest in the club. Stories emerged of coaching staff who lived outside of Wolverhampton sleeping in the boardroom on some nights if they had stayed working late. The club could not afford to put them up in hotels. Dougan resigned under pressure from other board members in January.

'By then the rot had really set in,' Harrison explains. 'There was a young player called Neville Hamilton, who had a heart murmur and collapsed up at the training ground. That was at the Castlecroft training ground, which was falling apart, it was riddled with asbestos. They were carting him off and putting him in an ambulance when Tommy's number two, Greg Fellows, went over and started taking his football boots off. Tommy asked him what he was doing and Greg replied, "Gaffer, we've only got 14 pairs of boots in the whole club, and we can't afford to lose these."'

Sammy Chapman was installed as caretaker manager for the start of the 1985/86 campaign. Bill McGarry, such a success in his first spell in charge between 1968–74, was tempted back in September, but he lasted just 61 days before handing the reins back to Chapman. The turnover of players was alarming. Saleable assets like Humphrey had left in the summer. In all, 33 players were used in the league. Supporters who lived through it regard the Third Division season as the hardest one of all that decade. The club had yet to bottom out, and so long as the Bhattis remained at the helm there were no signs of recovery.

'In that season we were being inundated with winding-up petitions,' Hope remembers. 'John Bird [council leader] was a well-oiled politician. He started off supportive, but when he saw which way the wind was blowing, he was very anti-Bhattis. I think they'd refuse to engage with him, which he got the needle about, and with some justification – you couldn't blame him. But the main concern was not going bust in the middle of the season, because if we hadn't fulfilled the fixtures the club would have been out of the league completely. It was gallows humour. We used to say "If it gets any worse, we'll have to announce the crowd changes to the team." That sort of thing.'

The club's lowest ever league attendance was recorded on 18 March 1986 when just 2,205 turned up for a Tuesday night encounter with Bury. A third successive relegation brought further problems off the field. In June, for the second time in four years, the club fell into administration, with Lloyds Bank again calling in the receivers to bring an end to the Bhattis' regime.

Unlike in 1982, the threat of Wolves' closure was not a long-running front-page story. 'This time there was an inevitability about it, that they were going to the wall again,' says Harrison. 'You kept your head down, you were almost embarrassed to admit you were a Wolves fan.'

The receiver did create one major front-page headline early on, though, when he came up with an enterprising plan to preserve the club's future. The proposal was to allow Wolves to enter the Conference as a part-time team, and hand non-league Enfield their place in the league. At the time there was no promotion and relegation between the two divisions, and the news was met with astonishment. Receiver Adam Stanway announced, 'If this is the only way I can keep the club in existence then I shall do it, subject to both leagues being in agreement. The only alternative is if local business and the public come forward and clear the debts to enable a new group to take over in time for the Football league kick-off on 23 August.'

Secretary of the Conference, then known as the GM Vauxhall League, Peter Hunter said, 'If Wolves can turn out 12 players on 16 August, we'll have them.'

In July a 200-strong group of supporters travelled to Newcastle upon Tyne to present a 3,000-signature petition to the Football League, who were at a hotel discussing the club's future. Their plea to allow Wolves to take up a place in the Football League the following season, regardless of whether a rescue package was agreed, fell on deaf ears. The Football League set a 31 July deadline to sort out the debts.

Sir Jack Hayward flew back from the Bahamas and announced he was willing to help the club on one condition. 'I am not going to bail out the Bhatti brothers, they have had enough out of Wolves already,' he said. 'I would be willing to help but only to save the club, and the last thing I want to do is put money in the Bhattis' pockets.'

Eventually, through club solicitor Michael Cooksey, the Bhattis broke their silence. With the receiver revealing total debts of £2.4m, including £800,000 to Allied Properties, the solicitor's statement claimed the Bhattis were owed £4m. Cooksey said the brothers were propping up 'gigantic debts' amassed by the club over the course of their ownership. 'They are fed up of being the butt of everything. They are misunderstood,' he protested.

The deputy leader of Wolverhampton Council, Dennis Turner, disagreed. 'I think this just demonstrates their attitude,' he said. 'They are jeopardising efforts to save the club. Nobody has been given any chance to validate any of these claims. Let them show proof.'

The Bhattis were eventually forced to cooperate with the receivers when a High Court ruling ordered them to hand over records of Wolves' financial affairs. Allied Properties lost its grip on the club when a Middle East bank called in the receiver, over a separate £700,000 debt, leading to the seizure and sale of Allied Properties' London headquarters. The way was now clear for Wolves' receivers to sell off the ground and buildings without the owners' consent.

The council stepped up to secure Wolves' future with a consortium fronted by Jack Harris and Dick Homden, proposing a property development deal to purchase Molineux and all the club's land. The council struck a £1.1m deal for Molineux and the remaining club property, including the Castlecroft training ground.

Asda agreed to pay £1.8m for the land behind the North Bank in return for planning permission to build a superstore, and the Birmingham construction firm J.J. Gallagher, fronted by Harris and Homden, purchased the club and rented the stadium from the council.

'I went back to being in business and took life a bit gently after that,' Hope adds. 'I vowed that I would have no more stress, because at the time, it was really stressful. We left a club for Sir Jack to one day rebuild. You could take a crumb of comfort out of that, but it was just sad. It's like a sinking ship, you know? We stopped it from sinking initially, but then it was run aground.'

Humphrey went on to enjoy the top division career Wolves might have provided had stability off the field existed. After five years at Charlton Athletic, the highlight came at Crystal Palace with a third-place finish to the 1990/91 season behind Arsenal and Liverpool. The sport is still his working life, in his role as head of football at Highgate School in north London.

'Wolves was my early years development, my first club,' he concludes. 'I always look back with fondness and it was a real rollercoaster. It was up, down, up, down. I had so many managers, but I enjoyed it. What I loved about this club was that it was one team, one town. You know, you go to London or Manchester and you've got so many clubs, whereas at Wolves the whole town was behind the club and I loved that.'

Humphrey was fortunate to miss the darkest times, the relegation to the Fourth Division, when that sense of the town and its folk being behind the club had long faded away. But soon enough, unity and pride started to return to the town's football club and its supporters as Wolves made their way back from the brink.

Chapter 9

The Eighties – Part Two

A RADIO studio at Mander House, in the city's shopping centre, is buzzing with conversation between two of the club's cult heroes from the 1980s revival. Alongside them is a former team-mate who they have cajoled into coming along for the ride, as a guest on their latest podcast. Andy Mutch and Robbie Dennison were key players in Graham Turner's team which won two successive promotions. They have remained close friends ever since and are enjoying being back in town with their *Mutchy & Denno* show, recorded at Wolverhampton Community Radio.

Tom Bennett is their guest on this particular Friday afternoon. He arrived at Molineux in 1988 from Aston Villa reserves, walking into a dressing room that had enjoyed two years of unparalleled success on the pitch. Much of the recording is taken up with Bennett's reflections of breaking into a team on the up, ending with a tale of his appearance in goal for Wolves during a hostile Black Country derby with West Bromwich Albion in 1991. The Scot was something of a utility player during his time at Wolves and when goalkeeper Mike Stowell went down injured five minutes into the second half, the more senior players turned the other way in the hope that somebody would be brave enough to volunteer between the sticks.

'Nobody put their hand up and, in my head, I'm thinking, "Well, I'm not playing very well, this could be an easy out for me," so I just put the gloves on,' Bennett explains. 'Robbie was warming me up, half-volleying shots into me and I'm dropping everything!'

'It was chucking down with rain,' Mutch chips in. 'You had these big gloves on, you were soaking wet standing there looking like a ten-year-old who'd been told to go in nets because no one else would do it.'

It was 1-1 when Bennett gave up his position at right-back to put on the number 1 shirt and he could take plenty of pride in a 2-2 draw at full time.

'Although, I honestly think if you'd stayed at right-back we'd have lost the game,' Dennison smiles.

The affection between the three men permeates the room. As a dressing room, it is harder to imagine a more enjoyable place to be than Wolves in the late eighties. Brought together partly through accident and partly by design, Turner's team overcame everything before them during two raucous promotion seasons in the Fourth and Third Divisions.

Mutch arrived at the club when it was still enduring its bleakest days. The Liverpool-born forward was signed for a pittance from non-league Southport in February 1986, with Wolves heading for relegation to the bottom tier. His seven goals in 14 games for a team that would finish 23rd in the Third Division hinted at the exploits that would follow.

'I played with Geoff Palmer in those early games,' Mutch explains. 'He was part of that legendary team of the seventies team and I was amazed that I was sharing a pitch with him. But I was shocked at the state of the place, with just 3,000 fans coming through the gates. I'd grown up watching Wolves on the television with top players like Kenny Hibbitt, John Richards, Willie Carr and Steve Daley. And it was shocking to see it like that.'

At Southport, Mutch had juggled his part-time football with a job doing deliveries and warehouse work at a refrigeration company. He was 23 years old when he was spotted by Wolves manager

Sammy Chapman while playing in a game at Kidderminster Harriers. He had been released by Everton as a teenager and a professional career seemed to have passed him by.

'I had the luck to be able to get into Wolves because we were that poor,' Mutch reflects. 'If I had gone to another club, I may only have played four or five games at best and not got a sniff. I remember after the first four games I rang my dad and told him I'd made a mistake coming here. I couldn't get a kick of the ball, the centre-halves I was up against were too strong. I didn't think I could handle it. But I kept getting opportunities in the team and I scored in the fifth game. I just got my head together and when that season finished, Brian Little came in as manager and brought in Ally Robertson and you could sense things were starting to change.

'Jack Harris and Dick Homden took over the running of the club in the summer and it wasn't long after that when Graham Turner came in. Everyone says a lot about what Sir Jack Hayward did for the club, it was fantastic and I can't say a bad word about him, but Jack Harris and Dick Homden deserve a lot of credit for slowly but surely piecing the club back together.'

Before the upward trajectory was established there was one grim chapter in the story that had still to be written. Chorley has gone down in the club's folklore and sends a shudder down the spine of those old enough to recall the episode. In mid-November 1986, Turner's men faced the Northern Premier League part-timers in the first round of the FA Cup.

Chorley's Victory Park ground did not meet the standards required, so the first game was played at a neutral venue, Bolton Wanderers' Burnden Park. Mutch scored in the 1-1 draw which forced a replay at Molineux.

That second game was a strange affair. A diving header from Matt Forman in front of the South Bank gave Wolves the lead, but the team from the third tier of non-league football equalised in bizarre circumstances, according to Turner. He claimed that a ball boy inadvertently played Chorley's goalscorer onside. The youngster on the perimeter of the pitch was wearing a yellow bib and was in the line of sight of a confused linesman who mistook him for a Wolves defender.

It set up a third encounter, and a second match at Burnden Park. Wolves capitulated, going down 3-0, to the delight of the non-league club's band of supporters and a number of Bolton fans who had turned up to bolster their support. The *Express & Star* headline was direct and to the point: 'Disgraced! Wolves sink to new low'.

Journalist David Instone's match report was just as damning: 'Wolves failed to produce a single shot on target all night, and the lowest ebb in their distinguished history bore more than a passing resemblance to a club in the death throes. They made Wolves look like a pub team at times and goalkeeper Ian Senior, the man whose heroics had made this second replay necessary, had the cleanest pair of knees in Bolton as he led his side's lap of honour.'

'Proper Chorlies' was the *Birmingham Evening Mail*'s take on the fiasco.

'Their attitude compared to our attitude was: top of the class versus bottom of the class,' Mutch says. 'It was one of the most embarrassing things I've ever been part of. I suppose if you don't have disappointments like that you don't enjoy the good times quite as much as we did. What made it worse was that I knew a lot of the Chorley lads. I'd played against these players for Southport and I was the one who was supposed to have moved on to better things. To come up against them like this and suffer that defeat was just terrible. I didn't know where to look. After that third game against them we just all wanted to get out of there as quickly as possible.'

It says a lot about the transformation of the team that only three players from that November evening were in the side that won the final game of the following season, when Wolves concluded their Fourth Division title season with a 2-0 win at Leyton Orient.

Mutch, Robertson and Micky Holmes were the three who will have enjoyed the success of 1987/88 all the more because of what had gone before.

While the newspapers went to town on the FA Cup shock, the reality was that Wolves were already on their way back. Bull and Thompson had just been signed, and watched the debacle from the stands. Soon enough they would be out on the pitch. Dennison would join them four months later with Wolves looking a team transformed. They won 11 of their final 12 league games. Bull's 16 league goals that campaign, accompanied by 10 from Mutch, helped propel Wolves into a two-legged play-off final against Aldershot, who had finished two places and nine points behind Turner's men. But a two-legged final ended in heartbreak with a 3-0 aggregate defeat.

Dennison had a more circuitous route to Molineux than Mutch. Between 1979 and 1985 he played in the Northern Ireland Football League for Glenavon, after being given his debut by Billy Sinclair, a tough Glaswegian.

'I was only 16 getting shouted at all the time, you either sink or swim,' Dennison recalls. It was a tough environment to grow up in, with The Troubles dominating Northern Ireland's landscape.

'Because you lived in amongst it, it was sort of accepted,' Dennison continues. 'So as a kid growing up I saw bricks being thrown at police and that sort of thing, so when there was trouble at games it didn't feel unusual. But when you were playing you knew you had to keep your mouth shut at certain games or when you were playing certain opponents. There were always tensions against certain sides, and I had to grow up pretty quickly. For me it was just a game of football and a case of keeping your nose clean.'

Concentrating on the football was enough for Dennison. The league was awash with players in no mood to be given the run around by a tricky teenage winger.

'Playing at 16, I had to grow up quickly because I was up against men and I used to get kicked around a bit. It was quite brutal, physically. You had to ride challenges against people trying to injure you. So when I came across to England, whoever I played against didn't bother me as I'd faced all sorts of opponents. It was part of the game for me to commit defenders, draw in opponents. You'd nick the ball past them when a challenge came in and that was a big part of the way I played.

'I had three trials around that age: Chelsea, Oxford and Brighton. I went across for two or three days at a time, but Glenavon wanted some money for me and it was hard to prove yourself, so it never happened. And then I got the opportunity to come across at 22 to Albion, which was a three-week trial. I thought the opportunity had gone so when it came up I knew this was the last chance to make it.'

Dennison did enough to secure a move and his professional career had begun. It was in at the deep end, though, with West Bromwich Albion toiling in the First Division during the 1986/87 season under the management of Ron Saunders. Appearances at Old Trafford against Manchester United and at home to Liverpool are still fresh in the memory.

'We lost 2-1 at home to Liverpool with Dalglish and Rush scoring,' he recalls. 'So, it wasn't a big deal giving up the First Division for the Fourth when Wolves came in for me, because like Mutchy, I wasn't playing enough games. Ron Saunders actually tried to sell me back to the Irish League, but I told him I didn't want to go because I wanted to prove myself. It had taken a while to get here so at 22 I wasn't going back.'

It was the day of the March transfer deadline of the 1986/87 season when Dennison crossed the Black Country. A meeting in the manager's office ended with the winger being told it was Wolves or nothing, but that was only half the story. The player still had to get across to Wolverhampton in time to sign the paperwork, which is where an unlikely hero in Carlton Palmer emerged.

'Carlton was sitting outside the office, because he's a bit nosey in that way,' Dennison continues. 'He wanted to find out what was going on in the meeting. I came out and told him that I had to get to Wolverhampton but didn't know how to get there, or where it was in relation to West Brom. He just said, "Come on, I'll take you over there in my car." So that was it, I got to Wolves, spent ten minutes sorting out a contract before the deadline passed and it turned out to be the best thing that I ever did.'

Dennison was reunited with two other Albion rejects, Bull and Thompson, as well as a fourth player from the Hawthorns, captain Robertson.

'There wasn't a lot of money in the game in Northern Ireland, the pitches and changing rooms weren't the best so coming into Wolves didn't feel too bad, as I'd seen a lot worse,' Dennison adds.

'Albion was a bit different as the players had their training kit laid out each day, but the first day I came into Wolves it was a lady called Mrs Clamp doing all the kit. I was sat in the dressing room and all I had with me was a pair of boots and a towel. When the kit appeared in a basket, the lads just wrestled each other trying to get some kit and it all went. I suddenly realised that that was all there was. So Paul Darby, the physio, went out and came back with a bright red new tracksuit still wrapped up. I don't know where it came from but it was my first day and all I wanted to do was keep my head down, and instead I'm training in a brand new red tracksuit. I'll never forget that.'

'When you look at that group, it was players who weren't getting games elsewhere,' Mutch continues. 'Bully and Thommo weren't playing at Albion, like Robbie. Keith Downing was not a household name. Phil Robinson couldn't get in the Aston Villa team and Floyd Streete was being left out at Derby. The only player with nothing to prove was Ally Robertson. He was initially an assistant coach to Brian Little but, once Brian left, he became one of the lads. It's to his credit that he captained us so well after 18 years spent at Albion playing mainly in the First Division with the likes of Laurie Cunningham, Cyrille Regis, Derek Statham and Bryan Robson. Ally had actually done something in the game, he was a shining example to all the lads.'

The opening day of the 1987/88 season will be remembered more for the trouble in the stands than anything that happened on the pitch. Newly promoted Scarborough, managed by Neil Warnock, had their historic day tarnished by the more unruly element of Wolves' support on a sunny August afternoon, with the club's Athletic Ground suffering extensive damage. On the pitch Wolves drew 2-2 with goals from Steve Stoutt and Bull. As the only ever-present outfield player in the league that season, Mutch proved to be the perfect foil for Bull.

'We had Bully, who could bang a few in, players who could create opportunities and then some solid experience in defence,' Mutch argues. 'So you had to be a good side to beat us. We had the odd bad day when we lost, but it never really crossed our minds that we would get beaten as we were that good by then. I actually said to Garry Pendrey, our coach, after we won the Fourth Division that we'd go straight on and win the Third the next season. It's a credit to all the players that they never took their feet off the gas. We just went out and did it the next season too. There was not a single player at the club who you thought was Charlie Big Potatoes, they were all cracking lads that just wanted to have a go.'

'When we won the Fourth Division, the players were better than that level,' Dennison adds. 'Once the gaffer had got us organised with a 4-4-2 system, worked on our shape so that everyone knew their jobs, we just clicked. It was a group of lads who worked their socks off and wanted to play for each other.'

Wolves visited Wembley twice during the 1987/88 season. The first occasion was in the Football League Centenary Tournament, held over a weekend in April. Teams from all four divisions won a place in the competition based on their league results during a qualification period earlier that season. The competition consisted of 16 teams: eight from the First Division, four from the Second and two each from the bottom two divisions. Matches were reduced to 20 minutes each way, and the Football League hoped that the event would capture the imagination of the public. The reality was very different, with a sparsely attended Wembley providing the backdrop.

'It was a massive incentive for me. I'd only seen the place on television, and qualifying for the tournament meant you were doing well in the league which is what we wanted,' Dennison says. 'We didn't actually get to use the changing rooms; we were bussed into the ground from a few hundred yards down the road for our game. We were drawn with Everton who were the reigning league champions. It was a great test for us, coming up against the likes of Neville Southall and Gary Stevens, who was the right-back I was up against.'

Wolves took the Merseysiders to penalties after Dennison's 30-yard effort secured a 1-1 draw.

'It was the best strike I ever hit, I knew I'd caught it well, and to beat Neville Southall who was one of the best keepers in the world, it's nice to have that memory. It was just unfortunate that there weren't many there to see it! We should have played more but Mutchy missed a penalty and we lost the game. I have reminded him about that! We stayed and watched a few other games and had some beers in the stands, then went out in London and had a few more. It was a couple of nice days away and a break from the season.'

The second Wembley visit came in the Sherpa Van Trophy Final, with opponents Burnley playing their part on an incredible day that saw a crowd in excess of 80,000 for a fixture between two Fourth Division sides. When Wolves wrapped up the league season with victory at Leyton Orient they had a three-week wait for the final at the end of May, so Turner organised a team-bonding trip to Majorca. By the time he returned to Wolverhampton, the town was in the grip of cup final fever.

The players were inundated with ticket requests. Thompson lived in a village outside Wolverhampton at the time and had supporters turning up at the door with carrier bags of money trying to persuade the player to sort them out with tickets.

The day itself was sun-baked and sweltering hot. For Mutch, a dyed-in-the-wool Liverpool fan, it was the opportunity to experience the occasion from the other side of the fence. 'As a young kid I did go to watch Liverpool at Wembley many times, it was almost a second home for us back then,' he explains. 'And I couldn't believe it, going down Wembley Way on the coach and seeing gold and black everywhere. It was absolutely amazing for the players. I think Burnley played their part as well because they brought the best part of 30,000 to make an 80,000 crowd. It wasn't the FA Cup, but it was a real cup final.

Mutch and Dennison scored the goals in a 2-0 victory and do not need a second invitation to chat about the match whenever the opportunity arises on their podcast.

'You go there to win the game first and foremost,' Dennison says. 'Then you look back, and they say it doesn't matter who scored, well it does! I've got this fantastic memory of scoring at Wembley and so has Mutchy. People still come up to me to this day and talk about that free kick in the final. Being a kid, growing up watching finals at Wembley, and to play there in front of a full house and score was just amazing. I've got a photo back home of us coming out of the tunnel at the start, with all the Wolves fans in the stand behind me, and it's one of my favourite photos.

'That experience is something you'll never forget,' Mutch continues. 'You felt like you were part of the DNA of the club on that day. The gold and black in the stands was phenomenal.

The club looked after us well, too. We stayed in a hotel out near Cockfosters and there was a big party afterwards.

'That day at Wembley gave the fans so much pride back after they'd nearly lost their club. The hope and belief returned. It's so long ago now and those days are gone. There have been different eras since, with different players and that's their time. But the supporters' love for that team is unbelievable because it felt like we were all in it together. There are fans of a certain era that come up to me and say those days were so good; scoring goals, winning games, getting promoted.'

In many ways, the final was a symbolic stage for a pair of careers that only three years earlier had been hanging in the balance. Their story didn't end there. Dennison was capped 18 times for his country and stayed with Wolves for ten years in all, twice missing out on promotion to the Premier League via the play-offs.

Mutch left Molineux after his final game on 1 May 1993, which was also the last time the old South Bank terrace welcomed supporters before its demolition. Changes were afoot on and off the pitch. Mutch joined Swindon Town for their only season in the Premier League, scoring away at the champions, Manchester United. He was also capped by England at under-21 and B levels.

'It was a big wrench for me when I left the club,' he admits. 'I came at a time when they were struggling and by the time I left they were supposedly going on to better things. I felt I should have been part of that, but it was days like the one at Wembley that I look back on with most pride.'

Over the past three decades Mutch has been an infrequent visitor to Wolverhampton on a matchday, but with the podcast has come the chance to reconnect with supporters once more. The two friends can be found enjoying a pre-match drink at The Lychgate on recording days, and have even found their way into more exclusive venues.

After a home game against Newcastle in January 2026, Mutch and Dennison headed through the corridors of the Billy Wright Stand in search of their old team-mate Thompson and found themselves at the door of the boardroom after bumping into vice-president John Richards. Moments later they were sharing a drink with Wolves chairman, Nathan Shi. Parachuted into the job by Fosun only a few weeks earlier, it was hard to know what the club's new man at the helm made of them both.

'We just told him that whatever he does, he needs to look after the fans,' Dennison reveals. 'They're the heartbeat of the football club.' Shi wasn't born when these two players were lifting the club off the floor, and is unlikely to have had any idea about what happened to Wolves during the eighties, let alone who the two former players in front of him were. But over time that may change. No other decade in the history of the club is filled with as many stories on and off the pitch, where lessons can be learnt and inspiration taken.

Chapter Ten

The Eighties – Part Three

'LADIES AND gentlemen, please welcome … the manager who helped bring the club back from oblivion … Mr Graham Turner!'

The audience at the Cleveland Arms rise as one to loudly acclaim the former Wolves boss as he takes to the stage to be interviewed by Matt Murray.

Even many years on, four decades on in fact, Turner remains one of the most popular ex-managers to have graced the Molineux dugout.

As was perfectly illustrated by that reception.

The Cleveland Arms is a well-known sports bar situated on the A454, between Wolverhampton and Willenhall and a ten-minute drive from the city centre. Famed for its events and Q&As with top names from the world of football, the regulars are usually Wolves fans with years of experience of supporting their club. Years of undergoing all the magnificent ups and the painful downs, who come to the Cleveland to relive their joy and misery in the close company of their heroes.

In a nutshell, they know their stuff. They know about, and lived and breathed, Turner's incredibly timely contribution. And so, this is the sort of night that hits differently.

And yet, it's worth remembering that Turner wasn't exactly a popular choice when he first checked in at Molineux in October 1986.

That wasn't necessarily to do with his own managerial credentials, although he had endured a difficult time during two years in the top division with Aston Villa.

Prior to that, he had established himself as a legend at Shrewsbury Town, initially as a player, then player-manager and finally manager, taking them into the old Second Division and twice to the quarter-finals of the FA Cup. Most definitely batting above their average. In that sense he was perfectly placed for the lower league rescue job that the position at Wolves entailed.

The problem was, Brian Little had been in caretaker charge at the start of that 1986/87 campaign, and had made a decent start. Although at just 32 years of age a relative novice, certainly in managerial terms, the Villa hero as a player, with two League Cup successes to his name, was getting a tune out of a Wolves team which had suffered the indignity of three successive relegations from First to Fourth Division.

Little had brought in the experience of Ally Robertson in the defence, the first of a number of signings from fierce local rivals West Bromwich Albion who would help reshape Wolves' history, as well as utilising club legend Geoff Palmer, also twice a League Cup winner, on his backroom staff.

Successive victories over Preston and Scunthorpe, with clean sheets to boot, made it four wins from nine league games, but Little's tenure was soon to end after just 36 days.

Dick Homden and Jack Harris, who had spearheaded the club's takeover in the summer with the support of Gallagher Estates and John Bird, the leader of Wolverhampton Council, were keen to bring in a more experienced manager to embark on such a crucial rebuild.

Having sought counsel from super scout Ron Jukes, Turner was the man they turned to, and, three weeks after leaving Villa, he was signing up to an altogether different challenge.

Speaking in the corner of the Cleveland Arms prior to taking to the stage, Turner admits that his boyhood allegiance to Wolves, and having a hero in Billy Wright, outweighed the many reservations he had about taking the job.

'If I wasn't a Wolves fan, I wouldn't even have looked at it,' he admits. 'I'd just left Villa, and I remember Jack Harris coming to see me at my house, and I was already a bit concerned as I knew they had got Brian in as caretaker manager.

'They said Brian's appointment was purely temporary, otherwise I wouldn't even have spoken to them about it. The only reason I did is that I was a Wolves supporter who had been brought up in Ellesmere Port, just down the road from Stan Cullis.

'As a kid, maybe aged around ten, I had written to Billy Wright to ask him for his autograph. No stamped addressed envelope, nothing, but Billy responded and sent me a programme where he had signed a picture inside, and I still have that programme today.

'Stan Cullis had lived down the street where my dad was born, and some of the family were still in the town, whilst there was also the ironworks there where many people from the Midlands actually walked to in order to get jobs.

'A lot of people from the town were either Wolves or West Brom supporters – my grandad was West Brom, so I think that is also why I chose Wolves. So that was the background, the scene behind why I took the job, because if it hadn't been the team I supported as a kid, I wouldn't have entertained it.

'Everybody who was around back then can remember the state of the ground with only two sides open, and the downward spiral with three successive relegations. There was an apathy about the place, an acceptance of the plight they were in, the state of the kit, the balls, the dressing rooms, it was all in a shocking situation.

'It was a rundown football club at its worst, and the only reason I took it all on was because I was a Wolves supporter.'

Winning the fans over was a tough first challenge given that following years of neglect on and off the pitch they were initially clinging to the small shoots of recovery planted by Little.

So too was there a challenge in convincing the players that he was the right man to take them forward.

Ultimately his reign would bring incredible success to Molineux and the revival which will forever remain etched in the history books. But not everyone came along for the ride.

Several players found life difficult under Turner for whatever reason, or reasons. Such can be the relationships between a squad and their leader. That's management, that's football and that's life.

'There were a few players who didn't seem keen on me coming in and I remember one lad saying something against what I was trying to do in a training match,' says Turner. 'So, my question back was to ask how long he had been here. "Four years" was the reply. And I think that set him up given what had happened in that time.

'There was definitely some resentment and it wasn't an ideal situation to walk into from a manager's point of view. But it was about winning them over and taking those with me who wanted to be part of the journey.

'When I first came in, the directors were very honest in telling me there was very little money available and I had to keep my powder dry. And at first the games were difficult. But eventually, the board managed to come up with some money, and told me I had a little bit to spend, but that I had to spend it wisely!'

Turner won his first game in charge, 2-1 against Tranmere thanks to goals from Andy Mutch and Matt Forman in front of a Molineux crowd of just 5,486.

Wolves would only win three of the next 15 league games, however, and included within that spell were three cup fixtures which led to that defeat against Chorley at Burnden Park, one of the most ignominious results in the club's entire 150-year history.

Ultimately, that was as low as it was to get. Thanks, in part, to the fact that Turner had indeed started to 'spend wisely', as decreed by the board.

It was on 20 November 1986 that Turner made his move and Wolves swooped to land young West Bromwich Albion duo, striker Steve Bull and utility man Andy Thompson.

Bull, then 21, had made a total of nine appearances in all competitions, including two in Division One which would prove his only ones in the top flight, scoring three goals for the Baggies in total.

Thompson, who had just turned 19, had enjoyed more experience with Albion in making 29 appearances, and was a regular in their Division Two side before joining Bull in heading up the A41.

Both had been recommended by ace scout Jukes, and both had little hesitation in deciding to join Wolves, even with the club's fortunes and facilities sitting well behind their fierce Black Country neighbours.

John Harris, son of Jack, revealed that his father and Homden both agreed to stump up the £65,000 needed to make the double signing.

'Dad wrote a company cheque out to make sure the club could sign Steve and Andy,' says John, who would eventually spend many happy years on the board working with his father, who would go on to become chairman.

'I think he had the money back from the club later once things improved, but it needed underwriting, and that was the commitment that dad and Dick showed towards Wolves at the time.'

Turner was certainly pleased to have brought in two young talents to help launch his rebuild.

'I'd seen Bully and Thommo play for Albion, in a Full Members' Cup tie against Chelsea at the Hawthorns,' he recalls. 'It was when I was at Villa and we probably had Chelsea coming up, who were fairly young, but had Micky Droy, an absolute beast of a fella, at centre-half.

'By comparison, Bully looked about 11 stone when wringing wet, but he knocked Micky Droy about from pillar to post. He was a bit erratic with his finishing back then, but he impressed me with his attitude, his bravery and his ability to get into goalscoring positions and on the end of chances.

'Thommo played wide on the left, and looked a very good footballer, and on top of the attraction of what I was seeing, Ron Jukes also confirmed they were both well worth pursuing.

'I phoned Ron Saunders, the Albion boss, who was reluctant, but eventually agreed a fee. The players came over, and we agreed terms, but I still felt something might go wrong, so I got in my car with all the paperwork and drove over to Albion to meet their chairman, Sid Lucas.

'He was nearly in tears as he didn't want to see two of their talented young players leave, but Ron was happy to see it happen, so Sid signed the forms and I stuck them in my pocket, chuffed we had got it done, and sent them off to the Football League.

'Their impact wasn't great to start with, but once they settled in, well, it couldn't have gone much better.'

Bull and Thompson, both cup-tied, were sat in the stand as Wolves were thumped 3-0 by Chorley from the Multipart Northern Premier League.

'I looked at Thommo and said, "What have we done?" was Bull's famous quote.

That game was two days after both had made their Wolves debuts, a home fixture with Wrexham in front of another sparse Molineux audience also ending in a 3-0 defeat.

Things could only get better. And they did.

The fixture that many supporters view as a key turning point and line in the sand following years of decline came on 7 February 1987 – a home game against Stockport.

Crowds had plummeted yet further – just 3,238 were inside Molineux that afternoon – and with 11 minutes to go, and Wolves a goal behind, the writing was on the wall.

Wolves were in 15th position in the Fourth Division table, pressure on Turner was already starting to build, and defeat to a Stockport side occupying third from bottom only four points off the basement was unthinkable.

But goals from Andy Thompson – a 79th-minute penalty – Micky Holmes on 87 and Bull on 88 clinched a comeback which many argue proved the catalyst for the entire revival which followed.

Including that win, Wolves were victors in 15 of their final 19 games of the season to surge into the play-offs where, amid the disappointment of defeat over two legs against Aldershot in the final, there was still much to be positive about.

In essence, one key defeat, 1-0 on a Friday night in Southend, was all that had stood between Wolves and automatic promotion, the Shrimpers finishing third, and ahead of Wolves, by just one point.

'Everything did just seem to click all of a sudden, but it wasn't an accident,' Turner says of that end-of-season run. 'We worked hard in training, found a system that worked, Bully and Thommo made a big difference, and it was about taking all that on to the pitch, which the players did.

'We had a great finish to the season and while it was a great pity about that Southend game, and then Aldershot, in the end it proved a blessing in disguise. It took us a bit more time and pre-season to get more solid foundations in place, bring in a few more players, and from there it was just a fantastic couple of seasons. The crowds started coming back, and the club was buzzing again.'

It certainly was. Those two seasons to which Turner refers, 1987/88 and 1988/89 were, indeed, truly magical. In 92 games across two seasons, they won 53 of them and drew 23, scoring 178 goals and collecting 182 points.

Bull, incredibly, reached a half century in all competitions with 52 and 50 respectively. His strike partner Mutch, who had preceded his arrival at Molineux, added 23 in each season.

There were so many highlights, including, as mentioned in the previous chapter, the Sherpa Van Trophy success against Burnley in front of a capacity Wembley audience, and the Mercantile Centenary Classic, also at the Twin Towers the month before.

In the campaign of 1987/88, promotion was sealed with a midweek 3-1 away win at Newport with their Welsh hero Mark Kendall in the Wolves goal, before the title was confirmed on the penultimate game of the season, a 2-0 home win against Hartlepool.

The following year brought a second successive league title, celebrated on an epic evening against Sheffield United when the 2-2 draw also secured the Blades' upward momentum into the equivalent of the Championship.

Wolves only lost one league game at home all season, the Easter Monday defeat against Bristol Rovers in which visiting assistant – and Molineux legend – Kenny Hibbitt received an emotional reception.

At one stage in November and December, Wolves hit 16 goals in three successive home fixtures, destroying Huddersfield 4-1, Preston 6-0 and Mansfield 6-2. Bull's returns in those specific games were two, four and three. Almost beyond belief.

Fans headed down Waterloo Road for kick-off pretty much knowing that even if Wolves went behind, it didn't matter. They possessed way too much firepower for any visiting team to cope with.

And yet, beyond the matches and the results, beyond the goals, the hat-tricks and the home comforts, it was more about a feeling and an emotion. A sense of belonging.

For younger fans getting their first taste of success, these were truly incredible times. Wolves could go on and win the Champions

League one day, and it would struggle to match what it felt like to follow that team and see them become heroes.

For those of an older vintage, those that had witnessed the team of the seventies, perhaps even the fifties as well, this offered a much-needed revival. Not players operating necessarily at the same quality as those that had gone before and won top division titles and cup competitions. But certainly, with the same heart, the same spirit, the same sense of togetherness, and the same pride in their club.

It was about, after the turbulence of the early to mid-eighties, being able to talk about Wolves with a sense of dignity and self-respect as opposed to shame and humiliation.

From almost going out of business, twice, and the tumble down the divisions, the comeback was on. And how the fans loved it, and embraced the new dawn.

Across the two lower leagues, up and down the country, the Wolves fanbase travelled in huge numbers, taking over stadiums, sometimes taking over towns. Attendances at Molineux, even with two sides of the ground still closed due to the regulations of the Taylor Report, soared as well.

From Turner's first game in charge, and that crowd under 5,500, by the time of the Sheffield United fixture two and a half years later it was 24,321, near capacity for what was available at that time. With the small matter of the 50,000 who headed down to Wembley for the Sherpa Van Trophy in between.

The success of those two years was achieved on a relative shoestring. Turner brought in Garry Pendrey as an assistant with Paul Darby as physiotherapist and highly esteemed chief scout Jukes was part-time.

Behind the scenes, Keith Pearson delivered an incredible job as club secretary, a vocation he followed with the utmost efficiency and professionalism through some very tough times.

All this overseen by that board of Homden and Jack Harris, supported by son John, until the arrival of Sir Jack Hayward in 1990.

'Sometimes having such a small group of people like we did then really helped,' says Turner. 'Everybody mucked in, and we all knew that if something didn't get done, then we would know about it.

'The players were the same as well, they were brilliant with it, because the state of the dressing rooms was appalling. They bought into what life was like, with two sides of the ground shut, no training ground, and having to beg, borrow and steal, even sometimes to find a bag of balls.

'I remember once phoning Mitre up to try and get some footballs, and I went across to get them and they were all sorts of colours, like beach balls. But they served their purpose!

'And when it came to the kit, I met a couple of people who owned a kit manufacturing business and sorted it with them that they supplied the training kit and the match kit. We all had to do what was needed, but that was fine. Because everyone bought into it, it worked.'

Within all that came a couple of other developments which became the norm for the time, but would cause utter consternation in the modern day!

First off, the Tuesday Club. A drinking club. Where, whichever players would fancy it, would head off after training to various hostelries in Wolverhampton or Birmingham to enjoy each other's company, and build bonds, away from the day job.

It was overseen by captain Ally Robertson, and Turner knew all about it, and had no issues with it, providing they didn't cause any trouble whilst out and all reported back in decent shape ready to train again on the Thursday morning. He had also run them hard on the Tuesday mornings. That was part of the deal.

And then came the car park training. Yes, for those that haven't heard this story, the team trained on the North Bank car park. On the Friday morning before the game on the Saturday. Imagine that in the modern day. Even in non-league? But again, it worked.

'Ally was the senior player and the likes of him, Floyd Streete and other senior players led things in the dressing room,' Turner adds. 'I knew about the Tuesday Club, and knew where they would go, but it was all about building team spirit. Then there was the training.

'We had lost Castlecroft by then so had to phone around for places to train. Ssometimes it would be Aldersley, sometimes in the middle of the racecourse at Dunstall, it was a crazy situation. We'd have to line all the players up and they would walk across the pitch and clear up any dog muck before we started – it would all go in a bucket.

'And then it all started one Christmas, the day before a game, when there was a bit of snow on the ground. We went and had a look at the car park at Molineux, and realised that if we moved a few cars out of the way, there was enough space for a five-a-side.

'So, we bounced a few cars out of the way – people soon learned that would happen if they parked there – and trained. All the staff played as well, and if you fell over you ended up with gravel in your knees, but again, it just set the standard even higher in terms of togetherness.

'It was a laugh, and at the end of the session the players would vote for who had been the worst, and they would have to wear a yellow jersey the following week. I am fortunate to say that I never won it, no one was brave enough for the gaffer.

'But the day after that first time we did it, because of the weather, we played ever so well and won the game, and so the next week, the players said, "Come on gaffer, let's go on the car park again."

'That started the tradition, a tradition which you couldn't in the slightest way look at as a professional person and think it was good preparation for a game of football. However, it was good fun, brought a good feeling, and just cemented that team spirit among a squad which had so many great characters.

'Bully was actually one of the quieter ones back then, he was just so focused, but then there was Mutchy and Thommo who were louder, and those experienced ones like Ally, Floyd, Mark Kendall. Not only good players but good characters and personalities, they would police the dressing room themselves.'

Indeed they did. Such special times and a story which deserved a happy ending. A promotion all the way back to the Holy Grail of the top division, soon to be the Premier League. But sadly, painstakingly, it didn't happen.

After the back-to-back promotions, Wolves had five attempts at another one on Turner's watch. Finishes of 10th, 12th, 11th and 11th, and then 8th after he departed in the March of 1994, showed they were not too far away from the play-offs, but ultimately not close enough. For Bull, despite 13 England caps and a World Cup for his country in Italy, his only top-flight experience would remain with Albion, and not among his 561 appearances for Wolves. The price of loyalty.

For Turner, his incredible successes made it a tricky dilemma as fan frustrations grew. Had he reached the end of the road? Or did he deserve more time?

Such was the lack of a collective will among the fanbase at the time that the popular *A Load of Bull* fanzine printed one edition with two free badges as a giveaway. One inscribed with 'Turner Must Go' and the other 'Turner Must Stay'. Covering all bases.

As for the man himself, he was given an early sign of the increased expectation after defeat in the second leg of the Sherpa Van Trophy Final at home to Torquay which prevented a second successive trip to Wembley and potential second successive lower league title and cup double.

Wolves had won the first leg 2-1 thanks to a late Bully brace, and the return, the first game in England to be played in front of terracing after the Hillsborough disaster, was expected to be a procession.

But Wolves fan and former Molineux striker Dean Edwards, one of those who hadn't necessarily seen eye-to-eye with Turner after his arrival, ended up with a goal in each leg and a 2-0 victory in the return took Torquay to Wembley.

'So, we were well on the way to the second successive promotion, and were trying to get to Wembley again to achieve another double,' says Turner. We lost the second leg to Torquay, and the lads were all devastated, sat around the dressing room, heads down.

'All of a sudden, the windows came in. I looked across and there were players with glass on them after something had been chucked through the window from outside.

'It just showed the impact that we had made, the expectation we had built. And well, that was it.'

There were more highlights, the league double over West Bromwich Albion in the first season back in the Championship including Bull's epic last-gasp winner at the Hawthorns, and back-to-back runs to the FA Cup quarter-finals, the latter of which against Chelsea proved to be Turner's penultimate game in charge.

But the Holy Grail of promotion proved elusive.

One season when it really felt like it might all come together was that 1993/94 campaign which ultimately proved Turner's last.

It was the season when the Molineux redevelopment masterminded by Sir Jack reached its conclusion, the opening of the redeveloped South Bank in the December as the Jack Harris Stand following on from the Billy Wright (Waterloo Road) Stand and the Stan Cullis (North Bank).

With the spectacular redevelopment completed, finally bringing a previously dilapidated Molineux to the forefront of modern stadia infrastructure, Sir Jack loosened the purse strings in terms of improving the squad.

'I was given some decent money to spend, and, once again, I thought I had spent it wisely,' Turner recalls. 'We brought in Geoff Thomas, Ned [David] Kelly, Kevin Keen, Peter Shirtliff and

Cyrille Regis. Then we had bad injuries. If you really wanted to sabotage that team, you'd have got rid of Bully and Geoff Thomas, and that's what happened. I remember the first game of the season, we beat Bristol City at home, and the atmosphere around the place was fantastic. It really felt like something was happening – that this might finally be the year.

'Geoff had come in and been brilliant for us, but he then got injured not long after scoring a great goal away at Sunderland. The lad then went right through him, and I remember him lying on the treatment table in the dressing room with his knee completely opened up.

'I don't think he was ever quite the same player after that and that was a massive blow because he was such a big influence on what we were doing.

'We lost two big players, and the crowd had become restless, it was my seventh full season and you could sense things were changing.'

Wolves lost that FA Cup quarter-final 1-0 at Stamford Bridge on the Sunday, and then were somehow tasked with facing Portsmouth in the league at Fratton Park just two days later, being comfortably despatched 3-0.

That was to prove the end of the line. Albeit the end of a line in which his seven-and-a-half-year tenure had been such a pivotal and game-changing one in the club's history.

'We never turned up at Portsmouth and I think everyone was still really down after going out of the cup to Chelsea,' Turner explains. 'And then [Chairman] Jonathan Hayward came into the dressing room afterwards and berated the players.

'They couldn't have felt any worse about everything without Jonathan coming in and when that happened, I just felt it was the end. You can't have a chairman, a director, any sort of outsider, coming into the dressing room and subjecting the players to that, particularly in those circumstances.

'So I asked if I could meet him the next day at the ground, at 8am, and told him I couldn't put up with that – it was the end. I always got on well with Jonathan and Sir Jack, but I did feel that an undercurrent was creeping in, you get word that there is a bit of moaning going on.

'When it does come to an end like that, I am not sure you ever completely get used to it. But I could certainly understand the anxiety and the drive to get over that final hurdle and get to the Premier League – I understand it because I had four years of trying to achieve it.

'I felt bitter at the time because I think I brought the club back into respectability, and so it hurt. Looking back now though, all these years on, I just see good times … so many good times.

'There is that sense of pride at playing a part in helping the club achieve something again and come back from where they were. It was a broken-down stadium when I walked through the door, and was magnificent when I left, and while that wasn't down to us, I think the efforts of everyone at that time certainly helped.

'And I got to work with Billy Wright! After I had sent that letter to him asking for his autograph as a kid, he later came in as a director. No matter what the result on the Saturday, he would always phone me on the Sunday to catch up – obviously he knew his football and to have someone like Billy calling me on a regular basis was absolutely brilliant.

'In summary, there is so much pride in what we achieved. But also, what crosses my mind is what we failed to achieve, the last step and what might have been. But the positives far outweighed everything else, without a shadow of a doubt.'

That is probably the story of Turner's Molineux reign, and those latter years of the eighties and early ones of the nineties.

A decade that started with a League Cup victory, and then somehow descended into a hat-trick of relegations and twice going out of business, ended with a revival which continues to stir the soul of all who were fortunate enough to witness it.

A group of staff and players who rolled their sleeves up, worked hard and played hard, and took Wolves back to the brink of the top flight only for that final push to prove a bridge too far.

They didn't win a major trophy, or play in the Premier League, or hit the giddy heights of Wolves teams that had preceded them.

But in so many ways, they achieved far more. They rebuilt an entire club, and reinvigorated an entire town.

Which the audience at the Cleveland Arms, and Wolves fans in general, will never, ever forget.

Chapter 11

The One Hit Wanderers

PRESTWOOD ROAD West, situated in Wednesfield in Wolverhampton not far from New Cross Hospital, is like so many of the busy main roads that make up the city.

And yet, if you drive down it, there's every chance you wouldn't be aware of the football pitches that are almost hidden away, tucked behind a small drive in between two of the houses. This six-acre facility used to be the home of Wolverhampton United Football Club, one of the many non-league clubs which had flourished across the region.

Established in 1976 by a merger of Oxley and Whitmore Old Boys, Wolverhampton United boasted several honours during its history, including winning the JW Hunt Cup in their first season, before folding in 2019.

The club may sadly have gone, but the pitches remain, and are still very much serving the local community.

Because they are now leased to the New Park Village (NPV) Football Development, a Community Interest Company launched in 1998 to support the neighbourhoods of New Park Village and Heath Town.

In essence, those were two communities in the city deeply affected by gang activity, poverty and social deprivation, where opportunities for young people were limited and the negative impact on family life was proving considerable.

The brainchild and founder behind the project is Joe Jackson, once of an elite band of Wolves players – perhaps you could call him a 'one game Wanderer'.

He is among a group that in some ways everyone would love to belong to. And in other ways, no one would want to belong to. Those who have lived the dream of making one first-team appearance for Wolves. But then, when no doubt feeling they had plenty more to offer, made no more.

Jackson's footballing story, even before the extraordinary impact he has made with NPV, is already an extremely powerful one.

Because via his one and only first-team appearance for Wolves, away to Notts County in the First Division on 1 May 1984, he became the first black player to come through the ranks at Molineux to represent the first team. An accolade he views as a huge honour.

The team were already relegated, and caretaker boss Jim Barron gave several young players an opportunity. Wolves lost 4-0 in front of a crowd of 5,378. All these years on however, the result really doesn't matter.

'Despite the result it was a fantastic day personally,' he reflects. 'I had played the majority of my time at Wolves in the youth set-up, but I was 18 when I got that opportunity in the first team.

'The result wasn't great, but for me, I was a young lad from the local community getting that opportunity to wear the gold and black, and it doesn't get much better.'

Although Jackson's time at Wolves was limited, and he admits there weren't the support mechanisms in place to help when he was released by the club, he did go on to forge an impressive career at non-league level, both as player and manager.

He later took up a role as football development officer at Bilston College, now the City of Wolverhampton College, before deciding to move in a new and even more purposeful direction by launching NPV, which continues to flourish with the strong support of wife Debbie.

Community tensions are nothing new, and were well known to Jackson growing up in multi-cultural Wolverhampton in Whitmore Reans. But that was very much part of his motivation, believing it is important for those who have the opportunity to try and make life better and provide more opportunities for young people.

'My professional career didn't last long and might not have turned out the way I liked but being in that environment opened my eyes to the world of football,' he says.

'Racism was rife, throughout my career it was a problem, and it still hasn't gone away. How did I deal with it? I didn't. I reacted, and I would get sent off.

'That is the nature of the person I am, I will always fight back, but I think what we are doing now with NPV is another way of fighting back. We set up back in 1998 because of the gang situation in the city, the culture which had developed.

'Youngsters around Heath Town and New Park Village were at loggerheads, and we needed to set something up that produced some sort of intervention. We are saying that there is a different way that we can operate as human beings, and we can try and show these young people that there is a place they can go in football where they interact with others and recognise that we can all be friends.

'You look at our teams and our sessions, all the different cultures playing together, enjoying it together, and that is what it is all about.

'We can talk about breaking down barriers and working cohesively but talk is cheap – we need to get out and do it. I was born and bred in Whitmore Reans – and we know that is practically Wolves anyway – so the club always felt like home.

'We have now had almost 30 years of being consistently out there in a community where one of the biggest issues has been inconsistency, and that leads to a situation where people become vulnerable.

'We'll never know what different journeys our young people might have taken, but if I'm honest, we've all had times when we've not been that great, but then we become adults, when it's natural to mature and learn from your mistakes.

'And then, if you can become a person who can be a light for another group of people, particularly the next generation, I feel that is what all our jobs should be.'

Not everyone who made only one appearance for Wolves, and indeed those that didn't make any at all, have gone on to support the community in a similar inspirational way to that of Jackson.

But it's fair to say that all among that number still nurture and cherish the opportunity and experience that they received.

Across 150 years of history, there is a rich tapestry of players who have made just a fleeting impact, each with their own story and experience to remember.

Many of them, perhaps unsurprisingly, hailed from Wolves' early years. With the club, and the Football League, only just having started, there was plenty of learning to be done on all sides.

In that very first season, wing-half Jack Benton made his one and only appearance in the club's second-ever game, a 4-0 defeat at home to Everton, whilst Bob Dudley made his only outing in the last fixture, a 2-1 victory against Notts County.

Jimmy Hill – no, not that one – had actually made his one and only Wolves appearance in the fixtures played before the formation of the Football League, a 4-1 FA Cup win against Long Eaton in 1883. As did Jack Waldron, in the following round of the competition, as Wolves lost 4-2 to Wednesbury Old Athletic.

What stood out among those 'one game Wanderers' of the early years, summing up the embryonic stages of league football at the time, was how many players moved on to other local non-league clubs after their brief Wolves impacts.

Benton later assisted Willenhall Pickwick, where Herbert Bailey and Bill Howells played after representing Wolves in 1891 and 1900 respectively, whilst Dudley left for Warwick County.

Jack Pickerell, who played his Wolves game in 1890, left for Dudley Town, Frank Lester, who appeared in 1894, joined Fallings Heath, and two others from the same season – Winston Crump and Jack Roberts – headed to Hereford Thistle and Ewells FC Wednesbury respectively.

Even moving into the 1900s, as the game started to develop, there were very few big transfers between clubs and many of those who chalked up a solitary Wolves appearance drifted back into local football after their moment in the sun.

Arthur Arrowsmith, who played in a 1-1 draw with Birmingham in 1908, moved on to Willenhall Swifts, Arthur Price, who made his debut against Chesterfield a couple of seasons earlier, left for Acocks Green, whilst Charlie Pilsbury, whose first and last game was in 1903, departed for Bilston Swifts and later, Tipton Victoria.

Pilsbury is also part of another elite group relating to those who appeared only once. He also scored in his solitary appearance, finding the net in a 6-1 defeat to Manchester City.

Others to boast a 100 per cent scoring record include George Swift, who struck against Grimsby in 1901, Bert Shinton, who netted against Stockport in 1909, and, later on, forward Bobby Thomson, who found the net against Newcastle in 1957 before later becoming a prolific marksman at both Aston Villa and Birmingham. And then, more recently, back in 2011, James Spray, having been an unused substitute in the Premier League at just 16, came off the bench to score in a League Cup win against Millwall.

There are other stories relating to those one-game personnel. Ernie Whittam, who appeared against Blackburn in 1936, was actually blind in one eye, whilst goalkeeper Billy Walker, handed his debut in a local derby with West Bromwich Albion in 1929, had a proper afternoon to forget.

He broke his leg in the first half, Wolves lost the game 7-3, and he was never seen in the first team again.

Fellow keeper Chic Brodie, between the sticks for Wolves against Manchester United in 1961, had his own story to dine out on a few years later.

He became a taxi driver in London and was involved in a minor collision with a white Jaguar, which turned out to be driven by England's World Cup hat-trick hero Geoff Hurst. Standard 'fare' for Brodie, whose professional career had come to an end in 1970 when with Brentford, as he collided with a sheepdog which had run on to the pitch and severely injured his knee.

Brodie isn't the only Wolves player to have made his one and only start against Manchester United. In 1939, not long before football was suspended due to the war, Alan Steen, at just 16 years and eight months old, played and scored against United in a 3-0 win at Molineux.

And then, in 1967, came the last part-time player to appear in Wolves' first team, a 22-year-old accountant, close to completing his qualifications, who was called up to play against Manchester United in front of over 50,000 at Molineux.

To come up against the Holy Trinity of Best, Charlton and Law, and the reigning First Division champions who were top of the table and a few months away from beating Benfica to win their first ever European Cup.

That was the task facing defender Stewart Ross, who, while pursuing a career in accountancy, had progressed at Wolves from the fourth team playing in the Worcester Combination, to the third team in the West Midlands League, and then the reserves in the Central League.

He had been scouted by George Noakes, and invited in to train at the age of 14 by boss Stan Cullis, but even with the progress and potential of a footballing career, he opted for the stability of chartered accountancy, with BDO Stoy Hayward and Muras Baker Jones.

But what a story he had to tell his clients, the day he took on the mighty Manchester United!

'I remember I was meeting a client at the time, not long before Christmas, when I got a call from the manager Ronnie Allen, asking me to report to the office at Molineux,' says Ross.

'The team had lost their previous game 4-0, and I was brought in to replace Dave Burnside, although I hadn't done a single training session with the first team. On the day of the game, my parents drove me in, and we had lunch at the old Molineux Hotel.

'We walked down the alley to the ground, and not many people knew me at that point, I could walk straight through!

'With over 50,000 inside Molineux I was very nervous as you can imagine, and then it was just about coming up against Best, Law and Charlton!

'There are parts of it I can remember, including a couple of tackles on George Best, winning the ball and getting support from the crowd for doing so!

'I was playing in midfield, and we were actually winning at half-time, and then in the second half Graham Hawkins was injured and I moved into the back four.

'I can remember just after half-time, Bobby Charlton played a one-two around me in the middle of the park, I never saw him, and he went straight down the other end and scored! It was a special day, although we ended up losing 3-2.'

Quite the story. It was to prove Ross's only start for the first team, although he did make a couple of further appearances as a substitute. There have been times since when he has sometimes wondered what might have happened had he pursued a career in football, but ultimately, he remains completely comfortable in the choice that he made.

Trying to break through at that time would have been particularly challenging given the quality of players at Wolves' disposal, which was undoubtedly a factor for many in the preceding decade as the team conquered all before them in the 1950s.

Take full-back Joe Baillee, who made one appearance in a 6-4 win against Huddersfield in 1955, otherwise proving unable to get in front of the excellence of Bill Shorthouse or Eddie Stuart.

Centre-forward Harry Middleton was Wolves' first-ever player to pick up England youth honours, but his only appearance in the gold and black came a year after Baillee, deputising for Johnny Hancock at Everton.

Wing half Les Cocker was another England youth international and also part of Wolves' FA Youth Cup-winning squad of 1957/58.

He would spend several years as a reserve at Wolves behind the likes of Ron Flowers, Bill Slater and Eddie Clamp, breaking into the first team just once, against Blackburn in 1961.

Fast-forward a couple of decades to the eighties and players were making the odd appearance for very different reasons.

The chaos that befell that decade saw a revolving door of players come and go as Wolves often had to beg, borrow and steal to put a team out as various financial crises took hold.

Several players came and went on loan with little fanfare and little action, including an appearance for Nicky Sinclair in 1984 and Brian Caswell three years later.

Anthony Kernan had come over to Wolves from Donegal but saw his Molineux career curtailed by injury after playing against Coventry in the March of 1982, whilst Steve Blackwell was from much closer to home, the Wolverhampton-born striker later flourishing in non-league after his one Wolves outing as a substitute in 1985.

A couple of months prior to Blackwell's appearance, Cavan Chapman joined his brother Campbell in the team just once, for a goalless draw at Cardiff. Later, Matt Hellin played his only Wolves game in the curtain-raiser of 1985/86, the club's first ever in the

Fourth Division, and Mark Turner, son of Graham, stepped out at Derby on the final day of 1992/93.

But what was it like to make just one appearance for Wolves, especially in that turbulent spell in the 1980s? Another two who did just that, and went on to success at different levels in their career afterwards, were defenders Graham Rodger and Darren Wright.

Rodger arrived at Wolves as a schoolboy, alongside fellow Kenilworth-based hopeful Tim Flowers, and, later becoming a full-time apprentice, was one of so many to benefit from the coaching and 'tough love' provided by youth team coach Frank Upton.

And then, at the tender age of 17 years and 20 days, injury to John Pender opened the door for a senior debut against Ipswich.

Previous boss Graham Hawkins had not long been sacked with Jim Barron taking caretaker charge, with Wolves on a run of four consecutive defeats and in a period when they scored just twice in ten games.

They lost, 3-0.

'I can't remember much about it, but maybe I've tried to block it all out, because it was a really bad day at the office,' says Rodger. 'Yes, I was only 17, and one of the club's youngest ever players, but I really thought I'd be able to go out there and hold my own.

'As it was, it just showed that I wasn't quite ready for that level and so what could have been a really massive day for me turned into a disappointment.

'It was to prove my only game for the club – at one point there was talk of a three-year contract, but it never came about and I moved on.

'It was a difficult time at Wolves. Initially there was a good feeling, with Derek Dougan banging the drum and saying the club was going places, but for whatever reason that never came off and the club ended up in freefall.

'While there was disappointment that it turned out to be my one and only Wolves senior appearance, I think I will always be more disappointed that I didn't really perform to the standard I wanted to, both for myself and the fans, who always wanted to get right behind young players.'

Life certainly improved for Rodger after swapping Wolves for Coventry City, where he came on as a substitute in the 1987 FA Cup Final and was involved in the Sky Blues' winning goal in a dramatic 3-2 victory against Tottenham.

What might have been in terms of a career at Wolves? A question which also applies to Wright, brought up in Great Bridge in Tipton, and another to have learned so much about the game from his time as an apprentice under Upton.

His one and only senior appearance came about 18 months after Rodger's, but with Wolves in similarly testing times, and finished in a 3-1 defeat, away to Plymouth.

He was also just 17 at the time, and an injury to Ricki Herbert opened the door for his inclusion, manna from heaven for a lad who had stood on the South Bank with his dad and also been to the 1980 League Cup Final.

'Being taken on as an apprentice by the club was the dream of every lad like me – my heart definitely ruled my head!' Wright reflects.

'Bill McGarry was the manager then, in his second spell at the club, and he had watched me play for the reserves against Coventry before telling me I was travelling with the first team the following weekend.

'It was a strange one as we were playing a friendly against Truro City the day after the Plymouth game and I thought I was travelling just to carry the kit and stuff and then play in that one instead.

'It got to the Friday night, at the Holiday Inn in Plymouth, and the gaffer told me to watch what I was eating and drinking as I was going to be playing the next day.

'I was straight on the phone to my mum and dad as you can imagine! I can still remember running out before the game to do the warm-up and seeing the fans behind the goal, where I would have been watching myself just a few years earlier.

'It was so surreal to be running out with the shirt on getting ready to play a first-team match for Wolves, almost unbelievable really.

'We lost the game which was disappointing, but for me, at 17, I'd made my first-team debut and was thinking this was the start of my career in football, my career with Wolves.

'But things often don't work out like that, in football it changes dramatically in no time at all, and I never played for Wolves again.

'There were a lot of changes at the club and that was it really – there were five or six of us apprentices, and at the end of the season none of us were taken on.'

Wright, who now lives in Cornwall a few miles south-west of the scene of his only Wolves appearance, went on to play over 100 games with Wrexham which included European experience by virtue of winning the Welsh Cup.

He will always cherish that afternoon at Home Park.

'Of course, I wish it could have been more, and of course I wish it had been at Molineux rather than away at Plymouth,' he admits. 'But it was still an unbelievable feeling and one I will never forget.'

As time has moved on, the provision for young players following in the footsteps of Rodger and Wright has changed to such an extent that academy graduates are given a far more all-round learning environment, well beyond football.

And that means that even those that depart with just a solitary appearance, or a few more, or even none, often do so with much appreciation and gratitude of their formative years.

Much of that is down to the people they have met, the scouts, the coaches and managers, the environment, it all comes together to deliver memories which they continue to cherish.

Elliott Bennett, with two Wolves appearances, and Sam Winnall, with one, both went on to enjoy impressive careers in the game after their Compton Park education.

'I get asked this question a lot and my answer is always the same – if those two games for Wolves turned out to be all I had in my career I would still have been happy,' says Bennett, who went on to make 59 Premier League appearances with Norwich City.

'That was always beyond my wildest dreams. To get those two appearances, in front of my family, including my dad who is no longer with us, that was the pinnacle of where I ever thought I could get to.

'I will always remember a chat with Terry Connor when Brighton came in for me, when I said I didn't want to go.

'He told me I needed to go, I needed to go to become Elliott Bennett the footballer and not just Elliott Bennett the academy kid from Wolves, to go and make my career.

'Thankfully that's how it worked out, and when you look at the decisions I made in my career, that was the best one. I will forever be grateful to Wolves as a football club for giving me the platform to go and become a footballer. As a result, I ended up living something that I never ever thought was possible.'

Winnall adopts a similar mindset, admitting: 'It was probably a combination of reasons as to why it just wasn't meant to be for me at Wolves.

'But there was never any bitterness – everything about the club gave me such a good chance of making a living in the game. It was quite a daunting time when I had to leave – I think I was 22 at the time and it's all I had known having been there for ten years.

'I hadn't really made any sort of mark on the football world in terms of appearances, and it was the first time I had been out of contract.

'In the end, it probably turned into the best thing that could have happened for me, and the thing I needed most, to go out and prove myself.

'It also gave me the chance to put into practice everything I had learned in all those years coming through at Wolves, and that is why, even though I had to go elsewhere to build a career, I will always look back with nothing but good memories of my time at the club.'

Winnall now works as a counsellor, providing support in mental health, wellbeing and psychology to athletes, including academy scholars at Wolves.

And that's a similar area to Johnny Gorman, another 'one game Wanderer', who has now completed a master's degree in psychology at the University of Bath, with a particular interest in the lived experience of former athletes.

So many others with fleeting impacts at Wolves have gone on to achieve much in careers both inside and outside of football, and go back a bit further and Marlon Walters is, like Jackson, another example of providing support for the community.

Walters, a good friend of Carl Ikeme, was one of the first to sign a Premier League contract when Wolves first went into the league in 2003, and, even though never making a first-team appearance, was a regular captain of the reserves.

Having gone on to enjoy a good career at non-league level both as a player and assistant manager, Walters then set up his own company – MW Impact – which provides a range of support for young people across the Midlands.

In mentoring children and young people, and addressing issues which affect mental, emotional and physical wellbeing, as well as areas such as knife crime and gang culture, Walters is delivering a service way beyond what you might expect from a former footballer.

It is also delivered with a powerful backstory, as a tribute to son Marnell who passed away at the age of three and a half months, and remains the steadfast motivation behind all that he does.

'I was distraught when I had to leave Wolves, but looking back now, in truth I wouldn't have changed it,' he says. 'I think this was more what God's plan was for me, and I can make more of a difference doing what I am doing now.

'I don't think I was ready for football, but I took away some absolutely wonderful memories from Wolves and am so grateful for the experience. Losing my boy left me with so much mental trauma and I wouldn't say I have recovered completely and maybe I never will.

'But the way to recover was to do something positive, and now I feel I know what it takes to help people bounce back. When I think back to Wolves, and people like Mike Smith, John Perkins, Terry Connor and Keith Downing – I have taken bits from all of those and how they worked and dealt with people and used that in what I do.

'I think I am living proof that if you can develop a mentality, and have a group of people behind you and supporting you, then you can come through anything and try and make it into a positive.'

There are many similarities between Walters and Jackson in their approach to community support, and, even though they only have one Wolves senior appearance between them, their respective spells with the club have clearly shaped their lives in ways which they both very much understand. They are also powerful role models within their local communities.

In the summer of 2026, Jackson joined Wolves' League Cup winner George Berry, and fellow pioneer Don Gardner – the first black player to represent Wolves who made three appearances in 1975 – in attending the unveiling of a permanent monument in Wolverhampton to honour the Windrush generation.

Another pivotal and powerful show of strength and support, and a sign that when it comes to Wolves, sometimes it isn't just the number of appearances that displays the true contribution to the club and community.

Returning to Bennett, he was part of a reunion event organised by former academy assistant director Glyn Harding in the summer of 2026, to mark the 25th anniversary of when Wolves won an Under-21 tournament in Japan dubbed by FIFA as the 'Junior World Cup'.

Bennett was the only one of the seven players in attendance who had gone on to play regularly in the Football League and indeed Premier League, but for all of them, there was no bitterness or regret or tales of what might have been. Instead, just a collective sense of joy and appreciation that they got to appreciate the academy journey together, even if it didn't ultimately lead to the first team.

For the 'one game Wanderers', and indeed those that didn't play at all, their impact and their memories extend way beyond what they delivered on the pitch.

Now that's what you call a team picture! One of the earliest Wolves line-ups, from the 1890s.

Stan Cullis, then captain, and later the most successful manager in the club's history. Wonder where this signed ball ended up?

What a captain, Wolves' best ever. Billy Wright leads out the team at Molineux in 1949.

So many Wolves legends in one photograph. Stan Cullis and the squad with their first league championship trophy in 1954.

Another two Wolves greats, as Ron Flowers is given a few words of wisdom from former player and then coach and scout, Joe Gardiner.

And now it's a chance for Richards! King John fires home the winner at Wembley in the 1974 League Cup Final.

Emlyn Hughes, who days later would lift the League Cup trophy, given a 'lift' by his team-mates ahead of the 1980 final.

One man and the Molineux Mound! John Humphrey in action against Manchester City in 1981.

The Wolves bug bit early for our two co-authors!

Over four decades ago, Paul Berry on Waterloo Road outside Molineux getting an autograph from club legend John Richards.

Paul Berry runs out as mascot with Kenny Hibbitt against Cambridge during the promotion-winning season of 1981/82. Johnny Phillips wearing his Wolves shirt as a young Wolf!

Associated with the Shropshire Star

Tel. Wolverhampton 22351

Friday, July 2, 1982

£2.5m debts force club to stop trading

WOLVES HAVE GONE BUST

THE TICKET OFFICE IS CLOSED UNTIL MONDAY 5th JULY 82
WE APOLOGISE FOR ANY INCONVENIECE CAUSED

The sign outside the Molineux ticket office this afternoon

WOLVES went bust this afternoon with debts of a staggering £2.5 million.

The receiver has been called in, the club has stopped trading and the possibility of soccer at Molineux next season is in doubt.

A sign has already gone up on the ground's ticket office saying it is closed.

Doug Ellis, chairman for just a fortnight, made a dramatic statement at a Press conference. He said that Lloyds Bank — owed £1.8 million by the club — had decided they could no longer continue to support the Molineux outfit. The directors had no alternative but to ask the bank to appoint a receiver.

In an eleventh hour bid to stave off the receiver, Mr Ellis revealed that he and vice chairman Malcolm Finlayson had offered to bank £250,000 of their own money.

But he said this had been refused because the bank was not prepared to accept the cash on a 12-month interest-free basis.

The shock statement revealed that last season, the club had a trading loss of £725,000. Even after a donation from the development association, this figure stood at £650,000.

The statement also showed that the club has liabilities of more than £2.5 million, and that the projected loss for the coming season — Wolves' first back in the Second Division — would be £540,000. Mr Eillis later said the Wolves were paying [illegible] a day in interest charges alone.

ALWAYS DANGER

After reading the statement announcing the club's grim [illegible], Mr Ellis said: "There is always a danger that there will be no football at the start of next season. But in this particular case I am hopeful there will be League football played at Molineux next season."

Mr Finlayson hit out at the way the situation at the club had been allowed to develop over the last few years. "It is one hundred years down the drain," he added.

Despite the club's tangled finances, £75,000 in advance season ticket sales has been deposited by the four-man board in a separate bank account and would not be touched.

The club accountant Keith Pearson said that season ticket money brought in before the boardroom upheaval last month would be a matter for the receiver. "As far as we are concerned the club is in limbo, waiting for the receiver to take over."

The receiver was expected to begin his investigations and control this afternoon. Mr Finlayson said the club's future would be completely in the receiver's hands.

He added: "My understanding of a receiver's job is that it is to keep the company going as a going concern."

[illegible] said that the board would do "everything to assist [illegible] to make sure league football will be continued next [illegible] at Molineux."

It was just a fortnight ago that Mr Ellis took control at Molineux after a fierce boardroom battle which ended with the [illegible] of Harry Marshall. Since then, £74,840 has been taken [illegible] tickets and for executive boxes. That money is in a [illegible] bank account.

[illegible] back page

Chairman Doug Eilis reads out the statement with Vice Chairman Malcolm Finlayson by his side and Director Malcolm Goody (left).

How Ellis broke the tragic news

News of the Wolves crash was broken by chairman Doug Ellis in a statement issued on behalf of the Board which said:

"When Malcolm Finlayson and myself were invited to join the Board 14 days ago we promised that a full investigation of the club's financial affairs be carried out.

We immediately requested the club accountant to prepare the club's draft accounts to 31st May, 1982 and to prepare a financial forecast to 31st May, 1983.

In addition, we appointed the international firm of chartered accountants, Peat Marwick Mitchell and Co., to examine these figures and produce a viability report on the financial affairs of the club.

For the last season alone these figures revealed a trading loss of £725,000 which even after a donation from the Development Association produced a NET loss of over £650,000.

For next season, as members of the Second Division, the accountants projected a further loss of £540,000.

The figures also show that the club had in excess of £2.5 million of liabilities as at 31st May, 1982 and could not continue to meet its debts as they fell due.

In view of the revelation of the seriousness of the financial position shown by the club's accountant's figures, supported by the independent accountants' investigation, our bankers felt they could no longer support the club. Under these circumstances the board has been legally advised that it cannot continue to trade.

It is therefore, with extreme regret that the directors have had no alternative but to formally request the bank to appoint a receiver.

We announced shortly after our appointment that in view of our initial concern over the club's possible financial position your directors were not prepared to accept monies for season tickets which might have been lost in the event of a receiver being appointed and football not being played next season. That money is deposited in a separate bank and a further announcement will be made as soon as practicable.

You will appreciate that it is with deep sadness that this course of action has had to be taken, but you may rest assured that I and fellow directors will do everything in our power to assist the receiver and to ensure that League football will continue to be played at Molineux if that path is available to the receiver or in accordance with his wishes."

A great shock — skipper Richard[s]

Wolves long-se[rving] club captain [illegible] Richards said that news of [the] appointment [of a] receiver was "a [great] shock."

But he hoped that t[illegible] would still be able to [play at] Molineux next season.

"At the moment [we are] waiting to be told w[hat will] happen. The playe[rs have] just got to hope for th[e best.]

"Wolves are one [of the] biggest clubs in Bri[tain and] were one of the b[est in] Europe — it was [a] shock to hear o[f these] developments. It w[ould be a] tragedy if they w[ent out of] business.

"Everyone in [Wolver]hampton — and [everyone] connected with [the club] will be hoping th[ey pull] through," he adde[d.]

TV star Paula's regrets — in tomorrow[illegible]

An Express & Star headline from 1982 as dark days enveloped Wolves with serious questions over the club's very existence.

ENFORCEMENT OFFICE
Barrington Road Worthing West Sussex
BN12 4SE

Telephone Worthing (0903) 502525 ext 246

Nearest Station: Durrington-on-Sea

Mr D Hope
Wolverhampton Wanderers Football Club (1982) Ltd
Molineux Ground
Waterloo Road
WOLVERHAMPTON WV1 4QR

Please address any reply to The Controller

Your reference

Our reference A/X976 282 003

Date 14th April 1986

Dear Sir

WOLVERHAMPTON WANDERERS FOOTBALL CLUB (1982) LTD

TAXATION ARREARS £169,435.85

I refer to the interview held with you at this office on 10 April.

I am instructed to say the Revenue is prepared to defer the present winding-up proceedings for a period of 6 weeks as from the date of this letter.

This is on the understanding that at the end of the 6 weeks period the company will be in a position to either arrange for immediate payment in full settlement of all liabilities or a substantial payment on account and detailed proposals for settlement of the balance of liabilities.

I will be pleased to receive the solicitors undertaking as promised at the interview.

Yours faithfully

D R PRATT

A much-needed stay of execution! Four years later and the club is in trouble again but Doug Hope secures a six-week delay to winding-up proceedings.

Wolves survived again, Brian Little coming in to take the caretaker manager's role and penning these programme notes for the season's opener.

Welcome To WOLVES 86

WELCOME TO WOLVES '86....A NEW SEASON - NEW PEOPLE IN CHARGE.

The fans have heard it all before but there is now genuine optimism about the place and things can only improve.

The next few games are important for me but far more important for Wolve There is a saying in football that the Club is greater than any individual and so it should be proved at Wolves. I ask the fans to be patient but realise the patient ones are here today and hope that you understand that everyone is working to put Wolves back where they belong.

The burden of not knowing whether there was going to be a football club w beginning to tell on the players, but I must stress that throughout the preseason and particularly this week they have really applied themselves to trainir and their attitude has been first class.

I am sure you will join me in wishing everyone that has left the club every success for the future, but in particular I would like to wish Sammy Chapman every success. He gave me an opportunity to stay in the game and I appriciate that.

So we go into these games this weekend against Cambridge United and Lincoln City hoping for wins that will be the sign of things to come.

Brian Little

Ultimately it was Graham Turner who was brought in to mastermind the glorious Molineux revival, at a time w. the facilities were also in muc need of sprucing up!

Chapter 12

Got There in the End – The Play-offs

NINETEEN YEARS, 13 days, 22 hours and 20 minutes after Wolves had been relegated from the top division back in May 1984, following an abject 4-0 surrender away at Stoke City, the club was back. Promotion to the Premier League on a fantastic day in Cardiff was met with jubilation by supporters who had waited so long for this moment.

The Millennium Stadium was written into Wolves folklore, following a comprehensive 3-0 win over Sheffield United in the Championship play-off final. And the significance of the running clock, counting down the years, days, hours and minutes? Immortalised on a banner, it became the iconic image of a great chapter in Wolves' history.

With the depiction of a toaster on the banner there was a quirky, arbitrary symbolism to the artwork and it certainly proved a hit with supporters as well as the wider national media, which featured it heavily in its coverage of the day.

Its creator, an artist and designer, prefers to remain anonymous but was happy to share where the idea came from. And this perhaps taps into Wolves' history with the play-offs which had, until this point, been a tale of despair and disappointment.

'An ongoing narrative of the build-up to the play-off final was how Wolves always messed it up and it had been so many years of struggles, going on and on and on,' says the man we will call Toaster. 'Back then it was seemingly a lifetime since we'd been in the top flight. We got talking about how long it had been and 19 years was easy enough to add up. Then I had a look at the last game we played in the top division and I remembered it being against Stoke City, when we lost. Wouldn't it be fun to work out how long it had actually been between the last kick in that match to the final whistle in Cardiff? It was easy enough to work out the years and months, then we looked at the days which got trickier with the leap years. We definitely didn't want to get it wrong.'

Toaster bought the material for his banner from Wolverhampton market on Peel Street and set to work once Dave Jones's team had navigated their two-legged play-off semi-final after a strong post-Christmas finish to the 2002/03 season.

'It was all a bit of a whirlwind as until we'd beaten Reading in the semi-final there were no plans for the play-off final, so it was all about getting tickets sorted at first. As a kid I used to take a small banner to games, and I've always been into European football culture. Those banners in Italy by the ultras and the tifo displays, which years ago I used to see snapshots of on the Channel 4 programme *Gazzetta Football Italia*, I was fascinated by that kind of thing. In Italy you could buy this magazine called *Super Tifo* from the newsstands and it would be collections of all the fans' displays from the previous few weeks and I used to love the choreography of it. Because I could paint for a living and could make letters and fonts I knew I was capable of doing a good size banner.'

And when the final whistle went in Cardiff and Toaster raised his banner, the ghosts of failures past had been well and truly laid to rest. The play-offs are now such an integral part of the English Football League (EFL) season that there is nothing unusual or strange about a format that does not always reward the best team over a whole season.

In December 1985, with English football at a low ebb, ten Football League officials representing all four divisions met at a hotel near Heathrow Airport to propose some ideas to freshen up their competition while reducing the number of teams in England's top league.

The idea was proposed by Brentford chairman Martin Lange, specifically designed to generate revenue for Third and Fourth Division clubs who were losing out on money from television deals weighted in favour of the top clubs, who had already been in talks about a breakaway league, which later came to pass with the inception of the Premier League.

As part of what became known as the Heathrow agreement, the old First Division would be reduced from 22 to 20 teams. In its first year – the 1986/87 season – fourth from bottom in the First Division competed with third, fourth and fifth in the Second for a final place in the top flight.

Both the semi-finals and final were decided over two legs, by away goals if necessary. This was a groundbreaking idea and it took some getting used to. After that first season of play-offs there were protestations across all the divisions. Swindon Town won the Third Division play-off final but their manager, Lou Macari, was unimpressed and called for the system to be scrapped. Oldham Athletic boss Joe Royle saw his side eliminated in the semi-finals on the away goals rule to Leeds United in the Second Division knockout, after finishing seven points above the Yorkshire club.

So there was perhaps a sense of frustration at Molineux when Fourth Division Wolves, after a late-season revival under Graham Turner, that saw the team win 12 of their final 14 league matches, finished in what would formerly have been the fourth and final promotion place, only to have to negotiate the new format.

Fifth-place Colchester United were seen off over two legs in the semi-final setting up a final against Aldershot, who had finished in sixth and won their semi-final against Bolton Wanderers, who had finished in 21st place in the Third Division.

'I remember the first leg distinctly at Aldershot, where the rain was absolutely pouring down,' Andy Mutch recalls. 'We had a few chances in that game. There were one or two shots where the ball got stuck in standing water in the six-yard box, it was that bad. It wasn't really fit to play.'

Turner's men went down 2-0 at the Recreation Ground but hope was not lost among home fans for the second leg, with a crowd of 19,962 turning up at Molineux. It was not to be, though, as the Shots ran out 1-0 winners.

'It was my first year at the club and I remember we all felt a bit aggrieved about having to go through the play-offs,' Robbie Dennison adds. 'We had Aldershot in the final and we finished nine points ahead of them, and there we were playing in a two-legged win or lose tie. There were 46 games in the league and back then we felt it should have been decided over that. But from our point of view it probably turned out for the best that we didn't go up that season, as over the next couple of years we got promoted, winning the league in both seasons.'

History would suggest Dennison was right, with Wolves enjoying two title-winning campaigns in the lower leagues before settling in mid-table in the Second Division for several seasons until 1994. What followed put Wolves firmly in the spotlight on the national back pages. Turner moved on and in his place came as high a profile appointment as anyone could have imagined.

After England were eliminated in the group stages of the 1992 European Championship in Sweden, they then failed to qualify for the World Cup two years later, missing out on the finals for the first time since 1978. The manager, Graham Taylor, was pilloried by the national press during and after his time in charge, which came to an end in November 1993. A Channel 4 fly-on-the-wall documentary, *An Impossible Job*, chronicled the qualification failure in painful detail, leading to further opprobrium being heaped on Taylor.

It was huge news, then, when just four months later he was announced as Wolves manager on 29 March 1994. The club sat 13th in the second tier of English football. Over 300 supporters assembled at the front of the Billy Wright Stand ahead of his unveiling. They were not all there to cheer the new man. There had been considerable opposition to his appointment amongst the fanbase at the time.

Inside the stand, a huge gathering of media had assembled in the Hayward Suite for the much-anticipated press conference. 'Some clubs approached me immediately after I left the England job, but I didn't feel the time was right,' Taylor said. 'I needed to recuperate. There were only a handful of clubs I'd have come back for and, though I flew in from Spain for Wolves, I'd have walked back if necessary.'

England winger Tony Daley and his Aston Villa team-mate Steve Froggatt were the marquee summer signings, with Neil Emblen also joining the club from Millwall. Wolves went into the 1994/95 First Division, a season when only the champions went up automatically, as one of the promotion favourites.

A derby win over rivals West Bromwich Albion in the third game added to the uplifting mood around Molineux. Taylor appeared to be building something special. During an emotional week in September, Wolves put in a performance that seemed to characterise the togetherness and positivity amongst players and supporters. Arguably the club's greatest player, Billy Wright, had died earlier that month. His funeral on 12 September was attended by the country's greats: Sir Bobby Charlton, Sir Stanley Matthews and Sir Tom Finney. The funeral cortege began its journey at Molineux.

The following evening Taylor's team, who had attended the funeral together, took to the field against Southend United and put in their best display of the season, a 5-0 rout.

'There was a vast amount of experience in the squad and at times it felt like it was men against boys,' Froggatt recalls. 'We were just battering teams. It was like an irresistible force pushing us on to promotion. We were a really powerful side. That Southend game, when we thrashed them at home, that's when people started to say, "These boys are the real deal."'

It had not been a trouble-free start to the season, though. Injury problems built up almost immediately. Talisman Steve Bull had been missing for the opening six games and Daley, the club's most expensive recruit, suffered a cruciate ligament injury that restricted him to just one substitute appearance all season.

'I played with Tony at Villa, I knew how devastating we could be as a pair,' Froggatt adds. 'I knew we would be a real force down the flanks. His career at Wolves just never got started. I don't think I ever started a game with Tony while I was at Wolves. He had horrific injury problems and that was a massive blow for the club as he was still at his peak.'

Froggatt succumbed to a season-ending injury of his own in December, when he was on the receiving end of a late and nasty challenge at Reading. The injury pile-up prompted Taylor to go on a round of mid-season spending, bringing in striker Don Goodman from Sunderland, young midfielder Jermaine Wright from Millwall, defender Brian Law – a free agent at the time – and veteran midfielder Gordon Cowans from Aston Villa.

But the stand-out capture was Dutch international defender John De Wolf from Feyenoord. Aside from being a Wolves headline writer's dream, De Wolf had played a key role in the Netherlands' 2-0 victory over England in Rotterdam, just over a year earlier. It was a defeat that virtually ended Taylor's hopes of taking England to the World Cup finals. The match was also the centrepiece of the documentary that came to define the most difficult part of Taylor's career. The signing raised Wolves' profile higher. Some of the Dutch press came over to Molineux for his photocall and followed his progress throughout the remainder of the campaign.

'I remember Wolfie,' says Froggatt. 'He was a six foot four Adonis-looking figure. He wasn't very quick but he was very commanding in the air, decent on the ball and the fans took to him straight away. He had that commanding presence and he became a real cult favourite.'

After an inconsistent run of results during December and January, De Wolf's first career hat-trick on a quagmire of a pitch at Port Vale in late February took Wolves back into the play-off places. The month began with an FA Cup fourth round tie that remains one of the greatest nights the redeveloped stadium has ever hosted.

Taylor's men were drawn away at top-flight Sheffield Wednesday. After a goalless game at Hillsborough, the teams returned to Molineux for a replay. Owls boss Trevor Francis's side was full of internationals, including England quartet Chris Waddle, Des Walker, Andy Sinton and Mark Bright. The match finished 1-1 after extra time, with goals from David Kelly and Bright. The Wednesday goalscorer was also responsible for squandering an incredible chance in front of goal with less than 30 seconds of extra time remaining.

The ensuing penalty shoot-out is still talked about today. When Wednesday keeper Kevin Pressman belted an unstoppable spot kick into the top corner – arguably the greatest penalty ever taken – it put his side 3-0 ahead after misses from the usually dependable Andy Thompson and Robbie Dennison. But Wolves scored their last three spot kicks and the South Yorkshire side missed their next two. Waddle, taking his first penalty since his miss in the 1990 World Cup semi-final shoot-out against West

Germany, saw his sudden-death effort saved by keeper Paul Jones. It was left to Goodman to secure a remarkable Wolves win.

What is sometimes forgotten when that dramatic shoot-out is recalled, is the penalty save made by Jones from Chris Bart-Williams in the dying minutes of the first game in South Yorkshire. Without that, none of the Molineux drama would have taken place.

The FA Cup was one of three knockout competitions Wolves were involved in that season. Interest in the League Cup came to an end after a thrilling 3-2 defeat at home to Frank Clark's Nottingham Forest, who went on to finish third in the Premier League. It was one of many compelling evening fixtures played under the Molineux floodlights that season. There were also four Anglo-Italian Cup ties, a competition for second-tier teams from England and Italy. In all, Wolves played 13 cup matches.

After a late Bull winner away at Southend in April, Taylor's men sat six points behind leaders Middlesbrough with two games in hand, and nine games remaining. But the injuries and intensive fixture programme was starting to take its toll. With only one team earning automatic promotion, Taylor knew his team had to go for it in the remaining fixtures.

Throwing caution to the wind, Wolves' approach produced some captivating contests. There were three 3-3 draws away from home – to Luton Town, Derby County and Sheffield United. At both Luton and Derby, Wolves came from 3-1 down, scoring added-time equalisers. But at Bramall Lane, Wolves were on the receiving end of a last-gasp equaliser.

Taylor was involved in an ugly incident as he headed for the tunnel at the end of the Sheffield United fixture. A home fan stepped forward from the stands and spat in his face. It was a horrible reminder of the baggage that still followed the former England manager at the time, much of it caused by the treatment he suffered at the hands of the tabloids. Taylor was incensed and climbed into the stand to confront the supporter, attempting to make a citizen's arrest, leading to a scuffle involving stewards and police.

At Derby, Dean Richards's two late goals earned a point. The defender arrived on loan from Second Division Bradford City in the last week of March and supporters were immediately impressed by his authority and calmness on the ball. After signing permanently, he enjoyed a successful career at Molineux – one that could have been better had it not been for injury problems – before moving on to Southampton and Tottenham Hotspur. In March 2005, he was forced to retire from the game on medical advice. Six years later, at the age of 36, he tragically died.

'As a person, he was one of the nicest lads you'd ever wish to meet, such a lovely lad,' Froggatt remembers. 'But what a talent, and he obviously proved himself when he went to Spurs. He was just a top-class footballer. He was great on the ball, commanding in the air and quick. The boy had absolutely everything.'

Wolves finished the season in fourth place, level on points with Tranmere Rovers. With 77 goals, they were the division's top scorers, with ten more than champions Middlesbrough. But it was at the back they struggled, with 61 in the goals-against column, the most for any team in the top half of the table. It set up a semi-final play-off against third-place Bolton Wanderers, with the first leg at home.

Bolton were without their first-choice keeper, Keith Branagan. Manager Bruce Rioch took a gamble, and instead of turning to second-choice Aidan Davison he called up recent emergency signing Peter Shilton for his first start in over 18 months. The former England keeper was 45 years old, but he made a series of saves to keep a struggling Bolton side in the tie, with dominant Wolves winning the first leg 2-1.

'We are going into a 90-minute game with a one-goal lead, when does that ever happen?' Taylor said in the tunnel, after the match. 'It's great news, isn't it? I'd pick any game to have a one-goal lead before we kick a ball and that's what we've got.'

The tables turned in the second leg. Bolton were rampant at Burnden Park. Wolves supporters' pantomime villain was John McGinlay. The Scottish forward scored both goals in a 2-0 victory to take Bolton through 3-2 on aggregate after extra time. At 1-0, McGinlay and Kelly were involved in an altercation that led to the Bolton player punching the Wolves forward to the floor, after Kelly had initially pushed McGinlay in the face.

'He's got to go, the referee has no choice. McGinlay has got to go,' yelled Jimmy Greaves, commentating for ITV that evening. Referee Steve Dunn, who was only a couple of yards away from the incident, produced yellow cards for both players after they shook hands with each other. 'That's a cop out,' was Greaves's verdict.

'The way it happened was quite innocuous,' McGinlay explains. 'A corner went to the far post and was knocked back across goal. Mike Stowell came for the ball and took it as one of the Wolves defenders pushed me on top of him. David actually grabbed me first and my reaction was to swing my arm and I connected. The referee was standing six yards away with an unobstructed view.

'Two thoughts flashed before me: Bruce Rioch is going to sack me and I won't be able to play at Wembley. I tried to shake David's hand and asked the referee not to spoil a good game. Then the referee showed us both a yellow card. There was no reason why he didn't show me the red card, and David probably should have been shown one as well.'

'I was sat watching from afar feeling helpless really, and couldn't do anything about it,' Froggatt recalls. 'That season just ended in enormous disappointment because we were absolutely flying. We were fighting on a lot of fronts. The two main signings of the summer were out, Tony missed the entire season and I missed half of it. If Graham had kicked a black cat a hundred times he wouldn't have had any more bad luck than he had that year.

'Everyone could see at the start of that season what a good team we were. Sometimes injuries are the difference between success and failure. To have four or five players go down, not just with a little hamstring injury or something like that, we're on about cruciate knee injuries and ankle ligaments, massive injuries that kept players out for a long time, you couldn't have predicted that.'

A subdued summer followed. Wolves had squandered their best chance of promotion since returning to the second tier. The permanent signing of Richards, for a club record £1.85m, was the only incoming transfer. When the club accepted a £1.5m bid for Bull from Coventry City it caused much anger amongst the fanbase. At the time, Taylor was held responsible for agreeing to the sale, but Bull has since gone on record to say it was a decision made by the board. Nevertheless, there was less goodwill going into the 1995/96 season.

Wolves did not win any of their opening three games, and were on the back foot from then on. A humiliating 4-1 defeat at home to Stoke in October highlighted the lack of confidence in a team playing with the burden of fans' hopes. On a cold Sunday afternoon at home to Charlton Athletic on 12 November, with Bull dropped to the substitutes' bench, matters came to a head.

The match at Molineux was an incredibly tense affair. A large section of the support had lost faith in the manager, and patience was in short supply. Goalkeeper Jones kept Wolves level with an outstanding early second-half save, before the home side laid siege to the Charlton goal as the game progressed. The fine margins of success and failure were on display. A Goodman header deep into added time cannoned back off the crossbar. The visitors from south London escaped with a point.

A vocal set of fans gathered outside the Billy Wright Stand after the match, singing 'We want Taylor out'. The following day, they got their wish.

'It is with much regret that I have tendered my resignation as manager of the Wolves,' said Taylor, at a hastily arranged press conference. 'I am sad, because this is as much to do with matters off the pitch as those on it. Obviously the team has not been playing well but, only 13 weeks into the season, we are still in all competitions. Our recent run of only two defeats in 12 games is not as bad as our sterner critics claim.'

'In my entire career, it's my biggest regret,' says Froggatt, looking back at Taylor's departure. 'I was actually lying in hospital. I had a blood clot problem as a result of my ankle operation, and I was listening to the Charlton game in Wolverhampton on the radio, and I heard all the boos. Then the next day Graham got sacked, and I knew it was the worst decision the club could have made because there were still quite a lot of us missing.

'The boys that had come back from injury weren't match fit at the start of that season. All the players at the club knew we would turn it around, but unfortunately for Graham it didn't work out. I was devastated, it was probably one of the lowest points of my career. I was on the sidelines watching the team not get promoted and then the following season Graham gets sacked.'

Wolves turned to Leicester City manager Mark McGhee next. He joined the club in December, after an acrimonious departure from Filbert Street, and oversaw a 1-0 home defeat to Port Vale in his first game. He quickly strengthened the squad, signing Simon Osborn from Queens Park Rangers and Steve Corica from Leicester City, both for fees in excess of £1m. But Wolves' form dipped even further during the second half of the campaign. The club finished the season 20th in the table, just three points above the relegation places.

Iwan Roberts, Keith Curle and Adrian Williams were signed in the summer as Sir Jack Hayward made more money available for transfers ahead of the 1996/97 season. McGhee struck on a three-man defence with the emphasis on possession-based football. Without ever capturing the imagination of supporters in the same way as Taylor's team had, Wolves were in the hunt for automatic promotion all season. Again, Bolton were one of the clubs standing in Wolves' way and by now a real hostility was developing being the two Wanderers.

'If you read back into the history books there was a Nat Lofthouse, Billy Wright rivalry and respect, it was fostered back then,' McGinlay says. 'It was revitalised in our era. It was just a great atmosphere whenever we played, whether at Burnden or Molineux.'

In January 1997, Wolves lost 3-0 in a game dubbed 'The Battle of Burnden Park' after a 22-man brawl which involved Steve Bull and Gerry Taggart attempting to headbutt each other, while other heavyweights like Richards, Curle, Jamie Pollock and Nathan Blake flexed their muscles. Even the Bolton mascot, Lofty the Lion, was reported to the FA for inciting the visiting fans. Typically, McGinlay was on the scoresheet again.

'We had got to the stage with Wolves, where it was just meant to be,' the Scot continues. 'They had tried everything to beat us, and they were kicking us that day but we could scrap as well. I think that was an all-or-nothing game for them going for the title and they lost it that day.'

Bolton went on to win the division but Wolves came off the rails with only three wins in the final ten games and had to settle for the play-offs. Unfancied Barnsley pipped them to the second automatic promotion spot. McGhee had made few friends in South Yorkshire, with a comment made to the Birmingham *Sports Argus* during the run-in about which club was fit for promotion.

'I would guarantee that most of the Premiership clubs would like it to be Barnsley,' he said. 'They might fancy the prospect that Barnsley would be annihilated next season and thrown to the sharks. They probably think they would go straight back down.'

Barnsley's players admitted to pinning a newspaper cutting with the quotes to their dressing room wall to inspire them during the promotion run-in. It was not the first time McGhee had come across as arrogant, having written off Birmingham City as 'a very ordinary team' ahead of a local derby the previous season.

Wolves faced Crystal Palace in the semi-finals, who had finished five points behind them in sixth place. The damage was done in the first leg at Selhurst Park when two goals from substitute Dougie Freedman secured a 3-1 lead.

Supporters did their bit, creating an electric atmosphere at Molineux for the second game. Wolves won 2-1, as Palace withstood a barrage of attacks towards the end of the tie. McGhee later bemoaned Palace's third 'offside' goal in the first leg, before a nod to a depleted squad that bore similarities to the issues faced by Taylor. 'One refereeing decision has cost us, though given our problems with injuries we did well to get this far,' he said.

Sir Jack's patience had snapped, though. 'It is blackmail. The manager goes to my son, Jonathan, the chairman, and says he must have a player to strengthen the side,' he complained, the day after the second leg of the Crystal Palace semi-final. 'They've thought that the Golden Tit – me – would go on forever. Money has been wasted on players who have not come off or performed to their potential. A lot of clubs put the price up three times because it's Wolves and they laugh like a drain when we buy them. I see some players we have bought who do not have the commitment and are overpaid, with their sports cars and homes. They have let the fans down.'

It appeared that the days of spending were over. Wolves had taken its toll on the Hayward family, with disputes emerging over Jonathan's running of the club which ultimately led to his departure and a legal wrangle. But just as it appeared that Sir Jack was losing interest, he decided to give it one more shot.

As with Taylor's arrival, there were headlines around the appointment that Wolves made as they sought to gain that elusive promotion. In 1999, Dave Jones was manager of Southampton, in the Premier League, when his world was turned upside down. Between the end of his playing days and the beginning of his coaching career, in the 1980s, Jones was employed as a care worker at Clarence House, a school in Formby, Merseyside, for children with behavioural problems.

His accusers were all in prison when they claimed that Jones had abused them during his time there. One of them saw his photograph in the newspapers, and remembered Jones as the PE teacher at the school. An investigation had already begun into abuse at the school, called Operation Care. Jones's accusers were told that they could expect compensation should he be convicted. In January 2000 it was announced that the case would go to trial. Southampton chairman Rupert Lowe responded by putting Jones on gardening leave, before eventually replacing him with Glenn Hoddle.

'Football was my sanity,' Jones explains. 'When Rupert Lowe took it away from me at Southampton, my wife said to him, "You've killed my husband." What I didn't understand was why it had to go to court, but my lawyers said it had to go to court to reach the end. I called my autobiography *No Smoke, No Fire* because that's what the judge said.'

On the fourth day of the trial at Liverpool Crown Court, in November 2000, the case was thrown out by the judge, who instructed the jury that the Crown Prosecution Service's case had been completely discredited. He went on to praise the defendant for his dignity. So, did Jones return to work as a changed man?

'Probably I became a little bit more aggressive with the press. Maybe I became a bit less patient, I had more important things to do. I wasn't unfriendly to the press but maybe they just saw my manager's head on more. With the court case you've got to remember that the *Liverpool Echo* were gunning for me big time. They were on the police's side. It was the police that were drip-feeding the newspaper. I had a lot of support within the football world and when I came to Wolves nobody said anything bad, but you'd get chants from the opposition crowd.'

Seven players left during the summer of 2001, with Mark Kennedy and Shaun Newton coming in. As the season progressed, other signings were made. Colin Cameron, Nathan Blake and Alex Rae arrived during the opening two months of the campaign, with Kenny Miller and Dean Sturridge joining mid-season.

'He would bring in characters that should never play with each other really and he got them working with each other,' centre-half Paul Butler explains. 'Even in the bad times, where we got beaten in the play-offs and we were losing games, he used to stay calm. I've probably seen him lose his head twice, maybe three times, in all the time I've known him. His man-management was good and he had good coaches around him. I always remember him saying, "Managers manage and coaches coach."'

That play-off semi-final defeat to Norwich City at the end of the 2001/02 season went down as one of the most desperate moments for Wolves supporters in the club's entire history. It was not a low ebb – the eighties provided that – but it was the manner of the failure that hit hard. Not so much a dagger through the heart for supporters at the hands of their arch-rivals West Bromwich Albion, who pipped them to automatic promotion, more a painfully drawn-out death. Jones's men had an 11-point lead over Albion in March, which was squandered with just seven games remaining.

West Brom had a game in hand, won it and reduced the gap to eight. Wolves' lead still looked impregnable but on two occasions, in the space of three days, they showed their fragility. Against Nottingham Forest, on 6 March, they twice squandered the lead and had to settle for a draw. Next up, at Birmingham, they were pegged back for a draw after going two ahead. When Kevin Muscat was sent off during a home defeat to Grimsby Town later that month, the rot had begun to set in.

Albion secured the second automatic promotion place with 89 points, finishing three clear of Wolves. Losing out to sixth-placed Norwich – who finished 11 points behind Wolves – in the play-offs was a bitter pill to swallow. 'You've Let Us Down Again' read a banner in the South Bank as the final whistle sounded against the East Anglian club.

Jones had an issue with the banner. 'How could we have let them down again, we weren't here before?' It was a fair point, but supporters had lost the ability to distinguish between this and previous failures. In their eyes, it was one more in a continuous run of setbacks.

Butler acknowledges that the manager and players had messed up in the final run-in but reveals that within the squad there was no resignation.

'We had played so well to get where we did and then we just let ourselves down. We came back in to training after the summer and the fans were talking about that play-off semi-final as if the chance had gone. Sometimes it does go, but we just got our heads down.'

With the summer arrivals of Denis Irwin and Paul Ince, from Manchester United and Middlesbrough respectively, Jones acquired some serious talent and experience for another attempt.

'I came home one day and got a phone call from Dave,' Ince says. 'He gave me the sob story, and said something along the lines of, "This might be a yes or it might be a no, Paul. But last year we were top and looked like we were going up. I just need someone to come in and be a leader, help organise the players." He said he'd already spoken to Denis Irwin and I thought, "Are you sure? I'd better check with Denis first!"'

Irwin was two years older than Ince and had a CV which included seven league titles, three FA Cups, one League Cup, a European Cup Winners' Cup and, most famously of all, the Champions League in 1999 as part of an historic treble at United.

'I had a very good relationship with Denis and he said he was up for it, and it was about doing things right,' Ince continues. 'There was a core of players who'd come so close so maybe we were adding that little bit of icing on the cake. The decision was: do I go to Wolves or do I go into coaching and start getting my badges? From where I lived on the Wirral it was a straight journey down the A41, maybe an hour and a bit. It was ideal. If Wolves was two and a half hours away there was no way I'd have joined because I'd been doing so much driving up and down to Middlesbrough for the past three years.'

'We were doing our pre-season training at RAF Cosford in that second summer,' Alex Rae reveals. 'I was driving in listening to The Wolf FM on the radio and it announced, "Breaking news: Wolves have signed the midfield guvnor, Paul Ince." I remember thinking, "Not this clown!" Paul and I didn't really have a great deal of love for each other. He'd been at Middlesbrough when I was at Sunderland, we were similar, we didn't have a great deal of kindness towards each other at that time.'

Ince, too, was in the car when it dawned on him just exactly who his new team-mate would be.

'I'm driving to the training ground for the first time, and I'm thinking about all the players. I was going through them in my head, "I don't know him, I don't know him" and then I thought, "Alex Rae is there. I fucking hate Alex Rae." Every time we played against each other he was mouthy and narky, but a top player, don't get me wrong.'

Despite all that Ince had achieved in the game there was a tension in the air when he began his Wolves career ahead of the 2002/03 season.

'I walked into the training ground and there was a kind of silence,' he recalls. 'Having Paul Ince and Denis Irwin there was massive for them but it was massive for me too, having this reputation, people expect you to behave in a certain way. There's always a bit of nerves when you go to a new changing room, it doesn't matter how old you are. I remember walking in and seeing Alex there and I just looked over and said, "Alright Al?" and he went, "Alright Incey." To be fair, after day one we just clicked, we had a common respect amongst the two of us. Now we were teammates we became close straight from the off.'

'On the first day he was at Wolves a photographer took a great picture of the pair of us in stitches at training together,' adds Rae. 'Arms around each other laughing, and from that day we were great pals. He used to bollock everyone on the pitch and people would give it him back, and I think he liked that we were characters who did that.'

But the season did not begin as the players hoped. A 3-1 home defeat to Sheffield United on 5 October left Wolves 14th after 11 games. The team was barely keeping place with the promotion pace-setters but everything changed in the New Year.

The third-round FA Cup meeting with Sir Bobby Robson's Premier League title-challenging Newcastle United side is regarded by many of the players as the catalyst for the late season charge, which saw Wolves cement their place in the play-offs.

'It was the first time I faced a Premier League team who were good, they were Champions League standard,' says Joleon Lescott. 'Alan Shearer was a legend, the team was full of exciting talent. I was quite close to their midfielder Jermaine Jenas from the England youth set-up, too. That was a huge game and it was the start of me recognising what the Premier League was about.'

'There was a lot of animosity between the players,' Butler remembers. 'Craig Bellamy was pointing to the Premier League badge on his arm trying to wind up the fans. It was a real cup tie and you could sense it. Alan Shearer gave as good as he got. Me and Joleon tried to boot him up and down the pitch and he gave it back. To come out at the end of that and win 3-2, it kick-started our season because we walked off the pitch having done that to Newcastle.'

Blake was watching in the stands, having broken his foot in November. 'I remember George Ndah played in the game and scored the winner. The atmosphere at Molineux was outrageous. A lot of our momentum picked up after that game. In my own mind I knew I had to get fit, there was a real determination to get back in the team after that and I managed to get fit in March, just at the time that George got injured.'

'If you could give me just one or two games again then that day when we beat Newcastle 3-2 would be one of them,' Matt Murray says. 'Everything about that was sensational, Molineux was unreal that day. I really believe that kick-started our whole season.'

'We also built a cocoon, where the world was against us,' Jones adds. 'That's why I got the big black team bus with the wolf head emblazoned on it. The big heads are in town. I remember going to Walsall the next weekend and the pitch was rock hard. They had all these braziers on the grass trying to warm it up. They'd brought in tons of sand to get the game on, but they lost. The ball was rolled back to the keeper and it bobbled over him when he tried to clear it and George nipped in to score. We had to produce on that pitch, we were the ones being knocked off the perch. We had to live that life and that's why you needed the characters who didn't care about that.'

Wolves were winning again. After losing three league games in December prior to the Newcastle cup tie, they lost just twice more during the remaining five months of the season. The team surged up the table and finished fifth on 76 points, ten fewer than the previous season. For a club with such a torrid play-off history – four failures in four attempts dating back to the very first season of the play-off system in 1986/87 – Wolves made remarkably light work of the job.

'There was always the feeling that Sir Jack had put a fortune into the club just to see them in the Premier League so we felt a duty to deliver,' says Blake. 'When we came here it felt like there was a specific job to do. It was great for this crop of players knowing that we delivered what he always wanted. To break the duck is always the hardest. If you're the first to scale Everest you're the main man – we were the first Wolves team to get them up in the Premier League era so it was an achievement in itself.'

'Fans always go back to that team for the simple reason that there had been a lengthy period where they hadn't been successful,' Cameron adds. 'You're never forgotten by that generation. People always talk fondly about certain things that hadn't happened for a while and that's why we'll always be remembered. I'm very proud of that – as a professional footballer you want to be remembered.'

'To get Wolves to the Premier League was a great achievement in my first year there,' Ince reflects. 'Of all the things I won that was the greatest achievement of my career. I'm coming to the end of my career and now I had a chance to be part of the Wolves team that got promoted. I still see fans now who talk about it. When you speak to Wolves fans you see the glint in their eye when they remember that year.'

Forty years on from the first season of the play-offs, Wolves could once again find themselves involved in the format as a Championship club. With the EFL play-offs now controversially stretching down to eighth place in the league, there will likely be another chapter to write in a story that provided so much heartache before that golden day in Cardiff.

Chapter 13

Merlin the Magician

MICHAEL KIGHTLY wears a sparkling smile at the same time as ruefully shaking his head.

'In some ways, when you watch it back, it just doesn't seem real,' he admits. 'What a time it was – one that none of us will ever forget. I mean, we lost 6-0 at home to Southampton, and were given a standing ovation as we left the pitch! Imagine that these days – it would never happen.

'It's always great when you are winning games, but when you lose how the fans react can be massively important. That gave us such a lift that day, it told us the fans were with us and we really had to try and do something good and achieve something for them.

'Thankfully we did, we were on the crest of the wave and went on to win the Championship and reach the Premier League a couple of years later.'

Kightly has just returned to the Green Room at the University of Wolverhampton at the Halls. The Wulfrun Hall, as most still call the venue, situated next to the renowned Civic which has played host to so many incredible nights of entertainment since its construction was completed in 1938.

Queen Elizabeth II actually visited in 1962 to enjoy lunch with civic leaders whilst musical royalty has certainly followed.

From David Bowie to Elton John, Queen to Nirvana, Take That to Oasis to Blur, a prominent 'who's who' of top stars have graced the famous stage down the years.

And when it comes to football, and Wolves, the esteemed venue played host to a civic banquet in 1959 to mark Billy Wright's 100 England caps making him the first player to reach a century for his country.

It was also the scene of a vitally important 'Save the Wolves' meeting in the 1980s, chaired by legendary television broadcaster David Coleman, who was helping to rally the troops in protest at the actions of the infamous Bhatti brothers, who owned the club at the time.

So maybe this particular night, in which Kightly and former team-mates George Elokobi and Matt Jarvis were joining their former gaffer – Mick McCarthy – had a tough act, or acts, to follow.

But Kightly's response and expression during the half-time interval was a palpable sign not only of how much fun the audience were having, but the participants too!

After all, there can sometimes be a danger in looking back that an air of strong nostalgia can overstate the importance of a particular spell or era.

On this occasion, when thinking back to McCarthy's spell at Wolves, that is never the case. Which is why the 700-strong audience at the Wulfrun are captivated by the camaraderie, the humour and the memories, good, bad and indifferent, and sometimes poignant.

'I loved my time at Wolves, and feel privileged that every time I come back, I receive a warm welcome,' said McCarthy, who had spent the afternoon visiting a Molineux Memories session run by Wolves Foundation for people with dementia and their carers.

'They were great days, one of the happiest times for me, and everyone at the club worked so well together.'

The evening comes not far short of 20 years since McCarthy arrived to take the reins at Molineux.

Inheriting the hotseat of a club which had become beset by apathy, fuelled by a lack of progress since being promoted via the play-offs under Dave Jones, and having failed to adequately strengthen to prevent an immediate return to Championship purgatory.

Former England player and manager, and indeed mercurial midfielder, Glenn Hoddle, had replaced Jones, incredibly presiding over five successive 1-1 draws to launch his managerial tenure.

An identical sequence followed not so long later, meaning that 10 of Hoddle's first 13 league games ended in stalemate. And yet, that second batch of draws were part of what would turn into a 21-game league unbeaten run for Wolves under Hoddle, the longest in the club's history, albeit one where the inability to turn those one-point returns into three meant they missed out on the play-offs and finished ninth.

Four wins in five at the end of the season, including excellent performances against Reading and Sheffield United, had the crowd singing 'sign him up' due to Hoddle initially having put pen to paper on a six-month contract. He duly did indeed 'sign up', on a one-year rolling deal, but the collective sentiment 12 months later was very different, after the team proved unable to build on the initial progress.

It had been something of a strange spell, with some players such as Lee Naylor and Joleon Lescott effusive in their praise of Hoddle's coaching and methods, but others finding it difficult to work with him or live up to expectations.

As it happened, Hoddle himself was no longer as engaged in the process, and with the loss of parachute payments after two years away from the Premier League, and the need for the club to cut their cloth accordingly, the job very quickly became less attractive a proposition.

So infamously, on the first day of July in 2006, ahead of a World Cup quarter final between England and Portugal in Germany, Wolves' CEO Jez Moxey was enjoying a leisurely trip around the lake in a rowing boat at West Park when Hoddle called to say he was resigning.

'I feel my expectations and the club's have drifted too far apart and this decision has been made early for the benefit of the club,' said Hoddle.

Relations had already been strained after Moxey's frustration as the play-offs drifted out of sight saw him describe the 2005/06 season as a 'complete disaster', but by the time they had reached the summer, the tone was more conciliatory.

But Hoddle's subsequent decision prompted the need for a speedy managerial search, with the team flying out for a pre-season training camp in Spain a few days later.

Current skipper Paul Ince, and assistant Stuart Gray, were both very much in the running, but the more experienced and former Republic of Ireland boss McCarthy, on holiday in Portugal at the time, was also available having left Sunderland four months earlier.

'As soon as I heard from my agent that Wolves were interested in talking to me, then of course I came back from holiday and met Jez and Sir Jack [Hayward] at an apartment in London,' says McCarthy. 'We had a good chat for a couple of hours and I came out thinking, "Let's see what happens," but before I'd even got back to the airport, I got the call telling me I'd got the job. I spent the final weekend of my holiday in Portugal really looking forward to getting back and getting started.'

Whilst he was away, McCarthy entrusted his regular lieutenant and assistant Ian 'Taff' Evans with going to watch the team play in a pre-season friendly away at Swansea.

The team drew 1-1 – a certain Rob Edwards grabbing Wolves' equaliser – but the report back to McCarthy suggested, that with the depleted squad and players available, he was going to have his work cut out.

'I asked Taff to go and have a look because it was good to know what we were heading into and he was going to be coming in with me,' says McCarthy. 'I took some notes on a piece of paper which I kept for a long time as a reminder, but suffice to say it wasn't overly positive.

'Most of those that were half-decent were preparing to move on, and others weren't so great, and it was all in a bit of disarray. But it just needed some leadership and fresh direction, and getting some new players in and some form of structure.'

The budget was meagre, hence Hoddle's departure, but McCarthy and Evans, and particularly their renowned chief scout Dave Bowman, set about doing exactly that. Bringing in new players.

A substantial amount of talent and experience had either left before or shortly after Hoddle, and, aside from the arrival of McCarthy's former Sunderland captain Gary Breen, the replacements were largely of the more fledgling variety, but many with a point to prove.

Little wonder that the suggestion, at his first press conference, that Wolves could reach the Championship play-offs, was met by the immortal reply: 'MM stands for Mick McCarthy, not Merlin the Magician.'

But over the next two years, 'young and hungry' became a much-adopted strapline for the Wolves squad, to the extent that the club eventually took the decision to try and move away from it when needing to change that approach in the Premier League.

But in McCarthy's first three years at the helm, how it reaped such wonderfully successful dividends.

None more so than Kightly, the first guest to take to the stage in front of an adoring public at the Halls. Spotted by Bowman, he was playing for Grays Athletic in the Conference, having previously been released by Tottenham as a schoolboy and Southend as a young pro.

Wolves was certainly to prove third time lucky.

'I remember it to this day, that the Grays manager Mark Stimson phoned me to say he'd had a phone call from a top manager and a big club saying they wanted me,' says Kightly.

'I had a release clause of £25,000, so I knew straightaway I was probably going to be on the move, but then he asked me to start guessing which club.

'I tried a few in League Two that I thought it might be, and he came back saying "No, even bigger than that, with a proper manager."

'I just couldn't guess it, and when he told me it was Wolves, I was like "wow" – I just didn't believe it. I came up from Essex for the talks, and remember turning up at the training ground, and the gates opening to come up from the drive, and from that moment I was blown away by the facilities.

'And the gaffer, from the very start he made me feel special, when I had come up from Grays and was thinking that nobody would know me. I remember asking in his office if I was going to be part of the first team, and he told me that if I did the business in training, I would play.

'I knew that would do for me, and I was ready to sign there and then. By this time, Nottingham Forest were also interested and I was due to go and visit them on the way back from Wolves. I never even went to Forest, I just knew Wolves was the club for me.'

'I remember his first day in training,' McCarthy interjects. 'He just went in there and ripped it up straightaway, and Breeny came up to me afterwards, and said, "Who the **** is that"!?

'I was always a manager who would play someone if I knew they could do it, none of this nonsense where you bring them in for six months and see how they go. With Kights, I just knew from the start he would have an impact.'

Kightly's final appearance for Grays came in front of 1,163 at home to Cambridge. His first Wolves goal, a winner away at QPR came in front of 12,323 in his second appearance at Loftus Road.

He went on to blaze a formidable trail over the next couple of years, and certainly until the arrival of untimely injuries which hampered his progress.

His was just one of so many memorable tales relating to the squad, and the recruitment of that time, which in some ways, provided just as much of a story as the results, and Championship title, which eventually followed.

Take Wolverhampton-born Karl Henry for example, out of contract at Stoke, who thought he had been asked to come for an in-house training game by McCarthy.

Until phoning his stepdad the night before to discover it was Steve Bull's 20th anniversary testimonial in front of a near full house against Aston Villa.

Arriving at Molineux with his boots in a bag, Henry was sent on inside the first ten minutes after Mark Davies was injured, by half-time McCarthy had decided to sign him, and a few years later the midfielder born and raised in Ashmore Park was lifting the Championship trophy for his home-town club.

And then there was Elokobi, another guest at the Wulfrun alongside Kightly and Jarvis.

Growing up in Cameroon, in 1996, over a nine-month spell when he was just ten years old, Elokobi lost his dad, his uncle and his grandfather. All of his male role models.

Shortly afterwards his mother moved to London, Elokobi initially staying in Africa with his grandmother before himself coming across at the age of 16, and being spotted by a Sunday League team having a kickabout on Kennington Park.

That led to a move to Dulwich Hamlet in Division One of the Isthmian League, the first time he had ever been properly coached, before Colchester United and then, on transfer deadline night in January 2008, the culmination of his dreams, and a switch to Wolves.

'It's an incredible journey, a journey when I never stopped believing, and one I am super proud of,' says Elokobi. 'To come and work at such a marvellous club, and with the gaffer, the backroom staff, TC [Terry Connor] and Taff, it was a dream come true.

'That deadline day is one I will never forget. I was waiting for terms to be sorted out and there were agents involved but I couldn't give two shits about that side of the deal, especially when it was prolonged and started dragging on.

'I was in the canteen at the training ground and remember watching the deadline day clock counting down on Sky and I started panicking. I needed to grab the bull by the horns so went into the office where the negotiations were taking place and told the gaffer, in front of everyone, that I wasn't bothered about money and just wanted the chance to play for this fantastic football club.

'The gaffer followed me out and spoke to me for a minute and told me not to worry and he would get the deal done, and he did. I was back in the canteen when I saw the confirmation go through on Sky, and when it dawned on me what was happening, I just started crying.

'I knew just how much hard work it had taken to get to that position, and yes it was the start of the really hard work to come, but they were tears of joy and tears of pain because of everything I'd been through.'

In footballing terms, the rags to riches tales of Kightly and Elokobi were two of so many experienced by McCarthy's players during such a groundbreaking era.

Aside from captain Henry making it into the Premier League, so too the likes of Sylvan Ebanks-Blake, Richard Stearman, Kevin Foley and Dave Edwards, who were snapped up from the lower divisions.

Goalkeepers Wayne Hennessey and Carl Ikeme had both come through the academy, Irish pair Andy Keogh and Stephen Ward emerged from lower league and the League of Ireland respectively. The experience of Jody Craddock and Chris Iwelumo helped calm any nerves at different times during the 2008/09 promotion-winning season, and Craddock went on to flourish again in the top flight previously experienced with Sunderland.

What happened was that McCarthy's management, coupled with the coaching of Evans and Connor, recruitment acumen of Bowman, and such a skilled and dedicated backroom staff, came together to create an environment, and a group, which was always so much more than the sum of its parts.

Along with the collective progress, leading to that Championship title and three years in the Premier League, individuals also developed to the extent that many of their own personal ambitions were also realised.

Notably that included Jarvis, whose appearance for England off the bench against Ghana in 2011 made him the first Wolf to wear the Three Lions since Steve Bull some 20 years earlier.

'I don't think you get many groups like we had back then during a career,' says Jarvis. 'A lot of us were of a similar age, we were all hungry, desperate to prove ourselves and get to the highest level.

'Working with Mick and his staff at that time was absolutely perfect for us, and that is why he is the best manager I ever worked with. He got the right people in the building, and the way he handled the players and staff, and the way he made everyone at the club feel, was a masterclass in leadership.

'He showed that you don't bring a winning culture from the top down, you build it from the inside out, where every single person in the building feels part of something. For me, it took me all the way to the England team, an incredible honour, and one I will never ever forget.'

What a game-changer this proved to be! An historic snap of Bully and Thommo on signing day in November 1986.

He's in there somewhere! Robbie Dennison has just delivered one of his trademark free kicks and 50,000 Wolves fans are in dreamland at Wembley in the 1988 Sherpa Van Trophy Final.

Dennison and fellow Wembley goalscorer Andy Mutch have remained close friends and are pictured here at the WCR Studios in Wolverhampton for a 'Mutchy & Denno' podcast recording with former team-mate Tom Bennett.

The legends! 500 Wolves goals between them, Steve Bull and John Richards meet up for a cuppa!

A matchday at the Great Western, and an incredibly loyal quartet among so many in the Wolves fraternity. From left, Steve Bishop, Tyrone Newland, Peter Abbott and Tony Cowley.

The open-tour bus parade which followed Wolves' play-off triumph in 2003 was one of so many in the club's history which brought the city to a joyous standstill. Winning boss Dave Jones and owner Sir Jack Hayward enjoy the occasion.

Paul Ince, seen here with Roy Keane after Wolves had beaten Manchester United, was an inspirational captain at Molineux.

Mick McCarthy walks out for his first game as Wolves manager, Steve Bull's anniversary testimonial against Aston Villa in 2006.

By 2009 Wolves had won the Championship title with Karl Henry and Jody Craddock lifting the trophy at a delighted Molineux.

Kenny Jackett led another Molineux revival restoring pride and respectability – and the 2013/14 League One title – after back-to-back relegations.

Talking of key managerial appointments ... Nuno had a dream. And at the end of his first full season in charge Wolves were back in the Premier League.

Wolves captain Conor Coady and legend Steve Bull help open a new Wolves megastore in Shanghai as part of a pre-season tour in 2019.

These were truly Golden times, and players such as Ruben Neves took Wolves to a whole new level.

The late, great Diogo Jota. Forever to be remembered blazing a trail in Fields of Gold at Molineux.

Mateus Mané is seen celebrating a goal for his Portuguese junior side Barreirense as he talks through his childhood memories with Johnny Phillips.

The first team picture of Wolves Women, as Heathfield Rovers, including founder members Jane Hill, Gill Spilsbury and Jackie Pickup.

Tasting silverware a few years on with a trophy shoot at Molineux.

Fast forward a fair few years and Dan McNamara was the manager who led Wolves Women to professional status and WSL 2.

Wolves' 150th anniversary year offered a chance to shine a light on the club's position in the community and return the city crest to the home shirt. Mayor, Councillor Paul Singh, and Leader of the Council, Councillor Steven Simkins, have a great view of Molineux from the Local Authority offices.

An historic 2026/27 season got underway with something of an historic goal. Raul Jimenez, returning to the club where he previously enjoyed such success, tucked away an added-time penalty to secure a point against Blackburn.

When Jarvis referred to 'every single person in the building', he wasn't wrong.

McCarthy made it his business not just to shake hands with every player and staff member on a daily basis, but to get to know all who worked at the club, whatever their role, and show a genuine interest in their lives away from Molineux or Compton.

Dan Morgan, then a cleaner at the training ground, was chastised by the boss on the first-day introductions when greeting him with, 'I'm Dan, I'm just a cleaner.'

'Never say you are just a cleaner,' McCarthy retorted. 'There is no such thing as just a cleaner – you are as important as anyone else. If the staff and players didn't have somewhere clean to work, they wouldn't be able to do their jobs.'

McCarthy, on later losing his job at Wolves, donated a substantial amount of furniture that he could no longer use to Morgan and his young family. He even delivered it himself, causing much excitement when driving a big van around the close-knit community of Ashmore Park.

Morgan was one of many staff perhaps sometimes previously ignored who felt far more part of the team during McCarthy's spell. Chris Lane was an apprentice groundsman back in 2008, another to feel a million dollars thanks to the attitude of the manager, not to mention earning some vital extra pocket money by being asked to help tend his garden. Ken Bates, at the other end of the experience cycle to Lane, recalls McCarthy popping to the groundsman's hut to share tea and conversation, and later wishing him well on his retirement, many years after leaving Molineux.

For some it might be termed a traditional and old-fashioned approach to management. For McCarthy, it was completely natural.

On the outside he could be seen as fierce and intimidating. He certainly had no qualms about making big decisions, often passionately defending his players in public even if it increased wrath among the fanbase. Making ten changes for a Premier

League fixture at Manchester United which secured not just vitriol from the travelling Wolves faithful but a fine for fielding such a dramatically changed team from the FA, he remained unbowed. Winning the games either side of the trip to Old Trafford away at Tottenham and home to Burnley, taking six points from three games, in his mind, made it absolutely the correct decision.

On the night at the Halls, Henry was absent as he was undertaking a final training session as head coach with Boldmere St Michaels' women's team ahead of a play-off final, which they would win 3-0 less than 48 hours later.

He sent a video message to be shown, which started with a clip of him delivering a strong but perfectly timed tackle to defend Wolves' penalty area in another tussle against United at Old Trafford. The camera then panned to McCarthy on the touchline, celebrating like the team had scored a spectacular goal.

'And this is why we all loved playing for Mick McCarthy,' Henry began his message.

He then went on to highlight just why it was that he enjoyed the best time of his career under McCarthy, how he kept the group so close together by spending more time and attention on those who weren't in the team than those who were, and created a spirit within the group where everyone both demanded of each other and supported each other.

'I have been fortunate to work for so many great managers, and for me, you were right at the top,' Henry told his former gaffer. 'And I have spoken to so many other players who say the same.

'That period at Wolves was the best in my career and you were the best manager I played for. So, I just want to say thank you. Thank you for being such a wonderful manager, thank you for bringing me to Wolverhampton Wanderers and giving me memories that I will have for life.

'I've created friends from that club during that time that I will have for life, and just want to say thank you for everything that you brought.'

And that was the togetherness, the culture, which McCarthy and his staff brought to that young and burgeoning squad, to such positive effect.

A culture where they would work hard, very hard, but sometimes play hard as well.

A culture where, on granting the players a pre-season night out in Ireland, McCarthy and his staff would go along too. Just minutes ahead of a midnight curfew, every single player would text him telling him he was the best manager they had ever worked for. And could they have another hour! Sometimes they would even deliver a rousing version of 'Super Mick McCarthy' to extract a few more minutes out of the night.

And then once, when Stephen Elliott had flown over to the tour ahead of joining the club, he arrived back at the hotel a few minutes later than stipulated. To be met by his grinning manager.

'I'm gonna have to fine you Sleeves,' McCarthy said with a glint in his eye. 'I don't even think you've got a contract yet, but I'm still gonna have to fine you!'

There was no let-up when back on English soil, with McCarthy and his staff always first on the teamsheet at Wolves' annual staff parties, held, bizarrely, in February. Once again, letting their hair down, happily mingling and chatting to club staff, whoever they were, and cementing that sense of belonging and togetherness.

His early-morning bike rides were also the stuff of legend. McCarthy heading out down the disused cycle path at the back of the training ground, a despairing Connor usually in his wake.

Before returning to transfer from mountain bike to exercise bike and watch a re-run of the previous weekend's game, always with the club analyst, making notes, spotting weaknesses, suggesting improvements.

For all his status as a 'no-nonsense and direct' manager, McCarthy was always forward-thinking. He was among the first to make use of more detailed match analysis, and put complete trust in a talented backroom team famed for its commitment to strength and conditioning. Wolves were the first club in the country to have a sports science laboratory accredited by the BASES programme, offering state-of-the-art assistance to players both before and after injuries.

It was actually whilst on the static bikes and watching a game back that McCarthy discovered he was losing his job at Wolves after almost six years at the helm. Less than 24 hours after being on the end of a hugely damaging 5-1 defeat at home to fierce local rivals West Bromwich Albion, McCarthy was relieved of his duties.

Club CEO Moxey, with whom he always had a great relationship and personally wasn't in favour of the board's decision, was the one entrusted to break the news and bring an end to such a drama-filled tenure in the club's history.

It was an emotional time for many players who looked on McCarthy as something of a footballing father figure. Someone who had given them an opportunity to live out, and realise, their Premier League dreams.

McCarthy spent a few minutes sat in the training ground reception, revealing that having to leave Molineux by the back door due to fan unrest the previous evening was something that particularly hurt.

'Last night I was wondering if that was it, the end of the road,' he admitted. 'But this morning I was up, ready to go again, looking forward to getting back in to work to start putting things right.'

He wasn't afforded that opportunity. And after Championship finishes of fifth, seventh and first, and Premier League survivals of 15th and 17th – staying up after losing to Blackburn on a crazy final day – McCarthy was dismissed. Wolves had slipped into the relegation zone, albeit only on goal difference, but wouldn't win any of their final 13 games of the season, picking up just four further points as their three-year Premier League stay came to a sorry conclusion.

As McCarthy disappeared upstairs to his office to pack up his belongings, a procession of players, some individually, others in groups, went up to offer their best wishes and good luck messages, but, above all, their immense gratitude for being part of his team.

The boss would have had every reason to slip away quietly. But he didn't. Once finished at Compton, he headed over to Molineux, walking around each and every department across the stadium to pass on his own thanks and appreciation to office staff for the support he had received.

His was a Wolves team and squad which was by no means the most talented in the club's history. Nor did they achieve the top-level honours delivered by their predecessors.

But at the time in which they came together, and the situation the club was in following Hoddle's departure, and what was needed to revitalise the fanbase, they fitted the bill perfectly of what was required.

At the end of the night at the Wulfrun, a montage put together by lifelong Wolves fan and Sky Sports cameraman Alex Gage was played on the big screen.

Cut to the strains of 'Good Riddance' by American rock band Green Day, it was a montage of the joy and delight of fans, players and staff experienced on the Championship celebration party on the final day of the season against Doncaster.

It certainly was the time of these Wolves players' lives.

Chapter 14

Beyond the Subway

THE SUBWAY that facilitates an uninterrupted journey from the city centre to Molineux has been a feature of the landscape for six decades and counting. Built during the 1960s ring road development, it neatly frames the matchday journey for thousands of fans. Leaving St Peter's Collegiate Church and the buildings of the university behind on the city side, the walk through the subway is illustrated by imagery on the walls of Wolves down the years. The great and the good of the football team. Billy Wright, Steve Bull, Ruben Neves and more. And there, at the end of the short walk under the low ceiling, Molineux awaits. The Sir Jack Hayward statue to the fore, Steve Bull Stand behind, a handful of hot food stalls, Kelvin's 'car boot' selling badges and scarves, and with it all comes the expectation and hope of what lies ahead for the next couple of hours.

Today's subway is a safe, pedestrian route, leading out to a small plaza around the statue before the footsteps to the turnstiles continue. Families wander the pavements and colours are on display. It has not always been this way. It was once a focal point for trouble, particularly during the 1970s and 1980s when crowd disorder was at its height. The Subway Army was one of the hooligan firms who would kettle visiting fans into the small tunnel under the dual carriageway. In so many ways they were strange times. The post-war boom had been replaced with a recession and there were a variety of contributing factors to the hooliganism which blighted the sport.

Wolves were not unique in attracting individuals and groups looking for a fight during this era. A perfunctory search of the internet will reveal the many firms that, in some instances, have been mythologised over time. Stories grow legs and it is easy to attach a romanticism to a period that was anything but pleasant to be involved in. Documenting this era through the eyes of those involved in causing the trouble has become a cottage industry, with numerous books and films on the subject. Only rarely do those whose job it was to fight fire with fire offer any insight into the times.

Derrick Sanders is in his 80s now. He is accompanied by John Carrington, another of his retired colleagues from the West Midlands police force, when we meet up to discuss a colourful and sometimes frightening period in Wolves' history. Both men are born and bred Wolves fans and have vivid memories of experiencing the club from the eyes of a supporter, first and foremost.

'My introduction to the Molineux and Wolves was being taken there aged seven, to see Stanley Matthews play for Blackpool in January 1947,' Sanders recalls. 'Dad paid the old 3p for my entry to the North Bank but dad was locked out as it was a capacity crowd. Once inside one of the stewards took pity on me and stood me on the turnstile between the North Bank and the Waterloo Road Stand so that I could see the match. It was a 1-1 draw. Dad came in 15 minutes before the end when it was customary for the gates to be opened for leaving fans. Many outside took the opportunity to enter and see the last bit of a match when that happened.

'The 1950s were memorable. When I was around 12 or 13, I played football in the mornings for the grammar school. We'd finish around midday, go and get some fish and chips from Oak Street, head home to get changed and then drive with dad and park up at what used to be the Blind Institute car park. We'd be in the ground on the North Bank by two o'clock for a three o'clock kick-off. I went for four seasons and only missed one game, when we beat Chelsea 8-1 [26 September 1953]. I was poorly that day. They were good days.'

There is perhaps an irony that when the club was at the peak of its powers and attracting the biggest crowds in its history, in Wright's heyday, the management of those crowds was largely straightforward. Policing in the 1950s is, aptly, often referred to as the 'golden age' in terms of method and respect.

Forces up and down the country enjoyed the confidence of supporters with their hands-off, localised approach. Crowd disorder happened but was rare, and occasional forays from fans into a rival end of the ground were viewed more like high jinks than anything more sinister. As Wolves stormed to three league titles and held their prestigious floodlit friendlies, and later the European Cup ties, under the lights of Molineux, the policing was focused on the safe movement of many thousands of spectators and preventing crushes. Mounted police would be used to direct large crowds who were overwhelmingly cooperative. Minor disturbances would result in individuals being ejected from the premises as opposed to the targeting of large groups. Disruption was spontaneous rather than anything planned.

Wolves typified the strong local identity that existed in the community. Supporters often lived and worked in the same areas as the players. This civic pride played out on the pitch where a team was built in the town, with players taking public transport or even walking to the ground. Travel was harder so large numbers of rival fans mixed infrequently, which further enhanced the communal energy of supporters chanting and singing on the terraces.

Sanders joined the police in 1962, four years before the borough forces of Dudley, Walsall, Wolverhampton, and parts of Staffordshire and Worcestershire merged to form the West Midlands Constabulary.

'I first policed Wolves in 1962, it was a normal part of the job,' Sanders continues. 'You'd have specific postings around the ground. There were no cameras, no radios or anything like that. There'd be nothing to concern yourself with other than dispersing the crowd at the end of the match. Traffic volume wasn't the same so most motorists would just let the supporters clear anyway. You just had a pocket book and a whistle in the early sixties. I remember trying a walkie-talkie out for the first time when I was on a push bike on Cleveland Road.'

Gradually, though, youth subcultures developed across British society, and the landscape changed. The Teddy Boys emerged as a nationally visible movement in the late 1950s. This led to the creation of a youth street culture in Britain with various groups of young men identifying common traits based on locality, dress code, music and – inevitably – football.

By the 1960s, Mods, Rockers and Skinheads had replaced the Teds. This youth subculture sequence played a key role in shaping football terrace culture, with the hooligan firms becoming firmly established by the 1970s. The sport was a perfect platform to foster group identity and territorial rivalry, and as the means of transportation became much easier and more readily available, it paved the way for a greater home and away rivalry.

'RM' – a fan who spoke with a preference for anonymity – was 12 years old when he first witnessed violence at Molineux, early on in the 1969/70 season.

'Manchester United fans had filled the South Bank and there was my sister and me sitting on the front wall at the edge of the pitch,' he recalls. 'We looked on as a Wolves fan had been placed on a stretcher, his scarf hanging down from his wrist and blood-splattered face and shirt. Two policemen followed close behind along the side of the pitch escorting a United fan by the scruff of his neck, as another policeman walked behind carrying a broken bottle. That was my very first sight of football violence.

'After the game we both headed to the bus stop in Broad Street where we found ourselves being pushed into a shop doorway as around 1,000 United fans stampeded down in the direction of the train station. We were frightened to death then we realised they were actually being chased by a mass of Wolves fans, what seemed to be the entire North Bank, and we then felt safe to leave the doorway and catch the bus home.'

As a young teenager, RM found himself attracted to part of the subculture that had taken root in society and had become part of a matchday for some. 'It was Skinheads, Suedeheads, Smooth Heads and Tom Girls and a history of sharing identical experiences, as did my friends that followed Wolves. My mother would be in the kitchen asking to help, but I would always decline as part of my day was getting myself ready for the big day.

'Back in the 1971/72 season Dr Martens only started at size eight and a half, so monkey boots it was from Millets. I would buff and shine my boots for a good half hour. After all, these were going to be my bovver boots and I felt like a proper Skinhead – albeit with my long hair – in my white Wrangler parallel jeans as white skinners were not around then. I donned my Harrington jacket which I bought from Red House and my Brutus shirt from Lester's clothing shop in Market Street. I must have looked a right idiot with my silk scarf tied around my forehead and woollen scarf hanging down the leg of my jeans, but that was the football fashion and I went with it.'

As opposed to the much larger South Bank, the North Bank was the firmly established home end for Wolves supporters where the chanting and singing would begin and where various gangs would meet, not always on good terms, to defend the 'end' from rival visiting fans. Wolverhampton's notorious gangs, the Temple Street 'Mafia' and Queen Street Boys, would be joined by others from estates such as Heath Town, the Scotlands and further afield.

On 8 May 1972, when Leeds United arrived at Molineux for the final game of the season, needing a win to secure the league title, Sanders was one of many drafted in at late notice when it became clear that disorder was breaking out on the streets around the ground. Similarly, at the end of the 1976/77 season, when Wolves drew 1-1 with Chelsea, there was a large away support present and skirmishes took place on the huge South Bank, which housed both home and away supporters.

'Before the game over 1,000 Chelsea fans had been frisked by police for weapons as they arrived at the station off the football special,' RM explains. 'Inside the ground Chelsea fans grouped to the right-hand side of Wolves supporters in the South Bank. There was no fence segregation, only a line of police separating the two sets of supporters. Then Chelsea South Stand lads somehow sneaked past the police cordon and filtered in with Wolves supporters. A chorus of "Chelsea, Chelsea" came ringing out and a fist hit me straight in the side of my face and I realised I was stood in the middle of the Chelsea mob. Fists were flying from both sets of fans and eventually Chelsea moved back as they were getting attacked. It happened so quickly, and they took us by surprise.

'I took my jacket off and found it had slashes in it from a razor blade or a Stanley knife. It must have happened when I was amongst them, obviously they knew I was Wolves. I think I was very lucky it had only gone through my jacket. Police moved the Chelsea fans back to the right-hand side of the South Bank. The match ended in a 1-1 draw and both Wolves and Chelsea fans invaded the pitch at the same time. There was a fair bit of fighting between the two sets of supporters on the pitch, mainly small groups and scuffles, but most supporters from both teams were celebrating promotion.'

A year later, fences were erected at the South Bank end of the ground to segregate and contain supporters. By now, many clubs across the country had hooligan 'firms' attached to them.

Social and economic circumstances played their part alongside the cultural movements of the time. A sense of belonging for disenfranchised young men was also a key theme. Quite how Wolves' Subway Army was formed is the subject of conjecture but one story suggests that a performance by rock band The Jam at Bingley Hall in Stafford ended in a fight between fans who had come up from Wolverhampton and some of the locals from Stafford. The Wolverhampton crew joined forces and the Subway Army firm was born, so the story goes.

Whatever the circumstances, it was one more headache for the West Midlands Police who had their own issues to deal with away from football, with accusations of a heavy-handed approach to law and order becoming commonplace in society.

'By the 1980s it had become a bit of a challenge,' Sanders says. 'I can't be specific with the date but because of the issues, not just in Wolverhampton, it was clear there were groups at various clubs and we needed to be far more aware of what the potential for trouble was, and communications were improving. We changed things. There was a police constable who was generally on administrative duties who now had, built into his role, assessing football issues and the next home game.'

'We had football liaison and football intelligence,' Carrington explains. 'Liaison was the administrative side and I did that for a while. You talked to the club, because they were paying for policing and wanted it done properly. Then you had the intelligence officers who actually went and talked to the fans, had a drink with the fans and mixed with them.'

'You were trying to gauge how you were going to police the next match,' Sanders continues. 'We'd use the information that John and others had gained when we had a meeting early in the week of the match, so that the boss could determine what support he might need. There was a budget for everything and we had to be careful how many officers we took out of regular policing.

There was a pool of people you could draw on but if there were other matches in the West Midlands they might be needed there.

'There would be overtime to consider, too. We could also call on jockeys [police horses and riders], dogs [and their handlers] and Operational Support Units [OSUs]. But we also brought in two uniformed officers who could travel to away games and take with them their knowledge, and if anyone was getting known to us then they could point them out to the other police force.

'One of the issues in the 1970s was that many of the fans travelled to matches by train. The football specials were taken off in due course because of the damage done to them. We used to meet them at the railway station and escort the fans to the ground if we could, because they were so disruptive. Sometimes it was done for their own protection. If you had the big teams like Manchester United or Arsenal it was a real headache.'

'A lot of it was pre-planned violence by now and the match didn't figure in it, other than it started and finished,' Carrington adds. 'Matches were categorised as A or B and it was my job to find the bobbies to work on the games. When we had Manchester United you knew you had to get every single bobby you could. We had nearly 400 for one of their games once.'

Sanders moved to work out of Dudley in 1980 but by the time he came back to Wolverhampton six years later and was posted to football matches, Wolves were in decline. Crowds had dwindled but the hooligan presence had not gone away, with the Bridge Boys emerging during this period.

'When I came back in 1986, my role at the football matches was slightly different,' Sanders says. 'I was responsible for the outside of the ground pre- and post-match. And we were seeing these running battles. After a match I'd be leading baton charges. I was getting a bit fed up with all that was going on, it was a real headache. The ground was reduced in size by then and I thought it was about time we did something about it.'

In the wake of the Bradford fire, on 11 May 1985, both the Waterloo Road Stand and North Bank had been shut. Another tragedy that happened on the same day as 56 people lost their lives at Valley Parade occurred at St Andrew's. Hundreds of fans of Birmingham City and Leeds rioted during their final Second Division match of the season. Ian Hambridge, a 15-year-old Leeds fan, died after a wall collapsed on him during the trouble. Football, as a spectator sport, was going through its grimmest period in this country. Declining safety standards and increased crowd disorder kept many away.

The Public Order Act of 1986 specifically targeted hooliganism. The Act abolished the common law offences of riot, rout and unlawful assembly, and brought in a new list of offences relating to public order whilst also permitting the exclusion of certain offenders from sporting events. 'Section 5' arrests became commonplace, where individuals were arrested for disorderly, abusive, or threatening behaviour that caused 'harassment, alarm or distress' in public.

By 1987, policing in Wolverhampton had become difficult and relations with the public were at a low ebb. There was widespread condemnation for the force after the death of Clinton McCurbin, a 23-year-old black man who died from asphyxiation while being arrested at a Next superstore, on 2 February, for allegedly using a stolen credit card. The subsequent march organised by the family created a tinderbox atmosphere in the town, with an enormous and unwanted police presence.

The town's football club was starting to recover by now, but that brought its own problems for the police with a significant section of its more unruly supporters travelling in large numbers once more. On Friday, 24 April, a key Fourth Division promotion game at Southend United attracted a crowd in excess of 10,000 with upwards of 3,000 Wolves fans estimated to have travelled to the seaside town, many without tickets.

The local force were ill-prepared for such numbers and could do little to stop Wolves supporters finding their way into the home sections of the ground. Before and after the match, there was trouble between rival sets of fans and large parts of the town centre suffered damage. It was the worst trouble the authorities had witnessed involving Wolves for a number of years, but it was not the first time a seaside town had been targeted. Earlier that season there had been trouble at Torquay and at the end of the previous season there had been issues at Blackpool.

So, there was a certain folly from whoever was in charge of setting the fixtures for the opening day of the 1987/88 Fourth Division season. Newly promoted Scarborough, managed by Neil Warnock, were given a home fixture against Wolves on 15 August.

'Whoever set the fixtures that year was to blame,' says Robbie Dennison, one of those in the Wolves team that day. 'Scarborough had done their ground up for promotion and they were celebrating coming into the league. But it's a seaside town and Wolves fans were going to head up there in their thousands whether they had a ticket for the game or not. We got into the ground and it was clear straight away that all hell was breaking loose.'

The *Express & Star* sent their Wolves correspondent David Instone up to Scarborough on the Friday night in case any trouble began in the town on the eve of the game. 'The office asked me to keep an eye on it, let them know if anything happened,' Instone remembers. 'There was no problem on the Friday night, but the Saturday was a horrible, horrible day. Wolves had a crowd-control problem at the time and that was one of the games that told us why. It should have been Scarborough's proud day. It was crazy that the Football League sent Wolves there on the first day of the season. It was a stupid decision of theirs.'

'I remember a voice coming over the public address system,' Dennison continues. 'I think it was the Scarborough club secretary, it was halfway through the first half, and he was asking Wolves fans to get off the roof.'

A Wolves supporter fell through the roof of the Hinderwell Road Stand, where trouble had been taking place between rival sets of supporters, and was stretchered off by St John's Ambulance staff. Wolves fans were causing havoc elsewhere inside the ground. A newly refurbished refreshment kiosk was smashed up and stock taken, metal fences were pulled down, toilets ripped up, cisterns pulled off the wall and seats thrown on to the pitch. The kick-off to the second half was delayed for ten minutes, whilst manager Graham Turner pleaded with fans to restore order and helped clear the pitch.

The game did not just attract the unruly elements from Wolves' support, according to RM, who recalls the day vividly. 'I was outside a pub opposite the Scarborough train station when some Leeds fans arrived and the police had them up against a wall, searching them,' he reveals. 'They made their way to the ground and word spread that there would be Leeds on the terrace on the side. Once the Wolves guy with the flag fell through the roof all hell broke loose as Wolves fans had already mixed in with Leeds supporters.'

'We came out for the second half and on my side of the pitch there's the contents of a kiosk emptied on to the grass,' Dennison recalls. 'I had to help the stewards clear drinks, hot dogs, chocolate bars, everything like that. That was just to clear the pitch so they could start the second half. It was horrendous and obviously a lad fell through the roof. At the end of the game he was sitting on a wall outside the ground with a neck brace on and a pair of crutches. He was begging us to give him a lift home on the coach as all his mates had left without him. He was asking Keith Pearson, the secretary, and Graham Turner if he could come back with us. It was an unbelievable day, a mad day for the fans, it should never have been a fixture scheduled for that day in August.'

In total, 56 supporters were arrested, including 40 from the Wolverhampton area. Scarborough chairman Terry Wood gave an impromptu press briefing on the pitch after the game ended. 'I think they're a set of animals,' he said of the visiting supporters. 'I would urge Fourth Division clubs to ban all Wolves fans this season. Ken Bates [then Chelsea chairman] had the right idea in wanting electric fences. If farmers can use electric fences to get their animals in check, football clubs should be allowed them to halt soccer violence.'

The fall-out from the trouble was significant. Wolves supporters were banned from attending six away games, with the club adding a further two-match sanction of their own. Not that all supporters were deterred from travelling to those matches, with many feeling the ban was a harsh measure on the majority who stayed on the right side of the law.

'We played Manchester City away [22 September] in the League Cup not long after the ban was announced,' Dennison continues. 'We pulled up outside Maine Road and there were about 30 Wolves fans who we recognised, but they had been to the club shop and were all dressed up in Man City hats and scarves. They were just waving at us on the coach, giving us the thumbs-up as if nobody was going to know. I scored the winner with a few minutes to go, we won 2-1, and a cheer went up in the stadium. It was unbelievable, they may have been banned but some found ways to get in the grounds.'

In October, three fans went to extraordinary lengths to circumnavigate the ban for a trip to Carlisle. Mike Watkins, Bob Munn and Bert Clark travelled to Scotland the day before the game when they heard that police might be setting up road checks on the route up from Wolverhampton.

'Bob's sister-in-law, Evelyn, lived in Annan across the border so we stayed there,' Watkins explains. 'She paid to join the Carlisle membership scheme and bought three adult tickets for us and two junior tickets for her boys. We travelled down from Scotland on the day of the game and we just let the Scottish lads do the talking on the way into the ground as the police were listening out for our accents. There must have been hundreds of Wolves fans inside the ground. When Steve Bull scored the winning goal, we all cheered. The policeman stood next to us just laughed and said, "I knew you were Wolves fans!"'

Back in Wolverhampton it was clear to the local force that they had to get a grip on the hooliganism problem in perpetuity. It was not enough to move from game to game knocking pockets of trouble on the head – figuratively and literally. There had to be another way.

'Operation GROWTH started in November 1987 and we were done by March,' Sanders, who was by now chief inspector, explains. 'The plan was put together in two or three weeks. I remember vividly sitting down on the floor with paperwork everywhere about the incidents we had, and I drafted about a page and a half to [Chief Superintendent] Dave Ibbs and said it was about time we put a covert operation together. He agreed and sent it up to headquarters in Birmingham.

'I had to go and see Paul Leopold, who was assistant chief constable of operations, who I'd met a couple of times. I sat for an hour with him arguing my case. He was asking where I'd get the manpower, and I was hoping to get the OSUs. I came back to Wolverhampton and Dave got in touch and said it had been approved. He asked me to structure the team that I wanted, interview who I wanted. There were around 15 who were interested and I wanted at least eight or nine so it was just a case of interviewing the individuals.'

Operation GROWTH was an acronym for 'Get Rid Of Wolverhampton's Troublesome Hooligans'. Within the force, the plans remained secret with only those operationally required to know the details briefed. 'We were policing matches at that time, and we weren't aware what was going on,' Carrington admits.

The officers selected to work on Operation GROWTH were tasked with infiltrating the hooligan firms by socialising with them at matches and elsewhere. It was a high tariff exercise, where valuable intelligence could be gained but the cost would be considerable if they were exposed.

'A lot of evidence was visuals [eyewitness accounts] from bobbies who had become part of the hooligan groups,' Sanders reveals. 'Although, it was very difficult when aggro was going on to support these bobbies. The officers would get in there and become part of the gangs. We had a PC from Staffordshire and a guy from British Transport Police who helped link it all up.

'We only had one who was sussed and we took him out straight away. It could have put the whole operation in jeopardy. There were never any questions after that but there could have been. The officers needed to be very aware of what the dangers were and competent enough to recognise when it was time to disappear.

'As an example of how dangerous this was, one of the undercover guys from Birmingham was in a pub, in the group, and was accused of being a copper. The policeman stood up, smashed his glass and held it in the face of the hooligans and said, "Who are you calling a copper?"

'Two things made Operation GROWTH work. One was the use of HOLMES, which was the Home Office Large Major Enquiry System, a computerised database where we could analyse everything. If somebody had a red hat on and he was seen three months later with a red hat on you could immediately call it up on the system. The sort of thing you can do now with searches.

'And the other one, and a vital one which had never been done before, was agreeing with the Crown Prosecution Service [CPS], who were getting into making decisions, on cases to proceed with. That was more important than the police, we just charged folks.

We had a weekly meeting with the CPS. They would look at all the statements the officers put in over the preceding week. Before they finished, duty officers would be obliged to put a statement in. The CPS would look at these and decide if there was evidence.'

The collating of evidence on HOLMES and the dialogue with the CPS ensured that Operation GROWTH could move swiftly and secure the convictions it required to be truly effective. Dawn raids were used to make the arrests, with over 250 officers involved in charging 67 men in March 1988, with a further ten arrests made over subsequent weeks. This included a police officer who had become so embroiled in his undercover work that questions were asked about his behaviour during his time off duty.

'It was quite an operation,' Sanders reflects. 'The one that really got [prison] time was after a match against Cardiff when a bloke threw a lump of concrete off a bridge on to a passing car. The passenger of the car was badly injured. He got done for a Section 20 offence, serious wounding with intent, and he went down for a long time. There were 111 potential cases and because the CPS wanted the rock solid evidence we went on the ones we knew we were going to get. It was collective evidence over a three- or four-month period. One, believe it or not, was a policeman.

'One of the matches towards the end of the operation was against Bolton [on 25 February]. They had their group of hooligans and in the build-up to this we had two Bolton spotters come and join us. They had a serious stabbing at a previous match, knew who was responsible and he was likely to be travelling. And, also, they were planning a pitch invasion. I was on duty that day, we only had the South Bank and John Ireland stands open. The lower tier of the John Ireland contained the away fans, but way before the match the guy suspected of the assault was arrested. Dave Ibbs was the match commander and we had a horse at each end of the stand, a couple of dogs and every 15 yards a policeman facing the crowd. They were not going to get on to the pitch.'

By the time the cases went to court, in December 1988, there were only formalities to complete, with 65 people pleading guilty. The vast majority of cases were Section 5 offences and there were relatively few who ended up serving any jail time. All of those who pleaded guilty received five-year banning orders from football grounds. The scale of the operation meant that inevitably some of those caught up in the trouble had never been on the authorities' radar and it was a harsh lesson to learn in such a public forum.

Ibbs held a press conference to highlight the work being done to rid the club of hooligans, with the police force needing to be seen to have regained law and order around Wolves fixtures.

'They'd meet at certain public houses and as visiting fans came into Wolverhampton they'd be waylaid and attacked,' he said of the troublesome elements being targeted.

'And there were many instances of quite dreadful violence being perpetrated. Inside the ground they'd act as a team, they'd leave before the end of the game to create ambushes. The whole scenario was a disgrace.'

One of the trouble-causers called up a local radio station, Beacon Radio, in the aftermath of the Scarborough match. Speaking on condition of anonymity, he admitted, 'The football team aren't doing anything so the hooligans have to. Wolves haven't been in the papers, except for when we went down to Scarborough and battered them.'

It was a warped logic but it revealed the state of mind that had taken root among a significant minority. The decline on the pitch over the previous years had stripped some fans of their status. Causing disorder was a means to regaining it. As with all public disorder, there were deeper roots to it than just simply gaining notoriety. A sense of belonging, however misplaced, had a role when working lives were being decimated by state cuts and industry closures following the initial post-war boom. The seventies and eighties were tough decades for many and for some men finding a sense of identity led them down such paths.

Operation GROWTH appeared to be a line in the sand. Regular trouble at Wolves matches all but disappeared in the subsequent years, but this was arguably as much down to the changing landscape across the country as anything specific to Wolves. The tragedy of Hillsborough paved the way for all-seater stadiums. Football regained a more wholesome place in the national media following the stories that played out during Italia 90, a World Cup tournament that appeared to capture the imagination of so many who had previously shunned the game, particularly around the England team. And then came the Premier League in 1992, which was one more step into a changing world so removed from the previous two decades.

'I think Operation GROWTH worked in the sense that it brought home that football fans were being arrested in dawn raids,' RM believes. 'Following that, hooliganism retreated into the background for several years.'

Reflecting on a challenging episode in the club's history, Carrington believes that there were some undeniably tough times when it came to policing the troublemakers.

'It took up a lot of resources,' he concludes. 'You wonder if we had been able to have those resources elsewhere, if we could have sorted other issues out. It felt like you were never stopping planning. The match would finish and you'd have a debrief and start again. Stress levels could reach bursting point policing matches. It wasn't just policing, it was a career. During the football season it was always ongoing. Intelligence was so important, if you could nip it in the bud before it broke out then that was a success.

'In many respects football was just the conduit for violence, if it hadn't been football it would have been something else. A lot of it was reacting to stuff rather than being proactive. OSUs and

Special Patrol Groups got a bad name because they went in hard and arguably heavy-handed.'

The ring road subway was still the scene for occasional flashpoints. After a league match against rivals West Bromwich Albion in the mid-1990s there was significant disruption when rival sets of fans clashed in the vicinity of the underpass, but the improvements in closed circuit television coverage and other technologies, the more structured segregation of supporters and an all-seater Molineux meant that these occurrences were few and far between.

Nowadays, Wolves' matchday fanzone – which opens for supporters before games – is found almost adjacent to the subway, another sign of how the football industry has become a far more family-friendly environment than in days of old. There have also been discussions between club and council about the potential of further developments in this area between Molineux and the city centre, though none have yet come to fruition.

Today's subway barely evokes memories of a once notorious battleground. At times a very unwanted and unsavoury one, but still part of Wolves' fan culture and history. And on many occasions another palpable example of how football, and everything that transpires on the fringes of the sport, mirrors the anger and frustrations of everyday life. The regular incidents of violence and crowd trouble that for many years defined what remains a key landmark for both Wolves and the city, are most definitely a thing of the past. And the overwhelming majority are happy to keep it that way.

Chapter 15

Kenny Jackett – The Perfect Fit

PRESTON'S DEEPDALE Stadium was built in 1875 and has been in use since 1878, making it one of the oldest continuously used football grounds in the world.

And so, on the opening day of the 2013/14 season, the 125th anniversary of the Football League, it was perhaps fitting that Wolves should travel to Deepdale to face Preston, one of their fellow 12 founder members of the league.

The away support were occupying the Bill Shankly Stand behind the goal, with a sellout following of 5,000 heading up the M6.

Wolves and England legend Ron Flowers walked out with the match ball as part of the commemorations to mark the anniversary, on an afternoon which, whilst marking history, was also signalling a new dawn.

It was the first game in charge for Wolves head coach Kenny Jackett, and followed back-to-back relegations which had seen the club tumble, with no shortage of chaos and acrimony, from the Premier League to League One.

Wolves' final games of the previous Championship season, at home to Preston's Lancashire rivals Burnley, and away on the south coast at Brighton, had been rife in turbulence.

Against Burnley at Molineux, when defeat effectively condemned Wolves to the drop, a large group of fans invaded the pitch after full time, damaging the dugouts and nearby advertising hoardings, and prompting the players' tunnel to be locked.

Away at Brighton, as the second successive relegation was signed and sealed, there were flashpoints between fans and players, notably Jamie O'Hara and Roger Johnson, as a truly miserable 18 months or so reached its nadir.

That was the context into which Jackett arrived as head coach, after Mick McCarthy's departure just over a year earlier had seen short spells in charge for Terry Connor, Stale Solbakken and Dean Saunders.

For Connor, McCarthy's long-term assistant who would link up with him again later at Ipswich and several other postings, it was a hiding to nothing, albeit he had been ready to try and form a squad in the Championship after relegation was confirmed.

Instead, the board moved for Solbakken, opting for a completely new direction and new approach, but it proved a change too far despite a promising start to the season which saw Wolves third in the table after winning at Blackburn before the second international break in October.

Gradually, however, Solbakken's more patient style of play, which many players felt would have been more suited to the Premier League than Championship, perhaps became too familiar to opponents, and too easy to play against, and after defeat to then non-league Luton in the FA Cup, he was gone.

Right man wrong time would perhaps be a decent summation of Solbakken's tenure, not least given his impressive CV elsewhere, including guiding Norway to the quarter-finals of the 2026 World Cup.

Saunders' arrival after Solbakken suggested a return to the more traditional style of management and approach, but in truth he had nothing like the experience or expertise of McCarthy, and, albeit with a decent points total, Wolves were relegated.

With fans revolting, and the club in turmoil, the next appointment was crucial. The process was led by Kevin Thelwell, and was his first as sporting director.

'I had a bit of time and space from the end of the season to carry out the recruitment, and we saw a lot of very good candidates,' Thelwell explains. 'The biggest difference with Kenny to the others was that he came across as extremely caring about the club, he understood the problems that we had and knew exactly the job that he needed to do.

'He also understood that he had to go about the job in a certain way, bringing younger players through with a mix of experience, and also resolving the Group 3 dilemma of players we needed to move on.

'Right from the start, he was what I'd call a "proper fella", professional, extremely courteous and very knowledgeable – he knew the names and backgrounds of all our young players and what they could achieve.

'Even though Wolves fans might not have known a lot about him after his time with Swansea and Millwall, I just felt people would take to him and he would do a good job.'

Jackett was duly appointed, and set to work. On the very first day of pre-season training, several of the leaders among the playing staff, including long-serving pair Karl Henry and Stephen Ward, were told they were available for transfer and would no longer be part of the first team set-up.

Johnson and O'Hara, for many fans the scapegoats of Wolves' demise, were also deemed surplus to requirements, whilst other first teamers came and went from Group 3 during a difficult couple of months.

Jackett, however, had done his homework. Not just on which senior players he wanted to keep or lose, but also on a number of the younger academy graduates who would need to be given their chance. The head coach was very much prepared.

Speaking in 2023, he revealed: 'I had left Millwall after six years in the summer as I felt it was the right time to move on having enjoyed some really good times there. I put in not just for the Wolves job, but also Sheffield United, and had an interview there as well.

'The prospect of becoming Wolves manager was a fantastic opportunity and I was excited to be granted an interview. That interview process involved first meeting with Kevin Thelwell, then with Kevin and Jez Moxey, and then the third and final interview with those two and also Steve Morgan.

'I remember one of the big questions was about what I would do in the first 30 days if I got the job, so I knew they were looking for some decisive action to set the tone.

'Having a summer to work on a reset is always the best option, as it's bloody hard to do that during a season, so I knew there was the opportunity to take things in a slightly different direction.

'I had been in the league with Wolves the season before, and I knew Dean [Saunders] well and had spoken to him after we played them.

'So, with that and my own knowledge I could sit there and confidently say I knew the Wolves squad – good, bad and indifferent – and what I would change if I had the opportunity.

'As well as the first 30 days question I was also asked about my attitude to developing young players, and I knew a lot about that under-23 squad, and who might have a chance.

'When it comes to the senior players we wanted to move on, people can call it a "bomb squad" and that's fine, but I spoke to every one of those fellas and almost all of them said they completely understood it.

'I just felt there were some situations where people weren't going to win the crowd back, and with two relegations, whether that was right or wrong, the squad needed to be reshaped.

'Having come through all that process, I was delighted to get the job, and have the chance to try and put all those plans into place.'

So back to Deepdale. First game of the season. As Wolves warmed up, Jackett's regular assistant Joe Gallen, and the new captain he had brought in, Sam Ricketts, headed over to those 5,000 away fans packed into the away end. They led the squad in applauding those fans, and, after a moment of silence, the fans responded.

They responded not just with similar applause, but with the sort of roar which would normally greet their team scoring a goal. A deafening roar. The sort of roar which made people who were sat reading their matchday programmes look up and wonder what the hell had just happened. The sort of roar which, even in the press box, left the likes of later Wolves boss Rob Edwards open-mouthed at its noise and ferocity.

If ever there could be a symbolic gesture from a group of 5,000 people, then this was it. A turning of the page, of moving on from the desperate disappointments of two successive relegations, to what they hoped would be a far more positive new chapter. Wolves fans rarely forget, but they can often forgive. Give your all for the shirt, make more good decisions than bad ones, and that crowd will have your back, and drive you forward to heights that you may not have thought possible.

'Sam is a very bright bloke who always had some good PR around him as well as being a good captain,' Jackett would later reflect. 'We'd had a chat about it and it was then him and Joe that made sure that, before every game, the squad acknowledged the fans while they were warming up.

'It was about getting themselves together, as a team, to thank those fans, and the same at the end of the game, whether we win, lose or draw. It's not easy to do, especially when the fans aren't happy, but it's important, it shows togetherness and it shows how much you value the supporters.

'That afternoon at Preston, it really felt like it was drawing a line in the sand and moving on from the criticism which had followed relegation.'

'Kenny had spoken a lot about the club having lost its connection with the fans, and I remember him telling me to make sure we thanked the supporters and acknowledged them any chance that we got,' Gallen recalls. 'I have to be honest, I did wonder what reaction we were going to get before that game at Preston, because I knew how difficult things had become.

'And then that roar? Wow. To have 5,000 even there in the first place just backed up what I knew – that Wolves were a proper club. They had been struggling but for those fans to turn up in such numbers and make that noise in giving us their support? It felt like a new dawn, without a doubt.'

Wolves only drew 0-0 that day in a very hard-fought game, but yes indeed, that new dawn had arrived.

For the next two years, a swathe of attacking football, with a few recruitment tweaks from Jackett along the way, took the team to a record-breaking League One title and then within goal difference of the Championship play-offs. Such was their attacking power, had they crept into that top six, few would have bet against them going all the way.

And the fans absolutely loved it. Bringing back memories of the days when Steve Bull was rampaging through the lower leagues they travelled in huge numbers, filling out away ends and taking over towns. Taking nearly 10,000 to MK Dons as they marched towards promotion in March of 2014 was another hugely symbolic moment. That academy graduate Liam McAlinden came off the bench to head the only goal of the game in the 81st minute perfectly fitted the joy of the season.

Wolves clinched the League One title at Crewe with a mass pitch invasion and screams of delight, less than a year since fans had streamed on to the playing surface in a blaze of anger after defeat at home to Burnley. The 6-4 win against Rotherham at Molineux which followed Crewe felt almost surreal. Like it wasn't happening.

And it had all been orchestrated by Jackett's sometimes quiet but always methodical presence, with a strength and steel underneath which made him a personality not to be messed with. He was the perfect fit at what had been such an imperfect time.

Of course, this chapter, and looking back on Jackett's tenure, is a particularly poignant one, given his passing at the age of just 64 in the summer of 2026 after a long battle with illness.

That he is no longer here to savour the adulation he still holds amongst the Molineux faithful, not that he ever chased that adulation, is of the utmost sadness.

Especially so of course for the Jackett family, his widow Sam and sons David and Ryan who were such staunch supporters of his career, including his time at Wolves.

And so too for Gallen, who lost not only a close colleague, but a dear friend.

'Kenny had first asked me to go in as his assistant at Millwall, and I don't mind saying that to this day, I am still surprised that he did,' says Gallen. 'I even said that to him on the phone when he called. "Who? Me?"

'He was just so good as a coach and on the training ground, and I'd always remember thinking that if I could get even close to that sort of level, I would be happy. So, I just thought, especially with everyone who he played with at Watford, and all the contacts he had, that he would have had plenty of other people to turn to.

'I wasn't too sure what he saw in me, but I am mighty pleased that he did. Working with him was incredible. He has always been so clever with his thinking, and I'm not sure people fully realised how clever he was around people.

'In every meeting, he would be the smartest person in the room. He would make more sense than anyone. Not in any flash way, but just a level of intelligence that was so important.

'And then he was so organised. He'd be in at the training ground before anyone else, and there would be a meeting first thing where everyone was able to have their say, and he would set out what was going to happen.'

That second season, which ended in going so close to reaching the top six, included the delights of Dicko, Afobe, Sako. It was certainly magic, you know.

But then, not long into Jackett's third, came Morgan's decision to put the club up for sale. And effectively draw back on further investment. Which he was, after just over eight years as owner, completely entitled to do.

Jackett's brief, however, quickly changed. From going for promotion, the lack of further strengthening, and sale of Benik Afobe in the January transfer window, following the departure of Bakary Sako the previous summer, and knee injury to Nouha Dicko, it became more a question of treading water.

Jackett had to steady the ship in preparation for a sale, and that's exactly what he did, even in the knowledge, which managers often have, that a change of ownership would probably lead to a change of coach. He did so, even when Fosun came in, and there were several weeks when it was clear he wasn't their choice, and he would, as feared, be moving on. He carried himself with the utmost dignity and professionalism, even if, as was proved by the chaos that ensued when Walter Zenga took charge and Paul Lambert had to deliver another element of a rescue act, Jackett would surely have been the best man for Fosun's transitional season.

'I could see what was coming in that third season, as soon as it was publicly put up for sale, and they did a good job streamlining the club to appeal to potential owners,' Jackett said of the changing landscape of the time.

'I remember lots of people being brought in to look around the club and the training ground, and the difficulty in wondering whether they were genuine or not. And then, as a manager, if new owners come in, you just have to do your job for them and see what happens.

'I always said to the players, you are employed by a club and do your best for the club and then it's up to them. I remember some initial conversations with Fosun and Peter Kenyon was involved, then he wasn't involved and Jeff Shi came to the fore.

'While we had a few meetings over a couple of weeks, I knew where it was going, and it wouldn't have been to anyone's benefit to drag it all out. All I can say is that they didn't give me any false promises, they were professional and polite and didn't treat me with any disrespect.

'They have a right to pick whoever they want as manager, just as a manager has a right to pick who he wants to play, or buy or sell. If they want to pick a new coach, it might not be easy to accept, but you can't throw your toys out, and we all know how football works.

'What I would also say, is that Wolves is a brilliant club and a massive club and for me to have had the chance to manage there was fantastic.

'As a manager, you never really have the chance to do a complete journey with a club, unless maybe you're Sir Alex Ferguson! You have to be realistic, and if it's a relay race, you just get given a leg. Then you have to do everything you can to make sure it's a good leg, and to play your part – that's how I see it. I was always very proud of our time at Wolves.'

For all involved in those three years, it was certainly a special time, recovering from such a devastating double dip to immediately bounce back a level, and lay the foundations for what has followed since.

Without Jackett's calm and authoritative leadership, Wolves probably don't end up being sold to Fosun, which in turn leads to the arrival of Nuno Espirito Santo, and the club's most successful and exciting journey for 40 years.

It also led to memories, so many memories, which for those such as Gallen, following the loss of his friend and colleague, have become even more cherished.

'When it came to the job, I just had so much respect for Kenny, and when I was given a chance by someone of his stature, believe me I did everything I could to make sure I didn't let him down, not even for a second,' he says.

'And do you know what? If I ever suggested something, be it trying a different player, or making a substitution, and he went with it … even if it went wrong, he would never breathe a word about it.

'He would never ever blame me for anything, which is amazing really, in the heat of the moment and the emotion of everything in football, especially when the pressure was on.

'He was a man of such high integrity and he has helped so many people in football over the years. A hell of a lot of people. Kenny just took everything in his stride and was never bogged down with problems but was all about finding solutions,' Thelwell added.

'We sometimes use these words too loosely, but I would definitely say he was one in a million.

'In a football environment, with all the pressure and expectation, it is so easy to point the finger at other people when certain things happen, but he never ever did that – he just got on with his job.

'He was a true gentleman, very courteous, very professional and very respectful, and has been a proper inspiration to so many people in the game. I regard myself as being very lucky to have worked with Kenny and known him on a personal level.

'Wolverhampton Wanderers should also feel very lucky – and I know people connected with the club do – as being very lucky to have had Kenny as a manager.

'We really did have one in a million.'

Chapter 16

West Park to the WSL

WEST PARK is just a few hundred yards from Molineux. Its boating lake, gardens, conservatory and bandstand are familiar to many who pass by on their way to Wolves fixtures. Impromptu football games amongst the locals are a familiar sight, too.

Over 50 years ago, one such informal kickabout sparked the birth of Wolves Women, a team which has fought against the odds for many decades but is now an integral part of the football club and, for the first time in its history, has just gone fully professional.

'It was always five-a-side on a Friday night,' says Jane Hill, one of three founding members of the team. 'We used to meet over at West Park, as it was free to play there, and just have a kickabout. People used to stop and watch us, and were surprised that it was a group of girls playing. We used to just chuck our coats down and someone would bring a ball. We didn't have any money. In the winter we just about managed to pay to use a gym on a Friday night.'

'There were obviously no mobile phones so a lot of it was word of mouth,' says Jackie Pickup, another of the founding trio. 'People would come along after hearing that there were some girls playing down at the park.'

The catalyst for these kickabouts becoming more formal came when Hill spotted a few lines in the local newspaper seeking female players for a team.

'I was working at Noose Lane in Willenhall in a brass fittings factory, I started at 16,' she explains. 'I saw an article in the *Express & Star*, just a small piece, from someone asking if there were any girls out there interested in playing football. I cut it out to show a lady I used to work with whose daughter, Gill Spillsbury, played football over at Ashmore Park. We used to kick around with the boys sometimes. I rang the number up and we arranged to meet up at one of his sessions at a gym but he never turned up.'

The mystery figure had seemingly given up at the first hurdle but had left some kit behind at a previous training session. Hill, Pickup and Spillsbury ran with the idea of forming a team and gradually their own informal sessions – at the park or in the gym of Springfield Road School – became more regular and popular enough to take the next step and form an organised team.

'The first time we thought about forming a team was when we got 11 players to commit,' Hill recalls. 'We called ourselves Heathfield Rovers. One of the first games we played as a team was at Bilston Carnival, we lost about 17-0, I was in goal! But we were always thinking that if we could get accepted into a league we had something to aspire to. Then I saw a piece on television one Saturday morning, on a programme called *Tiswas*, where women were playing in a proper league.

'So, I wrote off to the television programme and asked about it, and they got back to me and gave me the details of this women's league called the Midlands Women's Football League. The teams that were in that league included Leicester City, Nuneaton Wanderers, Solihull and Birmingham. We played our first competitive games in that in the 1975/76 season. They had a first and second division. We rented a parks pitch from the council for our games. You'd get people walking past and stopping to watch – it was still a strange sight in those days seeing women playing football.'

Heathfield gained promotion to the first division, won the Vice-President's Cup, and reached the semi-finals of the Midland

Ladies' Cup during that maiden campaign and they were able to use the success to leverage more support.

'I worked at Wednesbury Tube, which was one of the best places you could work for as they had two football pitches and a cricket pitch,' Pickup explains. 'Jane came to work there later on so I asked if we could have some pitches to use and that was the start of when we became a bit more organised, it was fantastic. They had a social club there and sometimes people would drift over from that and watch us play.'

Their second season of Midlands League football saw them playing on their new home pitch and the club's name changed to Wolverhampton & Wednesbury Tube Ladies. A second name-change, to Wolverhampton Ladies, took place in 1977 and the team brought in their first proper manager, Les Bryan. One of the most memorable games took place in a cup competition, against the 1974 Women's FA Cup winners, that brought them to the attention of a wider audience.

'We played against Fodens, from Cheshire, and half of them were England players,' Hill remembers. 'We lost that one 8-1. They were very good with us as they knew we were a relatively new team and they invited us to go and train at their place.'

'We looked up to them,' Pickup adds. 'They were playing great football. I eventually moved on and played for them for a season or so.'

As Wolves supporters, the women had always been keen to strike up a formal affiliation with the club. A chance meeting with the 1974 World Cup Final referee set up one of their earlier attempts.

'We tentatively approached Wolves when I spoke to the referee Jack Taylor,' Hill continues. 'I bumped into him at Molineux once and asked what he could do. He said, "There's no women's football around here but what do you want from Wolves?" I told him that we wanted to be Wolverhampton Wanderers. It was the team we watched and where we were from. He gave me a couple of phone numbers of people to contact but it never amounted to anything.'

The team was constantly improving year on year, though, and made it to the FA Cup quarter-finals during the 1980s. They moved to the West Midlands League in the 1988/89 season, and finally got their hands on a Wolves kit when the club's shirt sponsor, Manders Paint & Ink, donated a kit to the team.

In 1990 they were invited to join what was to become the National Women's League in its inaugural season of 1991/92. Set up by the Women's Football Association, this was the first nationwide league for women's football and that meant new criteria – such as stadium facilities and adequate financial resources – had to be met by teams wanting to take part. It was clear that the women's team needed more support.

'We got in contact with Rachael Heyhoe Flint [who was involved with launching the club's charitable arm, Wolves In The Community] and she set up a meeting with Jonathan Hayward [then Wolves director],' Hill explains. 'I went with Eileen Burrell, our secretary, and she was exceptional at what she did. It was very difficult to get sponsorship for womens' football at that time. Some of the women couldn't even afford their subs and Jackie used to put in for them. Getting sponsorship was the biggest problem.

'We were aspiring to getting more teams out, a reserves and under-16s. It couldn't be done without money. When the parents came down with their children they wanted to see a structure and see that the kids were being looked after. So Rachael and Jonathan sent us away and told us to do a business plan and come back with that. We'd never done a business plan in our lives but we threw something together: a mission statement, our ambitions and why we needed the support, somebody to take us under their wing and give us some sponsorship. We went back with that plan and left it with them. They came back and gave us £10,000.'

'I went out to interview people to help with coaching after that,' Pickup adds. 'They needed to be CRB checked. We had to pay for coaches, as it was growing and growing. We needed more facilities. Parents were getting more involved, bringing children along, so we had to get everything in place. When we finally got the affiliation with Wolves and were able to wear the Wolves kit properly, that was something else.'

'I remember the first time Rachel Unitt [102 caps for England] came along, she was only nine years old and we were training at Ashmore Park that particular day,' Hill recalls. 'We couldn't find a team for her as we didn't have an under-10s or under-12s. She was so disappointed as she was there, all in her kit, but we said she could stay and help be a ball girl, to feel involved, and that carried on until she was old enough to play, by which time with Wolves' help we had been able to offer coaching to younger age groups.'

By now, finally playing as Wolverhampton Wanderers, the 1993/94 season saw the women win the Division One North title and earn promotion to the top division of the English women's game. Competing at such a high level proved a bridge too far for a group who were still paying their subs to play each week. Arsenal and Doncaster Belles were the big hitters in the women's game, with line-ups packed with international players. Wolves finished second from bottom in their first season at the top and were relegated the following campaign.

'It was too early for us to go up,' reflects Pickup. 'The second season especially was very, very difficult. But we had some great experiences over those two seasons, like playing against Arsenal at Highbury. They smashed us, but after the game [England international] Marieanne Spacey popped her head round our dressing room door and gave us some complimentary remarks which was nice.'

It was around this time that the player who would go on to be Wolves Women's all-time record appearance-maker was starting out playing the game she loved on the playground at St Joseph's Convent School on Sandy Lane.

'We played with the boys at primary school, me and Amber Quick, as none of the girls played football,' says Anna Price. 'They all played netball, but we broke the tradition, I guess, and played with the boys. We were stronger than a lot of the boys, as we didn't have a great group of football boys in our year so I think we knew early on that we could play. We were good enough because that's all we did. We just played football together all the time, just outside our houses or wherever we could. I lived in Claregate and Amber lived close by in Tettenhall.

'One day mum saw an advert in the paper for something called Champion Coaching, which fed into the Wolves programme. We just trained for a long time, or played in friendly tournaments, because we were only eight when we joined and the competitive teams didn't start until under-12s.'

In 1999, the club was incorporated under the Companies Act and this is where the story began for BBC Radio WM presenter Jenny Wilkes.

'I knew John Richards, who was managing director at Wolves then, because I worked at Molineux hosting matchday hospitality,' Wilkes explains. 'I used to interview injured players and entertain guests. I was interested in Wolves Women because I used to watch a friend's daughter play, Claire Hakeman. John knew I used to watch Wolves Women and asked if I would get involved to help them with finances.

'I was impressed with what they'd achieved. They had under-12s, 14s, 16s, reserves and a first team by then, which was a really good structure. One of the first things we did was set up an under-10s. Although we were getting money from Wolves there was no day-to-day help, so all the admin was voluntarily done in people's spare time.

'John wanted me to get a financial buy-in from businesses. We set up a limited company and that consisted of Rachael and me, and I brought some people from the Wolves commercial team on board too who had contacts with sponsors. The first main sponsor we got was J. Bishop and Co, who were a hygiene supplies firm. They gave us £10,000 and we applied to get sports match funding which helped a lot too. I remember when Rachael used to come and watch the games with her dog, who she would walk around the pitch while shouting encouragement to the players.

'The day-to-day running of the club was really hard, though. Wolves lent us a minibus once and a player's dad volunteered to drive it. We'd barely got to the motorway and it conked out. It turned out he'd filled it with petrol instead of diesel. When we played away at places like Newcastle we'd have to hire a proper coach and it took up a lot of money.'

Price was just 15 years old when she broke into the first team, making her debut on 15 November 2001 in a Birmingham County Cup tie against neighbours Aston Villa. Under the management of former Villa legend Dennis Mortimer now, Wolves were enjoying success on the pitch at the time.

'The standard of the players we had was really high,' Price says. 'We were playing tier two then and we were really strong. We had girls that play for England within the set-up in the first team because they didn't have the professional leagues then, so you'd find that the England girls were scattered across both leagues because there wasn't really that incentive to move out of your home or out of your area as such.

'I can remember the first season and being just pipped to the title. Unfortunately, we kind of yo-yoed a bit after, we'd go down a league and then back up – we still had players like Emily Westwood, who went on to play for England. But in terms of the set-up, we'd be paying subs still. The captain at the time, Anne Johnson, would have an A1 board at training and you'd have to hand over your £5 for the week and she'd tick you off for that session.'

'When Wolves Community Trust [now Wolves Foundation] got involved with us we didn't have to pay subs but we had to find sponsors to pay our £300 player fees for the season. And if you didn't find a sponsor you'd have to pay that £300 personally. We did things like bucket collections at Molineux, which really stands out now when you look back. The Trust would give us a nominated fixture each season and we would go and bucket collect and that money would go into the Wolves Women to help keep us going.

'I can remember when I was the captain collecting £30 off everyone and we went and bought our own matchday training top to put on over our kit. You look back on things like that. We got a discount at the club shop, something like 20 per cent! But we'd have to go and buy that ourselves and, you know, that's not even that long ago when you look back at that, it was when the shirts were sponsored by Sporting Bet.'

Price's longevity in the team has been impressive. She carried on playing for Wolves until 2024 – taking a three-year break to attend university in Sheffield – and eventually made 358 appearances, a record that is unlikely to be broken. As an amateur, she combined the later years playing for the club with full-time employment at Thomas Telford School in Shropshire.

'As I started to get older, I just started to take it a season at a time and see how I was feeling at the end of each season, where I was at and if I could still offer something to the team. There were a lot of sacrifices over the years. As I got older the girls coming through were getting younger and fitter. So, you know, I'd have to make sure I was training harder, probably sacrificing more than when I was younger.

'Work were great, my full-time job is a PE teacher. They'd always support me with any midweek games, even kit launches or media duties They'd always support me going, so that always helped, where I know some females in the past have had to give up because of the lack of support from their full-time job. They saw it as a massive bonus for them as well because of all the girls and footballers at the school I worked at. I had to balance the two, the full-time teaching and the training. By the time I finished, we were training four times a week, and then matchday on a Sunday, so doing full-time work on top of that was getting harder and harder.'

The trophies came thick and fast for Price in the autumn of her career. There was a league and cup double in 2021/22 and another Birmingham Challenge Cup for the cabinet the following season as Wolves went back-to-back in that competition. By now the team was under the management of Dan McNamara, a role he accepted in 2018 despite applying for another job at the club, heading up the under-16s regional talent centre. So impressive was his interview that he was elevated straight to the first team role.

Price was on the interview panel for McNamara along with one of the women's and girls' set-ups most loyal servants Andy Butler, and a previous manager, Steve Cullis.

Cullis, whose grandad's cousin was none other than the most famous manager in Wolves' history, Stan, had joined Wolves Community Trust as an apprentice, having initially enjoyed a two-week work placement whilst a 14-year-old pupil at Deansfield High School.

That role helped him achieve his aim of a pathway into coaching, initially with the girls' under-11s, embarking on a journey which took him all the way through the age groups to, eventually the reserves, and then the first team.

Resources were minimal – it was usually just Cullis, Butler, physio Malcolm Cowell and fitness coach Roy Williams delivering training sessions at Aldersley or Bilston College, but they brought in more young players, added some structure, and the fortunes of the club improved.

After a couple of seasons as manager, Cullis moved up to the role of technical director, and he was in that position when the three of them sat down to interview McNamara.

'Macca interviewed very well, really passionately as people who know him will imagine, and, when it was over, I said to Anna and Andy that we had to give him the job with the first team,' says Cullis.

'He was exactly what they needed at that time, the right person at the right moment.

'I had to call him to say, "Sorry, you haven't got the under-16s job, but do you fancy an opportunity with the first team instead?"

'He bit my hand off straightaway. He had the enthusiasm, the passion and the drive, and brought a different voice and a different perspective.

'We worked together for a couple of months which was effectively handing the team over, and the rest has been history – he has absolutely flourished and taken the club to new heights.'

Success didn't arrive overnight, however.

After his appointment, McNamara couldn't halt a poor start to the season and Wolves Women were relegated on goal difference which, along with a restructure of the women's football pyramid, placed them in the FA Women's National League Midlands Division One – the fourth tier.

The following season, McNamara's team finished runners-up, missing out on promotion. Misfortune followed again in the 2019/20 season when the team had all but clinched top place and promotion with 14 wins from 15 games, scoring 83 goals in the process, only for the season to be declared null and void due to the Covid-19 pandemic ceasing all women's football.

History repeated itself the next year as the team flew out of the traps with six straight wins, scoring 37 goals, only to suffer another pandemic-enforced end to the campaign.

A deserved promotion was eventually achieved via the FA's 'upward movement' initiative, with the team returning to the National League Northern Premier Division, the third tier of women's football, after a three-year absence.

The 2021/22 season saw Wolves secure a place in the promotion play-off to the FA Women's Championship, after winning the Northern Premier Division, but a 1-0 defeat to Southern Division winners Southampton ended their hopes of a place in the second tier. As if to illustrate the hurdles that came with a part-time role, McNamara was forced to miss the knockout match as it coincided with his job as a Royal Air Force corporal undertaking a mission at an undisclosed destination. The aircraft technician followed his side from afar through a stream of the game many miles away.

Wolves Women were then pipped by Nottingham Forest for the Northern Premier Division title on goal difference the following campaign and had to settle for a fourth place finish in the 2023/24 season. Price announced her retirement at the end of that season but left knowing Wolves Women were in a much healthier place than the club she had joined at the age of eight.

'We had sports science staff, a full-time physio and a training facility at the Sir Jack Hayward training ground by the time I left,' Price reflects. 'At first team level we were always lucky enough to have good staff – my first manager was Dennis Mortimer, but the backroom staff were always volunteers until those last few seasons. Now the players get four sets of training kit whereas we just had one that we had to take home and wash to get ready for the next session. I remember when we were based at AFC Wulfrunians, Macca's wife would volunteer to come in and make food. Our goalie, Beccy Thomas, her mum used to do a chilli for everyone after the game, but now it's all provided at the training ground.

'The contracts coming in was a big thing. Anna Morphet, Tammie George and Katie Johnson were the first three to sign them, so everyone was getting paid. It might not have been a lot of money but at least we were receiving some expenses to help with petrol so that was a big change from having to pay just to be in the squad.'

After more than six years at the helm, McNamara became the club's first-ever full-time manager in August 2024, being granted Elite Athlete status by the Royal Air Force, a first for a working service person in the force. Two months later, Morphet, George and Johnson put pen to paper on those first professional contracts at Wolves Women, further cementing the progression and growth of the women's set-up.

The club was involved in a promotion race with Nottingham Forest in 2024/25 which went down to the wire, but there was a bitter twist at the end of the season. With a mathematical chance of finishing above leaders Nottingham Forest going into the final day and a place in the Women's Championship (now the Women's Super League 2) at stake, the players did not know that the Wolves hierarchy, led by chairman Jeff Shi, had scuppered any chance of promotion. The club had declined to apply for the licence the team required to join the second tier of the women's game which had been due to be filed in February. The players were told in the dressing room after finishing second. The sense of betrayal was palpable.

'As a group we are absolutely devastated to finish the season this way and believe it speaks volumes about the club's ambitions for the women's team,' long-serving winger Beth Merrick wrote on social media. 'For our staff to have to deliver this news to us moments after [the final game] is astonishing. Our players, staff and fans deserve so much better ... It's not about the money, it's about the honesty and transparency – ironically not very apparent with the #OnePack campaign.'

The criticism from the players was loud and clear along with their dismay at being let down. The squad met with then sporting director Matt Hobbs and director of professional development Matt Jackson to air their grievances and somehow a pathway was created for the team to continue at the club with the assurances that there would be no repeat of the deception if Wolves Women were in contention for promotion again.

'What happened in the summer was probably one of the most devastating things that's happened to me as an individual, and us as a group,' McNamara reflected during the following season. 'When I was told that we hadn't put the bid in, I really questioned what I was going to do with that information. I was in tears. It was then almost like walking into a house that had burnt down and putting it back together. Once I got three, four, five of the senior players to buy into it, it rolled out from there.'

'It was a shock, complete disbelief,' skipper Anna Morphet adds. 'I remember not knowing what to say so I did not say a lot, I was just trying to digest it. Those moments bring you closer together. You look around and realise how special this group is and the characters in it. If we didn't have the closeness that we had before finding out that news I don't know if we would have come through as well as we have.'

Nine months on from sitting down with those first few names on a piece of paper, McNamara led his team into a one-off promotion play-off against Plymouth Argyle, who finished as runners-up in the National League Southern Division. Wolves Women had again missed out on the title on the final day, this time to Burnley, despite winning 20 of their 22 matches. But a restructuring of the football pyramid ensured that – for one season only – an extra promotion spot was available.

The match at the Pirelli Stadium in Burton, on 4 May 2026, could not have been more tense, settled as it was by a single goal from Charlotte Greengrass in front of over 3,000 travelling Wolves supporters. It was fitting, too, that the club's leading appearance-maker was heavily involved as a key member of the backroom staff.

'I have a player care role now and it was a really emotional day, like a dream come true to finally get it over the line,' Price reflects. 'During the last five or six seasons we've been so close, like when we won the league four years ago, but obviously didn't go up because you had to go through a play-off then. Every year we've used that as a motivation and it's been a very similar core group of players who have stuck together. To actually get it over the line was a relief as well, to say "We've done it!"

'To think that young girls now can dream of playing for Wolves as professional footballers, it's something that I never thought I'd ever say. So, yeah, it was emotional, and everyone deserved it from what they'd put in and what they'd sacrificed. We've been competing against teams that are full time over the last three seasons. I think it was great for people like Jenny Wilkes as well, you know, it's been so much of her life. We wouldn't be where we are now, if it wasn't for Jenny. So, for people like that it was a real special day. Finally, finally we did it!'

Cullis moved on from his role as technical director and is now fulfilling a very different service within a senior safeguarding role at Wolves Foundation that also crosses over into the club. But he, too, shares Price's delight and pride at how the women's team have continued to press forward and break down barriers.

'I can still remember sitting down with Kevin Thelwell when he headed up the technical side at Wolves and putting together a five-year plan, and it may have taken slightly longer to become professional, thanks in part to Covid, but the team have made it,' says Cullis.

'We always had the hope of making it to the professional ranks, it was always a dream, but it needed the resources and backing from the whole club. Once that happened, there was no stepping back.

'There has been plenty of heartbreak in recent years, but with Macca at the helm I always felt we would eventually get over the line.

'There are so many different people who have played a role in that journey, and if I have just played a small part, then that's fantastic.

'Now I just wish everyone all the best and hope they go on to bigger and better things. The women's team are going to be on

TV more, they are going to draw a wider audience, creating even more role models, and it is going to show young girls just what is achievable if you follow your dreams and work hard.

'Thanks to the collective efforts of so many, people have been given the chance to create history for the football club, and I'm just really grateful to have had the opportunity to be involved in the development of the talent pathway.'

Progressive moves over recent years have seen the women's team making full use of the Premier League men's team's Compton training ground facilities. And with performance coaching and physiotherapy roles also moving to a full-time basis for the first time, the players are now enjoying 24/7 support from the management and backroom team. Yet the move to full-time football is also a controversial one given the damage it can do financially, with many WSL2 players never realistically able to command the earning power to give up their working life outside of the game.

Merrick brought the curtain down on her long association with the club. The 30-year-old finished her career with 163 appearances and 62 goals, her last one coming on the final day of the regular season during a 3-0 win against Halifax, having initially joined Wolves' centre of excellence at the age of seven. She left to continue her employment as a secondary school teacher.

Jade Cross was another loyal servant who chose to retire, leaving the game having scored a remarkable 178 goals in 314 appearances. She made her senior debut in August 2012, alongside her twin sister Emma. After first joining the club at the age of nine, she cemented her place among the club's all-time greats.

'On and off the pitch, they've been legends for the club, and they've done so much for us,' Anna Morphet says. 'I will miss them a lot as mates but I understand their personal situations. I was so pleased for them, they both went out on the biggest high that they could have got. I think part of what made them so special and so adored by so many of the fans is they knew what it meant to play for Wolves. They were both top players, but it's a new step, a new era and we're looking forward to it.'

It is a step into a new world and Morphet becomes the first Wolves Women captain of the professional era. Alongside fans' favourite Tammie George and Player of the Season Georgia Marshall she signed her professional contract during the close season, ahead of their historic WSL2 campaign in 2026/27.

Morphet says it was an easy decision to pursue her dream and turn professional, but admits it was emotional to leave her job as a physiotherapist at hospitals in Telford and Shrewsbury.

'To say you have an opportunity to be a full-time footballer, you'd snap your hand off,' she explains. 'It was a bit more of a pull at the heartstrings than I thought it would have been, mostly because I'd worked there for almost four years. I'd come straight out of university, gone straight to work there and a lot of people had looked after me and taught me so much through that time, and become very good mates of mine, but they were so supportive and completely understanding.

'The players very much appreciate how tough this challenge is going to be, but we could see all the work that was done even before we came back in for pre-season. We saw the commitment from the first day from all the staff within the club and players as well. It's a good group with good people. The players that have come in have been great so it's really exciting.'

Exciting, and groundbreaking, times lie ahead then. And their progress will be watched with interest by a growing fanbase, including those who began this incredible journey over 50 years ago with their five-a-side Friday evening kickabouts on West Park.

Chapter 17

Aye Aye Captains

KARL HENRY is sat on the benches in the dressing room at Boldmere St Michaels Football Club, not far from Sutton Coldfield, and is making his final preparations for a game which kicks off in just over an hour's time.

He has his iPad at the ready, reminding himself of his planned tactics and any late tweaks which he will present to his team to ensure they are well versed in what to expect once the match gets started.

Henry is coming to the end of his second season as the head coach of Boldmere St Michaels' women's team, a season which, at its end, would bring, via the play-offs, promotion to the third tier of the national pyramid. Effectively League One in the men's equivalent.

It's a job which Henry relishes, and probably devotes as much time and concentration to as many managers in the Football League. Relentless analysis, detailed training preparation, many one-to-one conversations, and a touchline passion and vocal support which belies an unswerving commitment and determination to succeed.

It is also the latest part of a process, begun at junior grassroots level and nurtured by developing his own academy, that Henry sees as a journey which will one day lead to a role within the men's game.

He is convinced his time as a captain at Wolves, through the good times and the bad, has helped with that preparation and reminded him of the value of a good on-field leader.

'As a captain, I think you are there to help get the manager's messages across, and that's how it was for me under Mick McCarthy,' he explains. 'On the pitch, I felt I was responsible, like I was Mick's on-field lieutenant and, while some people might not believe it, I do have a lot of respect for authority.

'Mick was the boss, and we all believed in him, and I think that is the most important thing as a captain, you have to have that belief in the manager. Sometimes you don't have that belief, but we definitely had it in Mick, and my job was to try and help implement the gameplan which he had set up.

'Looking at it as a coach now, I value that input more than ever. When you're on the sidelines or in the dugout you can't get to every player, and you need that captain and leader, or multiple leaders, to be worth their weight in gold.

'You need them to help make sure that the gameplan, in and out of possession, is implemented, because there is so much happening on the pitch, so many nuances to any game of football, that you need those people out there.'

Henry loves a debate, even an argument. He loved his time as Wolves captain. But even he would acknowledge there have been more successful skippers than him during the illustrious history of the club.

Have there been any born just down the road in the tight-knit community of Ashmore Park? No. Have there been as many who were as proud to lead out the team? Perhaps.

It is most definitely a great list of captains who have worn the armband for Wolves down the years.

In recent times, and successes, it is also striking that at times it has felt like a 'two man job', with a handover process almost part of the promotions or good times that followed.

Henry, for example, initially took the armband when Jody Craddock was injured, the experienced defender then returning for the final few games of the Championship-winning 2008/09 season. Henry then became the permanent skipper in the Premier League, whilst Craddock continued to inspire in his own way, with his performances and professionalism.

Going back further, when Wolves so wonderfully won the play-offs in 2003, ridding themselves of the disastrous demons of the previous season, one of England's finest Paul Ince was the captain, having taken over from Paul Butler, who still carried a major impact in the success of that group.

Nuno's promotion-winners of 2017/18 had Conor Coady as their main on-pitch lieutenant, but Danny Batth, who would leave shortly afterwards, had been a crucial cog in helping the adjustment with the influx of so many overseas signings.

Frank Munro and Geoff Palmer are others, legends in their own right, deserving of honourable mentions for skippering teams to promotion to the top flight. Legendary strikers John Richards and Steve Bull also captained Wolves on occasions.

Head further back in time and Wolves boast an array of captains fit to grace any discussion of great leaders in the game.

The legendary Emlyn Hughes, who had won almost everything there was to win during a lengthy career with Liverpool, so perfectly completed the set by lifting the League Cup for Wolves in 1980, still the club's most recent major trophy.

Six years earlier it was Mike Bailey, Captain Marvel, another hailed as one of the greatest skippers Wolves have ever had, steering a path to another Wembley triumph.

That 1974 triumph was a particularly poignant one not just for the victory Wolves enjoyed against Manchester City, but the fact it was, at the age of 32, Bailey's first major honour.

For many of his team-mates, they took just as much delight in seeing Bailey lift the trophy, as they did for themselves.

'To see Mike go up there at Wembley and lift the trophy is one of my greatest Wolves memories, without a doubt,' says club legend John Richards.

'We had gone through a very difficult time losing the UEFA Cup Final and then two semi-finals in the years before, and I am sure Mike must have thought that his chances of winning a trophy with Wolves were dwindling.

'He was such a great captain, but there was the real prospect he was going to finish without a major trophy, and to go through his career and not win something really wouldn't have been right.

'So, to get to the final in '74, and go on and win it, I think everybody in Wolverhampton – all of the players, fans, anyone associated with the club – were so delighted for Mike because he really deserved it.'

'Every time I think about Mike walking up those steps and lifting the cup, it gets me going to be honest,' reflects fellow Molineux legend Kenny Hibbitt.

'It's quite emotional, and I can still see it now. That was one of my highlights at Wolves, seeing Mike with the trophy. It was an absolutely wonderful moment, and he was proud as punch. He was the greatest captain I ever played with.'

From the post-war period, Wolves enjoyed the captaincy of some absolute icons not just of Molineux but also the international scene, and the world of football itself.

In Billy Wright, Bill Slater and Ron Flowers were skippers befitting such a golden era, as the team lifted its only three top-flight titles to date, as well as the 1949 and 1960 FA Cup Finals.

All three are Wolves legends, all with their own unique stories, and yet, despite their extraordinary successes, and exceptional talent, a shared humility which remained untouched by greatness.

Like Wright, Flowers also captained England as well as Wolves, albeit not with anything like the same numbers as his Molineux team-mate. But he was part of the 1966 World Cup-winning squad and, even though he didn't get on the pitch, Jack Charlton's recovery from illness the night before the final denying what would have been a dramatic introduction, he did later receive a winners' medal.

His influence, and leadership, at Molineux, were qualities which rubbed off on all of his team-mates.

'When I started at Wolves, I couldn't believe I was training with players I had watched win the 1960 FA Cup Final, and Ron in particular – with his blonde hair he stood out,' said Bobby Thomson. 'Ron just put his arm around me, as the senior professional, and said, "We will try and help you and teach you the game. If you need to talk to me about anything, I will help you."

'He had got everything. He could head the ball, he could tackle, a tremendous striker of the ball with either foot, and a good engine. And he looked after players on the pitch, he gave advice, which I found very welcoming.'

In Flowers' first official game as captain, at the start of the 1962/63 season, Wolves beat Manchester City 8-1 at Molineux, with Ted Farmer scoring four. Not a bad way to start.

It was Slater who held the armband prior to Flowers, taking it on from Wright and, at the end of his first season in 1959/60, raising the FA Cup aloft at Wembley after the 3-0 win against Blackburn when Wolves finished as runners-up in the league and weren't far off achieving the double.

His is a unique story, given that he started out at Wolves as an amateur and, when he did turn professional, for nothing more than a £10 signing-on fee, he remained as a teacher and had to fit training and matchdays in around the requirements of the day job at Birmingham University.

Quite a schedule, even without taking into account turning out for Great Britain at the 1952 Olympics in Finland and winning 12 England caps, including four at the World Cup of 1958.

Cullis once said of Slater at a dinner staged in his honour at Wolverhampton's Victoria Hotel at the end of his Wolves career: 'I know of no one who created a greater impact on the players at Molineux than Bill – with his self-discipline, good behaviour and sportsmanship. I wish we had many more like him.'

So both Slater and Flowers were more than worthy successors to Wright, who was always highlighted by manager Cullis as the perfect example for younger players to try and emulate.

'Billy was a model professional,' Cullis told Wright's biographer Norman Giller, when he was putting together material for the *This is Your Life* programme.

'What I can tell you is Wolves and England had no greater servant. He gave 110 per cent.'

If Cullis felt fortunate to have been able to call upon Wright as his captain, he was also a pretty inspirational leader himself during his time with the armband, displaying all the qualities that would then ensure he stamped his name in Molineux immortality as a manager.

During the 1936/37 season Wolves suffered some difficult moments to the extent that, after a 2-1 defeat against Chelsea at Molineux in the November, with the team occupying the bottom two places in the table, around 100 fans stormed the pitch to initially surround the referee and then wait at the players' entrance.

This was partly due to some controversial refereeing decisions, but also the league position of the team and some disaffection at the amount of players being sold by Major Frank Buckley.

Wolves also lost a week later, to Stoke, but from there their fortunes changed, embarking on a vastly improved spell which saw them eventually finish fifth in the table, and reach the FA Cup quarter-finals.

Perhaps it was no coincidence that this sequence coincided with Cullis becoming captain midway through the season, at the age of almost 20, becoming the youngest skipper in the league.

Major Buckley was already a big fan.

'From the start I realised Cullis had personality and perseverance beyond his years which is why he was entrusted with the first team captaincy before he was 20,' said the boss. 'Stanley Cullis had a mind of his own and was always willing and anxious to listen and learn.'

Many years later, midfielder Keith Andrews became another extremely young Wolves captain, albeit just for one game.

Andrews, who greatly impressed in his first managerial role with Brentford during the 2025/26 campaign, was, at 20, the youngest captain since Cullis when he took the armband for the final game of the 2000/01 season against QPR.

At a very different end of the age spectrum, a couple of years later, came an immense contribution from one of Andrews' Wolves team-mates and pretty much mentor figures during his time at Molineux and beyond … the Guvnor, Paul Ince.

Ince, who had become England's first black captain for a fixture against the USA in 1993, was brought to Wolves, along with former Manchester United team-mate Denis Irwin, by Dave Jones almost a decade later.

Wolves had just suffered the great collapse of 2001/02, squandering an 11-point lead over fierce rivals West Bromwich Albion to lose the second automatic promotion spot in the Championship, and then miss out, yet again, in the play-offs.

Ince and Irwin were brought in to add not only their quality and experience, but also their leadership, and it was Ince who eventually led the team to the Holy Grail of the Premier League with promotion via the play-offs.

He might have been at the back end of his career, 35 by the time of the play-off final, but his commitment to the highest standards, both from himself and team-mates, was a huge factor in Wolves finally making it to the Promised Land.

And that was that despite the fact that Ince wasn't necessarily keen on initially picking up the threads as captain.

'I signed for a year at first. I didn't want to commit myself any longer,' he recalls. 'The hardest thing for me was that Dave was going to make me the captain.

'That was a tough one because Paul Butler was there and it's never nice when you've been captain to have that taken away.

'I said to Dave, "You don't have to make me captain, I don't have to wear an armband to be a captain." I didn't want to disrupt anything but he insisted on it.

'I had a conversation with Butts who wasn't too happy about it but after that it was fine, we became good mates and it became about getting the job done.'

Get the job done, Wolves did, and so too Ince. He was Wolves' midfield warrior and inspirational leader rolled into one, and, even with all his previous achievements both for some of Europe's biggest clubs and for his country, it meant the world.

Returning to youth rather than experience, one of Wolves' first-ever captains was, like Cullis and Wright who followed, also young in age but blessed with maturity. That was Harry Allen, not just of Wolves but also England, a centre-half who, at 22, was part of the club's first-ever official league fixture, the 1-1 draw with Aston Villa in 1888.

Allen played in the FA Cup Final defeat to champions Preston the following season, but then scored the only goal of the game as Wolves lifted their first major trophy, the 1893 FA Cup, defeating Everton at Fallowfield Stadium in Manchester.

Just to prove that modern day football doesn't have the monopoly on controversy, Wolves' first triumph was accompanied by a fair amount of drama on that March afternoon.

Although the official attendance was given at around 45,000, it was estimated that almost 60,000 fans were inside the ground, and the overcrowding not only delayed the kick-off but also led to several pitch invasions during the game.

So much so, that Everton unsuccessfully demanded a replay afterwards, insisting that the stadium – which only hosted this one FA Cup Final – was unfit for a competitive match.

When it comes to skippers, from Allen, through to Cullis, Wright, Bailey, Ince, Henry, Coady, and so many others, what is it that makes a good captain? Or has made a good Wolves captain?

Wright, who held the armband when Wolves won all three league titles, was unequivocal.

'I decided early on that captaincy is the art of leadership, not dictatorship,' he said. 'Respect is the hardest thing for a captain to come by and the easiest to lose.'

For Richards, Bailey is always going to be right up there, in his opinion in that same sort of mould as Wright, Slater and Flowers.

In the sense of earning that respect of which Wright speaks, and leading by example.

'Wolves had that period of 20 years or so where they had such outstanding captains, and Mike was up there at that level,' says Richards. 'He gave me – just as he did with all the young players coming into the team – so much help and guidance in training and matches on and off the pitch.

'There were so many little tips and pieces of advice and I remember how he first taught me how to come off defenders. He would say, "When I get the ball John, just push the defender away, come towards me, lay the ball off and then go again."

'There was so much advice that he would give to us all, and it had a massive influence.'

When you think about the most successful recent Wolves captains, it is also no surprise that Richards, who always chooses his words carefully, selects one who he feels was particularly close to following in Bailey's footsteps.

'As a style of player, the way he carried himself on the pitch, I would say Conor Coady can be compared to Mike. Conor is modest and genuine, a quality player who leads by example and you don't see him getting involved in skirmishes – he is above all that – and that's exactly how Mike was when he was playing.'

Coady was another who arrived at Wolves as a leader, but not a captain.

Ultimately, he was handed the role by Nuno, and ended up leading the team to their most successful spell in three decades with a Championship title, two seventh-place Premier League finishes, an FA Cup semi-final and Europa League quarter-final.

'It's great to look at it as I played a part in that success but most important to me is just being part of the club at that time,' said Coady. 'Everything came together, all the different sections at the club at the time, including the supporters, got brought together by Nuno and the players he brought in and those who had been there before wanting to step up.

'People all stepped up in their different areas and we all moved forward. And I am very proud of it all.

'I may have been the captain, but big credit to Nuno, he let the dressing room run itself – it wasn't just me. We had John Ruddy, Rube [Neves] in at a young age, Benno [Ryan Bennett] with all his experience, people who had played in the Premier League before, Doc [Matt Doherty] desperate to prove himself in the Premier League.

'Nuno gave the dressing room such licence to run itself, he never set a foot in our dressing room because he didn't need to. I just loved every part of being involved in that, it was amazing. Some of the best times of my life.'

It is perhaps a sign of Coady's influence, that, even with a season as skipper for the imperious Ruben Neves, his leadership hasn't been replicated since he effectively left Wolves in 2022.

The biggest sign of that weakness came when Vitor Pereira didn't name one specific captain during his time at Molineux, leaving a lack of on-field leadership there for all to see.

A reminder there, too, that being a captain is not just about leading through the good times and the smooth waters.

Sometimes, it is about rolling your sleeves up, ignoring the criticisms and guiding a team through the many obstacles and challenges that stand in the way.

It is surely no coincidence that in the times that Wolves tumbled into the lower leagues across the last half-century, on both occasions, the captaincy was given to players with plenty of experience and plenty of calm assurance.

In the late eighties, after Wolves had dropped from First to Fourth divisions, and almost out of business, it was Ally Robertson who crossed the Black Country divide and moved down several leagues from West Bromwich Albion to boost a fallen giant.

Initially brought in by caretaker boss Brian Little, Robertson became Graham Turner's on-field leader and off-field mentor, helping the team to back-to-back lower-league titles and the memorable Sherpa Van Trophy success at Wembley.

Then, at the start of 2013/14, when Wolves had again inexplicably taken a tumble, this time from Premier League to League One, new boss Kenny Jackett called on a familiar face in Sam Ricketts, who he had previously signed for Swansea from Telford United.

With Henry at that point on his way out of Molineux, it was Ricketts who was handed the armband as Jackett led the rebuilding job which would spectacularly drag Wolves out of their previous decline and launch the road back to respectability.

'I dropped down a division from Bolton to join Wolves, but I did that because of the size of the club, and because it was Kenny,' says Ricketts. 'I knew that Kenny would be successful, and I knew I would enjoy playing for him again and for Wolves.

'The captaincy was quite new for me though. That was Kenny's decision and, looking back, it was probably a good time in my career for it. When I was younger, I was generally quite quiet in the dressing room but, as I got older, I became more confident and understood the game more.

'By then I felt like I could hold an argument and back it up, and I loved the challenge of doing it and felt comfortable in doing it. Every player and captain has their own way, and I was fortunate to have a good manager and a good set of lads at Wolves.

'I just tried to get on with everyone, to talk and to help people, that was my approach. But we also had some very good senior players, like Dave Edwards, and Kemes [Carl Ikeme] who was a couple of years younger but was coming into that bracket.

'They were also a big help as we also brought a lot of young players through, and it proved to be the reboot where the club found its soul again, and the relationship between the players and the fans returned.'

It was tough on the departing Henry that he was effectively forced out of the club by being made part of the colloquially named 'bomb squad', one of a group of players immediately deemed surplus to requirements by Jackett on his arrival.

Ultimately it was a decision which reaped its rewards with how the team responded that season, but for a former proud skipper, the method behind the process wasn't well received.

It's another sign of the pressure of being a captain and one, in Henry's case, who didn't shy away even when the team went through two years of disaster.

Still the one who would front up to face the media in the wake of another painful defeat, still the one who would lead players on community visits even when the Molineux public were none-too-forgiving. All of that goes with the territory, and is part of the job.

'Being a captain when everything is going well is the best feeling, when the team is winning and everyone is telling you what a great captain you are,' says Henry. 'It's the same as a player, that when everything is positive and working out on the pitch you just think everything is easy.

'But when things aren't going well, that's when the pressure starts, and as captain it's tough because you take the brunt of it. It's when times are tough that you see the character of the players, and of a captain, and you have to step up and show yourself as a great leader, or you don't.

'When you're losing games, and fighting relegation, or are then relegated, it's tough, and as a captain I always felt that extra burden and extra pressure on my shoulders. After the manager, the captain is often the next in the firing line, but that's life, it's what you sign up to when you take the armband.

'If the team does well, you're a hero, and if the team does poorly you're a disgrace. But nothing that ever happened at Wolves will take away my pride from being able to captain such an historic club, but not only that, to captain them to promotion and play in the Premier League.

'Wolves still have such a history of success – even if it's a long time ago, that feeling is still there – and that makes it all the more special.

'To have captained a club that is so steeped in history, and has such a long list of great captains, is something that will stay with me for the rest of my days.'

Chapter 18

Revolution

HEAD WEST out of central Porto along Avenida da Boavista and after just over three miles the port city of Matosinhos is reached. Its long, wide beach is marked at one end by the huge Anemona sculpture depicting a giant fishing net and, at the other, the Port of Leixões where the fishing industry has played such a key role in the area's economic prosperity for so many years. It is here that some of the country's best seafood restaurants can be found, where fresh fish is taken off the boats and delivered straight to the kitchens.

It was in the spring of 2017, with his time as head coach of Porto coming to an end, that Nuno Espirito Santo and his assistant Rui Pedro Silva met up for an important conversation in one of Matosinhos's restaurants. They discussed the offer on the table at Wolves and whether or not the players earmarked by Nuno and his agent Jorge Mendes, who lives just a few streets away from where they dined, would be able to last the pace in a gruelling Championship season.

'Nuno was concerned that we didn't know anything about the reality of the Championship,' Silva recalls. 'He showed me the squad. Ivan Cavaleiro and Helder Costa were already there. He had plans to bring Willy Boly, Ruben Neves and Diogo Jota in. Nuno said to me, "Do you think Boly, Neves and Jota can play in the Championship?" I said, "If they can play for Porto they can play in the Championship."'

For supporters, that period was a hugely uncertain time. After Steve Morgan's ownership had ended the previous summer, following the buyout from Chinese investment conglomerate Fosun, the team had lost its way. Kenny Jackett had done an admirable job to keep Wolves in mid-table for the 2015/16 season after the sale of top scorer Benik Afobe in January had undermined any hopes of a promotion push.

Fosun began the following season with a huge outlay of funds on players. In excess of £30m was spent, with Costa and Cavaleiro the headline signings of a recruitment drive led by Mendes's Gestifute agency. But the plans were undermined when Julen Lopetegui reneged on a verbal agreement to join Wolves and took charge of Spain's national team instead. It left the owners' plans in tatters and, despite Jackett being prepared to see the new season through, former Italy goalkeeper Walter Zenga was appointed just a week before the opening game of the Championship season.

He lasted until October, posting just four wins from the opening 14 league games. After Rob Edwards was briefly promoted from the academy ranks for an interim spell in charge, Paul Lambert saw out the remainder of the season, guiding Wolves to 15th in the table. Seven points clear of relegation but 22 points shy of sixth-placed Fulham, the Premier League was a distant dream. Nothing about the new ownership had convinced fans otherwise.

Nuno's impact was seismic. Nothing would be the same again. There was a coaching revolution which changed the team beyond recognition, one that far outlasted his time at the club. Structural changes to the backroom staff set a new benchmark for how an elite football squad should be run. The playing personnel brought in to work within this structure were better than any others in generations. A promotion, Wembley in the FA Cup semi-final and European football. 'Dreaming is for free' Nuno famously said. For supporters, everything changed the moment he walked through the door in that summer of 2017.

So where did it begin? Pre-seasons are hugely important. They can make or break what follows. It would not be an overstatement to say that the pre-season ahead of 2017/18 was key. And not just in terms of the new signings. Jota, Neves, Boly, Alfred N'Diaye, Barry Douglas, Leo Bonatini and John Ruddy made Wolves contenders in the Championship. But Nuno did not write off those who were already there.

'Without a doubt I thought my time might be up,' Conor Coady reflects. 'I remember the first few days of training and he had set up in a back three and no one really knew what he was going to do. The only thing you are thinking about as a footballer when a new manager comes in – and if anyone tells you any different they are lying – is if you are going to be involved. He had such a plan, every single day, but we didn't know where it all was heading. I was in the middle of a back three and was thinking there is no way I'm going to play here. I was wondering if I was going to be part of it.

'We went over to Austria pre-season, a trip planned by Paul Lambert, so we hadn't chartered our own plane – that came in during Nuno's time. So we're getting on what you would call a normal flight and I notice there's an empty seat next to me. I can see the gaffer walking on and am just thinking, "Don't be sitting there, whatever you do," because all the lads are behind me and I can sense the eyes on me and just know all the banter that is going to be flying about. And, yes, he's sitting next to me for the two-hour flight.

'But honestly, it was one of the best conversations I have ever had, on that plane going to Austria. Because he told me everything he was going to do. And everything that he did in his time at Wolves, and the approach he took, he told me it all in that conversation. That's not an exaggeration. He told me he was going to play a five, how it was going to work, how he was going to do this and that. He told me it was his club now and he was going to change everything.'

Local boy Danny Batth had seen too many managerial changes over the previous 12 months. Nuno was the fourth permanent appointment in less than a year. Batth was, quite naturally, concerned at the turnover of coaching staff. Nuno sat him down and took out a sheet of paper from his notebook.

'He wrote down the word "player" and put a circle around it,' Batth reveals. 'Then he marked out all the different branches coming out of the circle, representing the various coaches, departments and infrastructure at the club. "We're here to make you better. It's all going to be around you," Nuno said.'

As a player, Nuno only ever watched football from two places, which has perhaps defined his work as a coach. During an 18-year career, which began at Vitória Guimarães in 1992 and ended with Porto in 2010, he spent most first-team games on the substitutes' bench. Here, he was in prime position to pay close attention to the work of the coaching staff who helped influence his career path. There was a three-year halcyon spell under the tutelage of José Mourinho, whose Porto side won the domestic Primeira Liga – on two occasions – Taca de Portugal, UEFA Cup and Champions League.

The remainder of Nuno's experience was picked up as a goalkeeper on the pitch, from the position of the goalmouth. This was perhaps the most formative part. Nuno's ideology for the shape and style of his team came from here.

'I think, because I was a goalkeeper, the way I see the game helps me realise the space, the movement and the distance between the players,' he said during that first season. 'I can really look and analyse it from there. The reality is on the side as well, but I already spend so much time there.'

Five at the back, with a central three and wing-backs pushing high and wide was nothing new in football, but Nuno put his own stamp on the formation.

'It was the idea of Nuno and when we were at Valencia, he did this,' explains Silva. 'There are two secrets to being a good coach – when you have such a clear idea in your head and how you know how to train that, and you also have the players, it is perfect. Nuno knew the squad he had when he made the decision for a back five, and was already hiring some of the players for that idea.

'Sometimes the secret is to start training your players and then identify the best system for your players. It might not be a back five. Don't put your idea in place instead of your best players. For example, if you have three fantastic midfielders and two great strikers then they must play and you then find the system for that. In that moment at Wolves, Nuno managed to bring an idea and he also had the players for that idea.

'That is why I sometimes say that football is about a moment. In that moment when we were in Austria, Conor showed us that he could play there, the communication with the team, the way he understood the game, the way that he could make quick decisions. The qualities were there.'

'He would never go and high-press a team, it would always be a mid-block,' Coady continues. 'A 3-4-3, or a back five, whatever you want to call it. A lot would be in a mid-block and you would force the ball wide then your full-back would be the trigger to press. There were certain phrases he would use. He would always say "let the ball circulate". You are happy with the opposition back four or five having the ball. Let them have it there and then force them into areas where we want it to be. If it came into the middle he would kill you. He'd go into overdrive. Don't let the ball go through the middle of the pitch. We would be so compact and narrow that they could only go wide. And then, when it goes wide on that circulation you would jump. The wing-back would jump, your wide forward would jump.

'Another of his sayings would be about controlling the game without the ball. Not a lot of people say that. Managers speak about controlling the game, but it's about when you have the ball. With Nuno, it would be about controlling the game without the ball. That would come from forcing the opposition into areas where we wanted them to be. That ball would never come through the middle. We knew it would kill us because we only had two in midfield.'

Coady's defensive colleague Ryan Bennett speaks about every defender knowing when the moment would come to press and put teams under pressure.

'People always called it a back three but when we spoke about it internally it was a back five,' he says. 'It always worked as a five, in our minds it was never a three. Don't get me wrong, the wing-backs were going high, wide and forward but if you looked at it defensively there was always that initial shape and there were certain rules within that and that's probably why it looked so good.

'We knew that when the other team had the ball at a goal kick or whatever, on the first phase when the ball went one side, we never chased it, we never chased the first one, we'd always know. Say it goes to the opposition right-back after the first phase and then across to the centre-back, we knew when it went back to him that Doc [Matt Doherty] is getting ready to go. You could hear the players shouting, "Not yet, not yet" and then as soon as it went back to their centre-half the left player of our front three would start chasing on a curved angle which made the ball go wide to a predictable side and that's when Doc or whoever was right wing-back would just go, "bang", and we'd all go.

'When it was worked back to their left-back, left-midfielder, whatever they had, Doc was going then we'd all shuffle across at the back. We used to work on that so much. We'd work on variations of that so if the full-back was out of play we'd move into a back four. Sometimes the opposition would get out of it and we'd have to reset. But we would never become disjointed, the ball was never allowed inside us. That was one of the rules of the team, everything was on the outside of us.'

Both Coady and Bennett likened the defensive shape to a net.

'If you imagine a net, it is always in place, it doesn't move,' Coady adds. 'You could change the players in front of the net – go to a three in midfield and two up top or two in midfield and three up top – but that net never changed. So, if our right wing-back went to press, Benno [Bennett] would move across, then me, then Boly, then Barry Douglas or Jonny at left-back. It was also like one of those swings, and your net would all move together and always be in place.'

'They could go around the outside of the net, but they would never come through it,' Bennett points out. 'That was one of his principles from minute one. We had ways of working where we would never all be on the same line. If you can imagine we were on a piece of string, if someone moved along, you'd move with him, and if he moved inside you'd move to the outside.'

'The way Nuno wanted to play was really good for the players we had at that time,' says Ruben Neves. 'For me it was just a case of trying to cover everything in the middle, make the opponents play wide, try to close the middle every single time and then when we won the ball go on the counter-attack. In the Championship we had a lot of possession because we had a lot of quality and the teams in the Championship are not so organised as they are in the Premier League. It's a fantastic league, I loved it, a lot of physicality, a lot of aggressivity and a lot of passion.'

'This obviously took months of work, years of work by the time we were in Europe,' Bennett adds. 'But this was implemented straight away by the players that were there when Nuno arrived and those who came in. In the end, these things came naturally to us. If the ball was worked out to the left-hand side of the three, I would not be looking at the ball, I'd be looking at Ruben. Wherever Ruben went would determine where I went. Sometimes I would go high as a right wing-back [inside out] if Ruben dropped into my position, and other times Ruben would go out as the right wing-back and I would tuck in. That was the sort of thing we were doing. If one player moved there were three movements off him. Teams struggled to mark it, especially in the Championship. They were wondering where everyone was going.'

That Championship season got off to a winning start, when Bonatini's goal edged a tight encounter with Middlesbrough at Molineux. So often keen to see the ball moved forward quickly, supporters showed patience during the opening games of Nuno's tenure. Winning helped, but the new players quickly proved their worth.

Bennett and goalkeeper Ruddy were tried and tested and had been successful at Championship level. Douglas arrived from Turkish club Konyaspor, having also had a spell in Poland, but was also well versed in the physical and competitive side of the game. But the capture of 20-year-olds Neves, from Porto, and Jota, initially on loan from Atletico Madrid, for what would eventually prove combined fees of over £28m, were the headline deals.

Along with those new faces, and loan arrivals Boly and Bonatini, Wolves still had gems from the glut of signings from the previous season keen to make an impact, including Romain Saiss, Costa and Cavaleiro. It had quickly become the most cosmopolitan line-up in the club's history. The player incomings and the links between Fosun and Gestifute lent itself to plenty of column inches and airtime about just how Wolves thought such an approach would succeed in the Championship. Suggestions that some players were joining purely to put themselves in the shop window, or that the squad wouldn't be able to cope with the fixture list in the league, or even the winter weather, were rife.

Jota, speaking in December 2022, remembered the barbs that were thrown in Wolves' direction not just verbally, but also physically, with his strong and single-minded running lending itself to some robust challenges from opposition defenders.

'Standing up to the physical side was really important for me,' he explained. 'Even my missus used to say it built me even stronger. I used to remember things that were written in the press that we shared in the dressing room. There was that statement, "How can they do it on a cold rainy night in Stoke?" That was something we used to prove to people that we could make it. That we were able to not only play football but dig deep and get the results we were looking for. We built a strong mentality and the tactics were innovative at the time, there were not many clubs playing with three at the back. In pre-season we beat [Premier League] Leicester 1-0 in a friendly so we could see from that moment what we could do.'

What was also evident early in the season was that Nuno and his backroom staff were no shrinking violets on the touchline. Even if perhaps mindful they were putting a few noses out of joint in trying to break up the normal status quo of Championship football, they didn't hold back, whether in celebrating every goal or berating the officials after a decision went against them.

As assistant boss Silva recalls: 'I felt a little bit the attitude that, "The Championship belongs to England. Don't try to come here and change the Championship because you can't." Early on people were saying that when winter comes there is no chance for us to play like that.'

Just after Christmas, Wolves travelled to one of their keenest pursuers at the top of the Championship table, Bristol City. On a fiercely partisan night at Ashton Gate, Batth was sent off for Wolves, and City went in front but then had keeper Frank Fielding dismissed, with Douglas levelling from the resulting free kick. In the fourth minute of added time Bennett met another pinpoint Douglas delivery at the far post to head home in front of the delirious Wolves fans packed behind the goal. Nuno had been sent off following his protestations at Batth's red card, and watched on from the directors' box, where some took offence to his over-zealous celebration of Bennett's last-gasp winner.

'That was a really important win at that stage of the season as they [Bristol City] were flying,' Bennett says. 'To win in the last minute like that just gives you a lift. I remember after the game there was a great atmosphere on the bus home, the manager was buzzing. Everyone had seen the video of him in the stands, that's what it meant to everyone. That was him, too, everyone knew what he was like.'

Two more away games during the Easter period at Middlesbrough, having been reduced to nine men, and then Cardiff City, after the hosts had been awarded two penalties by referee Mike Dean in added time, all but sealed promotion. The Bluebirds' manager Neil Warnock took offence at the way Nuno and his staff celebrated at full time, leading to the comical scene of him walking around the pitch and refusing to shake the hand of the Wolves boss who was in hot pursuit.

'That was a tough week,' Bennett reveals. 'Saiss had been ill for a week before that Middlesbrough game and there's a picture of him laid out on the deck at full time. He was genuinely struggling before the game and that finished him off. That's him though, the way he came through it, and that was the mentality we had. As for Cardiff, we knew if we won that we had a firm hold on promotion.'

'Sometimes you might even be accused of celebrating a game like it was the World Cup Final,' says Nuno. 'It is the World Cup Final for us because every week, every day of our lives, we prepare to compete, to play against very strong opponents. Of course you have to celebrate. And the better persons to celebrate with are our fans because this is what we work for. We work for them to be happy, to be proud when they see the shirts on the pitch. At the same time we suffer together, we are disappointed together. But when you have a moment of joy, when you score, when you win a game, let your happiness take care of you.'

And as the campaign came to its end, there was time for a magical open-top bus parade as tens of thousands of supporters lined Wolverhampton's streets and West Park.

'I remember getting on the bus and I couldn't believe that the crowds kept on going,' says Bennett. 'I was thinking it was never going to end. The amount of support that was there, it was incredible to be a part of it.'

Incredible was the word for a season of such consistent excellence and unforgettable support. All thanks to a talented and ambitious group of players, skilled and innovative backroom team, and above all else, a head coach who knew exactly what he wanted to do, and exactly how he needed to do it.

Wolves' summer strengthening was impressive in 2018. Joao Moutinho, Raul Jimenez, Jonny Castro Otto, Adama Traore and Rui Patricio swelled the ranks and would soon ensure Wolves became a force in the Premier League. There were eye-catching league wins at home to Chelsea and Arsenal, and a memorable day out at Wembley when Spurs – in their temporary home – were beaten 3-1 over the Christmas period.

Nuno had inspired a togetherness amongst the squad that was replicated in the stands and perhaps no game of his time at the club epitomised this more than the FA Cup semi-final on 16 March 2019.

'That game was one of the best I have ever been involved in,' Coady reflects. 'We understood what that game meant to Wolves fans and we could feel it in the city. We used to go for a coffee on the day of a game. Me, Doc, John Ruddy, Max Kilman and a few of the physios. There used to be a Costa café by the railway station and we'd walk there from the Novotel, get a bit of fresh air and stretch our legs. We went and had a coffee and the amount of people that came up and wished us good luck on that day was just another level.'

The victory set up Wolves' first FA Cup semi-final in 21 years. On 7 April at Wembley, in front of 80,092 spectators, Nuno's side took a commanding 2-0 lead through Doherty and Jimenez, two players who had played such a pivotal role in Wolves' progress to the last four.

'I have never watched the game back,' Coady continues. 'I say to this day, for 75 minutes it was the perfect performance. And then it just went wrong.'

At 2-0, Watford head coach Javi Gracia turned to the mercurial Spanish winger Gerard Deulofeu. His introduction changed the game. With 15 minutes remaining he clipped a superb curling shot past Ruddy. Jota and Neves were substituted in the minutes leading up to Watford's equaliser in stoppage time. Leander Dendoncker tripped Troy Deeney in the penalty area, allowing the Watford forward to smash home a penalty to take the game into extra time. The period that followed had a sense of inevitability about it as Wolves, without the players on the pitch to make a difference in attack, succumbed to a second goal from Deulofeu.

'It is the biggest regret I have got in my career,' Coady admits. 'How many games do you see like that when teams come back to win 3-2? And it feels like you just can't stop it. When it was 2-2 you are like hitting your legs thinking, "Come on, come on, get us through." But no matter how hard you try, you just can't seem to stop what's going on. For 75 minutes it was done. That will always be the one that got away.'

Despite the initial hangover, Wolves rallied in the remaining four games of the season, winning three of them to finish seventh. If Manchester City could beat Watford in the FA Cup Final, then Wolves were guaranteed a place in Europe. For Bennett, who had four Premier League campaigns under his belt with Norwich City, the achievement was a career highlight.

'When we got promoted I thought that was me done,' he remembers. 'I left Norwich and came to Wolves and didn't really play much at first. Then after promotion, with the investment from the owners, I thought I wouldn't play much in the Premier League. But that turned into the most enjoyable season of my career. I was close to reaching 100 games in the Premier League and I didn't think I'd reach it after leaving Norwich. So when I hit 100 I was determined to enjoy every game. I knew that once I left Wolves I wasn't getting back, that was the way it was. The shape and the way we played suited me down to the ground, with how compact we were. Would that have worked for me at another team? I don't think so, and I've got so much to be thankful for during that time.'

'When City beat Watford in the final, Nuno put a picture of the Europa League logo into the WhatsApp group,' Coady reveals. 'It hit home then just what we had still managed to achieve.'

For many years, new managers or head coaches were encouraged to bring only one or two assistants or coaches when taking the Molineux hotseat, and to give the rest of the backroom team time to prove themselves. Under Nuno that approach changed. He arrived with a more extensive group of backroom staff and their influence within the medical and strength and conditioning side of the club was considerable.

Fitness coach Antonio Dias brought a series of new methods and techniques which were at the forefront of the European game. It was also accompanied by a far greater level of investment in facilities and equipment than the club had previously seen.

The word used by staff already in situ was 'revolutionary'. For the first two years of Nuno's tenure, there were barely any injuries affecting the team. The new strength and conditioning programme, focused on iso-inertial techniques, utilising flywheels and pulleys to provide resistance as opposed to traditional weights and Nuno being prepared to back the staff and make sure the players carried out the work they needed to do, kept standards high and created a positive culture.

Never were the significant advances needed more than during the third season of Nuno's reign, with regular trips to Europe interspersed with the domestic league and cup programme making for a hectic schedule.

Sleep patterns were on the agenda. After returning home in the early hours of Friday morning after Europa League trips – always made on a private plane – players would be expected to report back to Compton later that morning for a training session shaped by how many minutes they had played the previous evening. Staff believed changing sleep cycles and altering the body clock would be detrimental to the players.

This was perfectly illustrated when Boly's last-gasp winner accounted for Besiktas in Turkey on a Thursday in October 2019, and Traore's late double disposed of reigning Premier League champions Manchester City three days later.

'Antonio is a guy who wanted to plan our season and try to prepare the team to be sustainable for the whole season,' explains Silva. 'The Championship season was one of our best years for injuries, we played with almost the same team every game for 46 league games. Then in the Premier League we even played one game without using any substitutions.'

'It was a step up and we hadn't seen anything like it really,' adds Coady. 'It was built for you and your position. Beforehand we'd be in the gym, bench pressing and building up our strength. That was what was pushing us. Then Antonio and Joao [fitness/ rehabilitation coach Joao Lapa] came in and it was more about us in our positions. Antonio sat down with us all individually and gave us all a specific plan. He said he had watched the way I had played and knew the times I needed to be strong in certain situations for when I was pressing and when I was dropping back. So the gym sessions were based around what we needed as individuals.

'Next minute the iPads are out looking at the forces we were pulling, how high we were jumping. Whatever it may be, they took it to another level. It was about us as individuals, making ourselves better. It was that Nuno mantra. You come with us, and everything is there for you to get better. If you don't, crack on and do your own thing but you won't come with us. It was such a step up from where we were that it helped us and motivated us. From top to bottom they were brilliant and understood what they needed to do.'

'There were no bench presses and squat racks, they were all gone,' adds Bennett. 'These little pulley systems came in, we're doing eccentric exercises, mobility actions and we were in the gym every day before and after training. They put a massive amount of work into every single player with individualised programmes, everything had a focus. If you had not done enough sprinting then you had to make that up, it was down to the tiniest detail and nothing was left to chance.'

Players' off-field preparation and monitoring wasn't just confined to strength and conditioning. No stone was left unturned when it came to having a healthy mind as well as a healthy body. Nuno also brought with him Julio Figueroa, a mind coach whose sports psychology work complemented the fitness knowledge provided by his colleagues.

'I always mention Julio, the mental coach, who was really important, because it was something different,' said Jota. 'It was the first time I had seen something like that. On the physical part Antonio and Joao Lapa were great workers with one of the best routines I've seen. That first season in the Premier League we only had three injuries all season and two of them were me!'

For Bennett, who had spent his career working his way up through the divisions in England, it was also transformational.

'Without previously mentioning anything Julio would tell you things about yourself and you'd be thinking, "Fuck, he's right!" He noticed everything, he'd have a little book with him. He never said too much during training but he'd speak to people individually. He'd take a few reset sessions, where you'd go into a room and lie down for 20 minutes and just concentrate on your breathing. Certain players had individual meetings with him, but he was also a massive calming influence for the coaching staff. A lot of the stuff he did was with Nuno, helping him understand players, how people can be and their different needs.

'He brought in the blue light glasses to help with the circadian rhythm, which are physical, mental, and behavioural changes that follow a 24-hour cycle. It would help trick the body clock into the best peak performance time related to when you were playing matches. We'd wear them every morning at breakfast before training and then depending on what time the matches kicked off we'd wear them on the game day at the right time to maintain the same rhythm. When we were travelling we'd wear them to help with the time zones we were crossing.

'Julio used to do a lot of stuff like that and he was an important character at the club without saying too much. He knew everything that was going on at the place and, when I left, he was one of the guys I was probably upset about not seeing any more because by the end of my time there we had a really good relationship.'

'We first met him at Valencia, he is the kind of guy who can read a group's mental state,' Rui explains. 'He would know when to have meetings so we could talk about things and clear the players' minds. He is a guy who is always looking for a player to achieve his best by being in the best mental state. He could work in both ways – with the player and also with the coach. That was important. He could say to us as coaches, "Look, I think you are losing your ideas. I think you are going away from your track, you need to get back on track."

'One of his worries once was that we were not taking things action by action, we were just preoccupied by what the result might be. What I mean when I say action by action is each moment in the game: minute by minute, each duel, each possession. He was a guy that was always looking at ways of putting us on the right path to be a professional player or a top coach. Sometimes he would have private conversations with the players that we didn't know about and we were comfortable with that. Sometimes the players would talk with him about personal matters that were messing with their head and they needed a clear head. We as coaches didn't need to know the details, we just needed to know that the player is being looked after. In football there are always moments where a player is struggling mentally.'

A trip to Northern Ireland to face Crusaders might not have been the stuff European dreams were made of as Wolves returned to proper competitive action on the continent for the first time since travelling to PSV Eindhoven in September 1980. Doherty was unavailable through injury, but the tie drew memories of his own development from across the Irish Sea and subsequent arrival at Wolves. He would ultimately make 302 first team appearances in a Wolves first team shirt, making him one of just 36 players to have joined the 300 Club. But the way he first came to the attention of the club, and the pathway he has followed since, has the makings of a half-decent film script about it.

At the age of 18, Doherty was working for his father Tom's carpet upholstery cleaning business in Dublin. He had been across for trials with several English clubs without success. Playing at Bohemians in the League of Ireland, he was yet to make a competitive start for the club but, in 2010, the Irish side had friendlies with Wolves and Aston Villa on successive weekends. And so, for the Wolves one, Doherty was in the team, after Mick McCarthy's chief scout Dave Bowman, who had been monitoring his progress, asked for him to be involved. He went up against Wolves winger Matt Jarvis, featured again against Villa, and was soon invited over for another trial, from where he clinched a move to Molineux for the princely sum of £75,000.

Knocked unconscious in one of his early appearances for the reserves, Doherty made his first team debut in an FA Cup tie at Doncaster Rovers in January 2011. After a couple more League Cup appearances at the start of the following campaign, his Premier League bow came against Liverpool, as a half-time substitute in front of a crowd of 44,942 in a 2-1 defeat.

'That was quite a moment,' he recalls. 'I remember being out on the pitch looking at the clock in the second half, and there were only three or four minutes gone! But I didn't look at it again after that. Honestly, if I could relive that 45 minutes again, I would love to do it. There are so many Liverpool fans in Ireland, so what a place to make my Premier League debut. It only took me another six years to get my next Premier League appearance!

'When I grew up, I was never a defender,' he reveals. 'I was always a midfielder or a right-winger. I was always versatile and I could also play centre-back or centre-mid, even striker. If I'm defending, and the opposition is putting a cross in, sometimes I'm not thinking this is getting flicked on to the back stick. Instead, I am thinking if we win the ball and it gets flicked out to our midfielder, I am already on the way forward, thinking I can get the ball up the pitch and in an offensive position.'

While watching videos after taking the Wolves job, Nuno identified those traits. As he introduced the new five-man back-line, he earmarked Doherty for the right wing-back position, one which he went on to fit perfectly. Not that it was all plain sailing.

'In one of the first few sessions with Nuno I remember him asking me how my body fat was,' Doherty explains. 'That seems a bit of a theme from my time at Wolves. I used to come back every summer with a high body fat figure, I just couldn't stop. I would always be training through the summer but I must have been eating so badly.

'The backroom staff had a completely different outlook [under Nuno] and once they came in everything changed. Maybe it was because they had been at Porto and Valencia but immediately we listened to everything they were telling us to do and our focus was there from the very start.

'We had gone from the Championship to Europe in a couple of years but it felt natural,' he adds. 'It didn't surprise us. We had such a good team and such a good first year in the Premier League and there were so many great things about that season. One of which was getting into Europe. They were such good days.'

That feeling of embracing everything about European competition, in defiance of the general footballing theories about the Europa League, filtered through all levels of the club. Each trip was meticulously planned, from both an operations point of view and a football point of view, with different departments coming together to ensure the players had the very best possible preparation for each and every tie.

'All the preliminary rounds, going to Belfast and Armenia, and people were saying it was going to be hard with the extra games and the travel. I was thinking "This is Europe,"' says Coady. 'I remember Burnley going out in those rounds a couple of years before and people were saying how tough it would be. But we were going the opposite way and thinking this is such a great opportunity. We'd been in the Championship the year before – this wasn't an opportunity we were going to let go.

'It was unbelievable. That European adventure and the travelling. Going to the airport after training, getting back in the early hours, getting your head down for a couple of hours and then going back in for training. It's what you want to do as a kid. Play footy constantly. All we were thinking about was playing football. Besiktas was my favourite. I'll never forget that week. We hadn't had the best start to the Premier League season, but then on the Saturday we beat Watford at home, then Besiktas away on the Thursday night, and Manchester City away on the Sunday. We won all three. If anything showed just how much the club embraced the Europa League, and how desperate we all were to play in the competition, that was it.'

The full list of sides despatched by Wolves in the preliminary rounds and group stages comprised Crusaders from Northern Ireland, Pyunik Yerevan from Armenia, Torino from Italy, Braga from Portugal, Besiktas from Turkey and Slovan Bratislava from Slovakia. That led to the knockout stages and a two-legged tie with Espanyol from Spain's La Liga.

The impressive run through the tournament was not only putting Wolves as a club on the map, but also individual players. For Doherty, who decided to employ the services of Jorge Mendes as his agent, it helped him later move on – at the conclusion of Wolves' Europa League run – to Tottenham Hotspur in August 2020.

From there, in January 2023, would follow a switch to a European giant in Atletico Madrid, the next step of a footballing rags to riches tale which continues to drive him forward. Speaking from a hotel room in Madrid at the start of that move, Doherty can reflect on what has truly been an epic journey which, from first being given a sustained run in the Wolves team by Dean Saunders, has seen him work not only with Nuno but also José Mourinho, Antonio Conte and Diego Simeone. Stellar names in the world of European management.

'When you think about all the managers I have got to work under – Simeone, Conte, Mourinho – I might be the only player who has ever worked under those three managers. And I was with Nuno when he was at his absolute best with Wolves. I managed to survive through it all and did well enough, so I must be alright.'

Doherty's Spanish connections began in the Europa League run-in. His penultimate goal for Wolves – the last would come against Spurs – came in the 3-2 away defeat at Espanyol which saw Wolves progress 6-3 on aggregate and into a last-16 clash with Olympiacos.

This was the end of February 2020, but little could anyone know that life was just a few weeks away from starting to look very different. The world was about to go through a dramatic transformation.

'After all those years of drudgery in the Championship – and the Championship is like trench warfare – we'd done all these away days at Oldham, Burnley and everywhere else and suddenly it felt like our time in the sun.'

Pat Russell is reflecting on the sunny February afternoon in Barcelona when thousands of Wolves fans took over La Rambla, the long avenue which leads up from Barcelona's port area to La Placa de Catalunya, the bustling square at the heart of the city. A home and away season-ticket holder, Russell is just about old enough to remember the last time Wolves were in Europe, the 1980/81 season.

'The older lads than me used to go on about that PSV Eindhoven game back then,' he continues. 'That was always something that was one of my ambitions, to watch Wolves competitively in Europe. The Turin game was probably one of my favourite games ever. Torino and Espanyol I did as day trips. I'd saved annual leave and had flexitime with my company so I was able to use that for the other trips. In hindsight, if I knew then what I know now I would have done Yerevan and Bratislava too.'

Coady recalls walking around La Placa de Catalunya and taking in the sights and sounds of Wolves in Europe. 'We went out for a walk on the morning of the game; me, John [Ruddy], Doc and a couple of others. I've got a photo with the lads who made a flag which had a picture of me on it with a cheesy grin on my face. Our hotel was right next to the Nou Camp so I met my family for a coffee near the ground. It was an unbelievable season in Europe, enjoying the feeling of what the family and fans were doing too.'

'All the Covid news was out by then so there was a little sense of what was coming, it seemed unavoidable,' supporter Nick Goff recalls, of that time in Barcelona in late February 2020. We didn't know what Covid was going to entail fully but the way it was going we thought this might be the last trip for some time. When were we going to see Wolves play in Barcelona again?'

For Nuno, the accomplishment of qualifying for Europe was a phenomenal one. But it was the fans who fully understood the magnitude of the achievement, particularly those who had lived through the 'drudgery' of the 1990s, to use Russell's terminology.

'There was only 900 of us there in Turkey, a lot of people didn't want to go because of what Istanbul could be like,' Goff admits. 'I'd never been to Istanbul before and it makes London look like a village, I wasn't really expecting that, it's just enormous. We took over an Irish bar and had a few flags up. There was never any sense of trouble. Besiktas seemed a bit of a middle-class team, the stadium was right in the city centre. The ground was only just over half full and the atmosphere was not like anything I've heard in England. The Wolves fans just couldn't out-sing them, it was so loud.

'But anyone I speak to who went to Turin says that was the best Wolves away trip they have ever done. We got there at lunchtime, the weather was fantastic and we were in the middle of the main square [Piazza San Carlo] and you looked around and saw everyone; the away day regulars, people you hadn't seen for years, some who'd come without tickets chancing their arm. The environment was brilliant and even though everyone was drinking all day there was no malicious element to it, it felt like a party.'

'It was so fresh and a new experience,' Russell reflects. 'That Torino away game was the best away end I've ever been in, possibly alongside the Hawthorns in 1989. Within a relatively short space of time from being in League One we were in Europe watching our team compete at this level.'

On 1 March 2020, three days after Wolves played Espanyol in Barcelona, progressing through to the last 16 of the Europa League,

Nuno's side travelled to London to face Mourinho's Tottenham. After Jimenez and Jota ripped through the home side they left the capital with a 3-2 victory and all three points. The win moved Wolves up to sixth in the Premier League, three points off a Champions League place. A point at home to Brighton and Hove Albion the following Saturday took Nuno's side up to fifth, with teams around them not playing until later that weekend. It would be the last occasion supporters watched Wolves play for over a year. That same weekend four cases of Covid-19 were detected in the UK population.

On Monday, 9 March, fans with tickets to the first leg of Wolves' round of 16 tie against Olympiacos in Athens – to be played three days later – were given the news they feared. The Greek authorities declared a temporary ban on spectators attending sporting events until 22 March. A statement from Wolves read:

> Unfortunately, the decision has now been confirmed and all parties must submit to the official ruling imposed by the relevant Greek authorities. We share the disappointment of all of our supporters who will be affected by this decision, and can confirm that all match ticket refunds will be processed over the next 48 hours.

'We'd booked it and there were four of us going,' Russell recalls. 'We had a really good Airbnb sorted in the middle of Athens and there was no option for a refund so we just thought we'd go out there anyway. On the morning of the game we got taxis from the centre of Athens down to the stadium to see what the chances of getting a ticket were and to have a look around. It was at about 10:30 in the morning and the Wolves coach pulled up and, as we had colours on, the players were waving at us.'

'I remember seeing loads of fans,' Coady says. 'There were big fences around the ground and they had to be outside the fences so we couldn't speak to them because the pandemic was just kicking off. Normally when they go all that way you make an effort to go and speak with them but you couldn't even do that which was a shame. To know they still went all that way with everything going on was great for us.'

But for Nuno, global events had by now surpassed any desire to play the match. Several members of the backroom staff remember receiving a Siren text from the UK government while in Greece, informing them of the dangers of travelling overseas. Quite simply, the head coach was appalled that the game was going ahead.

'I remember him doing the press conference beforehand and saying that we shouldn't be going,' Coady continues. 'Looking back on it now, it wasn't right that we went when we just got masked up and did it.'

That evening, just a few hundred yards from the famous Parthenon, a couple of hundred Wolves supporters congregated in The James Joyce pub to watch the match on television, singing songs and partying until the small hours of the morning.

'When we flew over to Greece there weren't a lot of people on the plane,' Russell continues. 'We went via Switzerland and on the way back after we changed in Zurich there were only seven or eight people on our flight. It did feel a sense of doom or dread, "What's gonna happen next?"'

The day after Wolves' 1-1 draw with Olympiacos, the Premier League suspended all fixtures until 3 April, with the decision to be kept under constant review. It was wishful thinking; the pandemic spread like wildfire across Europe and on 23 March the Prime Minister announced a national lockdown. Life would never be the same again.

'The biggest impact for the club from the pandemic was not financial, it was about Nuno,' chairman Jeff Shi reveals. 'He was hugely impacted by it. At some moments I think Nuno was ruined by the pandemic. Financially we took some losses, of course, but it was not the end of the world.'

Wolves' Premier League season resumed on 20 June with a 2-0 win away at West Ham United, but all the remaining fixtures that season were played behind closed doors.

'It was one of the things that brought us down,' Rui Silva, Nuno's assistant, says. 'We were used to Molineux with the fans in and with the pandemic, the empty stadiums, all that feeling and support from the fans, we lost everything.'

Perhaps even more disconcerting for the players and management, particularly the large overseas contingent, was the enforced isolation at the Compton Park training ground.

'Yes, it was crazy,' Rui adds. 'In that moment we had to adapt everything. In the beginning it was just physical conditioning, with just one player individually. We started working at nine in the morning and finished at six in the evening, it was mad. Then we trained with a group of five players as we had three pitches. I was a neighbour of Rui Barbosa [goalkeeper coach] in the same apartment block. It was okay for us and the club were great, they went to the supermarkets for us and made the meals for us. But we were used to things like a lunch together. It was an obligation at training that everybody had to have lunch together, you could not leave to eat elsewhere. Normally we would have a lunch together at 12:30pm and it was a moment of connection. That was lost.

'Even cutting our hair was impossible. At the beginning I tried to arrange with Jeff to put a barber in the club in a safe environment to cut all the players' hair. But then Neves invited me to his house as he organised a barber to cut all our hair. Apart from Jeff, his was a mess as his wife cut his! The rules then were tough and the medical department went by the book.'

The Premier League campaign finished on 26 July with a 2-0 defeat at Chelsea. Wolves' 2019/20 season had now been going for a year and a day, since the 2-0 home win over Crusaders in the Europa League second qualifying round. And still it had not finished. European football resumed with the latter stages of the competition condensed into a mini-tournament once the round of 16 ties had been completed.

On 6 August Wolves won their second leg, 1-0, against Olympiacos and progressed through to the quarter-finals. All eight teams travelled to Germany, where the competition was concluded. On 10 August, Wolves narrowly lost to Sevilla, who went on to lift the trophy 11 days later. The 1-0 defeat was tinged with regret after Jimenez missed a first-half penalty before Lucas Ocampos struck the winning goal with two minutes to go.

'If Covid hadn't showed up I think we could have gone all the way,' Jota said later. 'The chance to play the rest of the tournament at Molineux instead of just one game in Germany, it was a sad moment. The fans deserved it and we would have been so much stronger if we had the chance to play two legs in those knockout stages. Even in Armenia, miles away, there were fans there, it was unbelievable. The part of the season we played after Covid was not that good. We lost in the Europa League, we still finished seventh in the Premier League, but not playing as good as we were before.'

On 29 November, Wolves travelled to London to face Arsenal at an empty Emirates Stadium during the behind-closed-doors 2020/21 campaign. Inside the opening five minutes Arsenal won a corner and Jimenez came back into the Wolves box to defend the near post.

'We used to do set plays where we would do zonal marking,' Coady explains. 'Raul would always be the front space, I would be behind him in the six-yard box and then it would be Boly or whoever else was playing. We all went up and as we went up – and I'd never put blame on anyone – but David Luiz was travelling like he'd been shot out of a gun, he was going that fast. I understand you go to attack the ball, but he was flying.'

A sickening crack echoed around the empty arena as the Arsenal centre-back's forehead collided with the side of Jimenez's skull.

'As we've come down Raul dropped on his side,' Coady continues. 'I'm not a doctor but you always remember the recovery position is to be on your side. He was lying there on his side and then his nose started gushing with blood, but he was out cold, his eyes were gone. Leander [Dendoncker] was the nearest player and tried to pull him over and we all shouted, "No! Don't do it." It was the worst experience I had in football, seeing a friend like that, not just a team-mate.

'At half-time we never even talked about football. We just asked the physio team how Raul was. The only thing Nuno said was, "Let's get this game over and go." It was mad, a Premier League game, but we were so worried about him, it was horrendous. The game slowed down after that, for both teams. We won the game 2-1 but it wasn't about that. Everything just slowed completely and obviously we all felt the Raul injury, it was the worst experience on a pitch. And with the empty stadium, you heard the sound echoing around.'

'What happened with Raul, the way they reacted and saved him was brilliant,' Rui says of the medical staff who attended to him on the pitch, in the ambulance and in hospital. 'If he had been in another country, he may not have lived. It was one of the moments that marked everybody. There was panic in the dressing room as we were worried about his life and then when he recovered everybody was relieved, glad that he was okay, but football was the secondary part of this.'

'Raul's injury hit Nuno a lot as well, he was his everything in terms of a striker,' Coady reveals. 'What he was like before his injury, I don't think there was a better striker in the league at the time. He set everything up for us, he knew how to sit in a block, he knew when the time to go was. I think that had a big impact on Nuno.'

The psychological impact of Jimenez's injury was felt throughout the staff at Compton Park, who feared for the future of a hugely popular member of the squad. On the pitch, with Jota's move to Liverpool two months earlier, the team was looking short of options in attack. It was not long before Nuno was forced to turn to 18-year-old striker Fabio Silva. The Portuguese youngster, part of the Gestifute stable, moved to Wolves from Porto for a fee of £35m. The deal would later come under investigation from the Portuguese Public Ministry and Tax Authority, according to a report in the Lisbon-based newspaper *Correio da Manha*, in July 2021.

'Every now and then we'd have a chat and say, "What's up with the gaffer there?"' Coady admits. 'It felt a bit different and we just wanted everything to be how it was the season before and the season before that, when we had so much success. We were all asking, "Do you think he's lonely? Do you think he's this or that?" It was horrible to think that might be the case because we went into work with him and wanted him to be the Nuno of the previous three years. We were hating thinking that he was lonely at home going through tough times. It [the pandemic] was a tough time for everyone and looking back now it was horrendous, wasn't it? Imagine if we had to do it in Portugal on our own. I couldn't imagine being without Amie and my boys so I can't imagine what he was going through.

'It hit all the staff, not just the gaffer. Home is home. I felt so sorry for him. I spent a lot of time away from my wife and the kids but I could always go home. They couldn't. We all understood the boat he was in. When flights were cut off and they couldn't get home it must have been so hard.

'He knew how to be the manager of a football club and all of a sudden it wasn't football. I remember him saying to me quite a lot that there was no point playing football without fans. He used to say to me, "The game shouldn't be going on." I remember him saying, "People will get used to this, they'll start watching it on the television." If you remember, every game was live on television at the time, and he used to say he didn't like it because people would get used to it. He was such a manager for us first and foremost but also for the supporters, the people of Wolves, he loved them. He donated £250,000 to them.'

In late January 2021, Wolves Foundation launched Feed Our Pack at Molineux during the third national lockdown. A £500,000 project to reduce the effects of food poverty and support the most vulnerable people in the Wolverhampton community who had been affected by the Covid-19 pandemic, it was made possible by a £250,000 grant from the Premier League PFA Community Fund and a personal donation matching that amount from Nuno.

The head coach was famed for his terse and uninformative press conferences during his four-year stay at the club, but when he sat down in the Billy Wright Stand at Molineux for a socially distanced chat on that cold winter's afternoon, he spoke from the heart about why he had made the donation.

'Thank God that I am working, that I am able to go to the training ground in a healthy environment,' he said. 'I cannot even imagine what it is like to be at home not being allowed to do your job, not being allowed to collect your salary, and all the problems that come after that. I am fortunate and we are privileged in football. We have the luck so let us think about the other ones, not us, who are in real problems.

'When you think that you don't have food and you are not able to provide food to your family, that is the worst feeling someone has. I am a member of this society. I am someone who deals with this on a daily basis, because there is always someone that you know who is having problems. I will try my best to get this message across, be an example, and get people involved in this Wolves Foundation project.

'We [the coaching staff] arrived here and we cannot thank enough how people make us feel. From minute one we felt like we were home. And now I can say that I'm at home. It's my moral obligation to give something back, and this is the right moment to do it. Because what we see is that we are getting far away, people are isolating themselves. After that comes the health problems, after that comes the absence of bonds that we have built over so many times. These bonds we cannot break, even if we are not from the same household, we are still here and we are going to be here again. The world is changing and I'm really afraid that being selfish will be our worst mistake, and I cannot allow that.'

Football in empty stadiums had become tediously familiar. January 2021 was a tough month for Nuno's team on the pitch, with the nadir a 3-2 home defeat in the Black Country derby against West Bromwich Albion. For the next game, away at Chelsea, Nuno abandoned the four-man defence and returned to the five at the back which had served him so well in previous seasons. Wolves drew 0-0 against Thomas Tuchel's side, with on-loan striker Willian José coming on as a late substitute for his debut.

Three wins in February steadied the ship and Wolves were well clear of any relegation danger with three months of the season remaining. The campaign was meandering to a mundane conclusion when, on 25 April, Burnley arrived at Molineux. A first-half hat-trick from Chris Wood stunned Nuno's side, with the visitors eventually winning 4-0. The defeat had a profound effect on the club's ownership. Almost 6,000 miles away in Shanghai, Fosun chairman Guo Guangchang had invited around 100 people to attend a party to watch a live broadcast of the match. Chairman Jeff Shi agreed that the head coach had run his race at Wolves and, in circumstances nobody could have foretold little over a year earlier, Nuno's reign had ended.

By the final week of the season, with lockdown restrictions gradually being lifted, a small percentage of stadia capacity had been opened to spectators. Home supporters would be allowed to attend Wolves' midweek match at Goodison Park against Everton and again four days later at Molineux for the visit of Manchester United. There was a certain irony that by the time fans were finally allowed back in the ground, Nuno had already been dismissed.

'I remember the day he came in when it happened and he was dead upset,' Coady recalls. 'He called a meeting a few days before the Manchester United game, there were a couple of games to go, and he told us and gathered us all in the changing room. He was upset, it was hard to see it, especially for the lads who'd been there right through with him like Ruben [Neves] and John [Ruddy], it was tough to see him like that. It made us emotional seeing him like that but I was relieved for him a little bit that now he could go and be with his missus and kids.

'He left the changing room [at Compton Park] and went upstairs so I went up after him, all the lads knew I was going to see him. He was having a cigarette in his office. I sat with him for a bit and he explained what had gone on with the owners. It was hard, I was so close to him and loved him as a manager. His ideas, what he did for the club, where we were and where we finished. It was incredible and I just think how it ended it should have been with him finishing how he wanted to rather than being pushed. You saw what the lads thought of him, giving him a guard of honour [after the United match] and giving him a hug.

'I'm proud of being a part of that club at that time. Everybody came together, all the different sections of the club, they were brought together by Nuno and the staff and players he brought in. People all stepped up and we moved forward. Travelling around Europe, winning at all these big clubs. Being captain of that, credit to Nuno for letting the dressing room run itself, he never came into the dressing room, he didn't need to. We had a great mix of good professionals like Doc, John [Ruddy], Benno and Ruben. We only thought Ruben would be there for a year and he's still there now. I loved every part of that.'

Just 4,500 supporters were allowed into Molineux for Nuno's final game in charge. It ended in a 2-1 defeat to United. Long after the supporters had gone and the media duties had been concluded, three men gathered in the manager's office in the bowels of the stadium: the head coach, the captain and Adama Traore.

'He was really close to Adama,' Coady reveals. 'He loved Adama, he used to say to him, "There's no one else in world football like you." The two of us were the last ones getting changed so we just went in to see Nuno to say goodbye. We sat with him for ages and he looked a different man again; laughing, smiling, it was like he had just let out a huge sigh of relief and he'd done what he needed to do. It was quite funny, after a while he said to Adama, "No matter where I go, whatever club, I'm going to take you with me" and I'm sat there thinking, "What!?" I just said, "Fucking hell, I worked with you for four years, what's going on here?" and he just burst out laughing. It was good to see him like this.'

An intensely private man, Nuno's impact at Wolves was remarkable. It is hard to imagine a closer bond between manager, coaches and players. His relationship with supporters and support for the community through his donation to Feed Our Pack ensured his place as one of the club's managerial greats on and off the pitch.

Accelerated by the Covid-19 pandemic, the end of that era came far too soon. With each passing year since, Wolves supporters are reminded of just how special those days were.

It was a success story built in the northern Portuguese city of Porto and its surrounds, home to many of the lead characters and where the foundations were laid for one of the most impressive coaching revolutions Molineux has ever witnessed.

Chapter 19

Out of Darkness Cometh Light

THE MAYOR'S parlour sits at the top of the offices of the City of Wolverhampton Council, based at the Civic Centre, right in the heart of the centre of the city, and within a stone's throw of Molineux.

Walk out of the council offices, and within a few steps the Golden Palace comes into view. Head under and out of Molineux Subway, and you are pretty much there.

The close proximity of council and club is symbolic of the need for the two to have strong and constructive relations. Not necessarily always agreeing, certainly not in each other's pockets, but a healthy alliance based on open dialogue and a shared motivation to deliver what is best for the people of Wolverhampton. It's also always worth remembering that, back in 1986, it was the council, led by John Bird, who actually helped the club from disappearing into the abyss thanks to several years of mismanagement from the ownership.

The mayor's parlour carries a similar feeling of ceremony and the weight of history as it would for fans heading into Wolves Museum.

Photographs of previous mayors adorn the entrance. There are many historical artefacts contained within, and it has been the venue for many city events down the years, including the awards of the Freemen of the City to Wolves-related recipients such as Rachael Heyhoe Flint, Steve Bull and John Richards. Step on to the patio area outside, and there is a glorious view across all areas of the city, including, of course, Molineux itself.

The first-ever mayor of Wolverhampton, GB Thorneycroft, was elected in 1848, and, for the 2026/27 term, the 167th mayor is Councillor Paul Singh. Rather fittingly, the mayor's term of office coincides with Wolves' 150th anniversary, as he has been a loyal and committed Wolves fan for over 50 years himself.

The leader of the city council heading into the club's major anniversary is another Wolves fan, Councillor Stephen Simkins. Although he will, very quickly, as a proud 'Bilstonian', declare that he shares his love of Wolves with that of Bilston Town, the Steelmen, still going strong in tangerine orange at their stadium in Queen Street.

The mayor and the leader hail from different sides of the traditional political divide. The mayor is a member of the Conservative Party, and the leader, from Labour. Councillor Simkins is also the deputy mayor of the West Midlands. The leader of the Conservatives in Wolverhampton is Simon Bennett, another proud Wolves fan who once worked for Wolves Foundation, the club's official charity. Plenty of opportunity for Molineux chat within the corridors of local power!

Political differences disappear when it comes to all things Wolves. For all their debates and discords across the council chamber, mention the gold and black, and all are usually united. The same goes for the rest of the city, a one-club city. A pride in their club tends to break down all other barriers.

'It's a sense of belonging, isn't it?' says the mayor. 'For all of us from Wolverhampton. I know the game has changed but when Wolves play on a Saturday afternoon, there is still a real buzz about the city – we are all looking forward to it.

'When I was growing up, it was about meeting all the lads, and the characters of Wolverhampton, people like Ezra and the cowboy, it was just embedded within us. It was a feeling that you can't buy or sell – and was about watching football and making memories that we still talk about now.

'So, for me, as a big Wolves fan, being the mayor during this anniversary year is particularly special.

'We look at all the great things that are happening in the city, and all the great work that we see people delivering in sports and grassroots sports, but within all that, Molineux is still the heartbeat.

'That's so right – the football club is the heart and soul,' adds Councillor Simkins.

'We always want to work hand in glove with Wolves, because it is such a big part of our city, a big part of our culture. We wouldn't be the same without Wolves and I love the fact that Molineux is still in the city centre – and that we can still see the stadium from where we are sitting now.

'The game has changed, and I'm not a fan of all the statistics and VAR because I think we've lost that space where we can all have our own opinions, and turn into managers! All that is done for us instead.

'But when it comes to Wolves, that link between the club and the city, it is so important – it's like a glue which keeps us all together.'

As with all fans, the mayor and the leader have their own Wolves memories to look back on. Their own stories to tell. The conversation between them flows effortlessly with reminders of great successes, and, sadly, the failures. Recollections of games and certain players. Like the thousands who continue to turn up and follow Wolves, they are both on their own unique journey as supporters, but one which, as with all fans, contains so many similarities and shared experiences.

The mayor moved to Wolverhampton from the Punjab in the 1970s, initially living in Willenhall, and his support of Wolves followed pretty much immediately.

He remembers his first few games as a nine- or ten-year old, attending with schoolfriends, jumping on the 529 bus for a mere pittance and disembarking at the bus depot where St George's Island is situated now.

One of the early games which sticks in his memory is the 7-1 victory over Chelsea in March of 1975. And the impact of John Richards. As well as watching Bob Hazell, one of the club's first black players, who was such an inspiration in having to suffer racial discrimination and become a pioneer for the good of those who followed.

'Growing up and going to Wolves was just a magical time for me,' the mayor explains.

'Getting on the bus for a couple of pence back then, walking to the stadium with thousands of other fans, listening to the songs, atmosphere like a carnival.

'As a young Indian boy coming to the country, then standing on the terraces watching the game, it made me feel part of the community.'

The love affair with Wolves continued. The mayor still has season tickets in the South Bank with other family members, sitting in amongst fans who have also become friends.

For Councillor Simkins, his footballing education was actually quite similar to many others from his generation. His father was a West Bromwich Albion fan, and, even with the fierce local rivalry, a lot of supporters back then would go to watch Wolves one weekend, and Albion the next. Along with, of course, his beloved Bilston Town.

'My dad was obsessed with football, so we'd go to watch Bilston at Queen Street, where it was also about meeting other people, but I'd pick up all the passion and enthusiasm of the crowd,' he says.

'But then, with dad being the biggest Albion fan in Bradley, we'd have to go to both, although all my mates were Wolves fans so that was always where I was going to end up when I was older.

'Going through the eighties, when Wolves were in the lower divisions, it actually felt really good going to places like Aldershot, Northampton and Scarborough. Often driving somewhere on a Tuesday night in a Ford Escort van with a hole in the back of it and standing on some rain-sodden terrace!

'They were good times though, with some great players. I knew Bully from when he was playing at Tipton Town, and then obviously with the Albion. Seeing him then do what he did for Wolves, and still be so heavily involved with the club now, is brilliant.

'It just gets in the blood, doesn't it? Especially in working class communities. Watching football quickly becomes infectious, and although there were issues with fans during those years, in so many ways it brought people together, for the love of the same club.'

Aside from the love of Wolves shared by so many councillors and employees over the years, there are also occasions where pleasure has crossed over into business.

There have, of course, been many moments of delight shared over the last 150 years. Civic receptions to mark specific successes such as the winning of major trophies or tributes to players such as Billy Wright, upon his retirement.

Open-top bus parades where thousands upon thousands of supporters flooded into the city to salute their heroes, again, including cup final wins through history, and, even in the last half century, successes such as the Sherpa Van Trophy, play-off glory in 2003 and promotion under Nuno Espirito Santo in 2018.

More recently, previous chairman Steve Morgan worked closely with the local authority on the extensive plan to develop the Compton Park training ground, in a multi-partner initiative also involving the relocation of St Edmund's Academy and City of Wolverhampton College.

But perhaps, as alluded to earlier, one of the most dramatic link-ups between local authority and club came in 1986, when, for the second time in four years, the club was close to going out of business and disappearing forever.

There were debts of £2.4m – a considerable sum at the time – a threat of being expelled from the league and the genuine possibility of extinction.

Owners the Bhatti brothers were nowhere to be seen and, at a crisis meeting, Wolves Supporters' Club chairman Albert Bates outlined plans to get the Football League to charge the Bhattis with bringing the game into disrepute.

A 3,000-strong petition was handed to the Football League begging for leniency, but they wouldn't budge and gave Wolves four weeks to prove they could fulfil their fixtures for the following season.

'I fear the worst and am extremely pessimistic about the future of the club,' were the words of Council Leader Bird.

Finally, however, thankfully, a deal was done between the council, Gallagher Estates and Asda to save the club, with the council buying Molineux, and Gallagher Estates and Asda agreeing to pay off debts subject to the supermarket chain building a store next to the ground.

'There was a lot going on with the council back then, with John Bird leading the bid to save the club, but needing people to overcome their political differences to vote with him,' says Councillor Simkins. 'Things got quite heated, but, with the help of partners, the council were able to acquire the club on a community-based process.

'Even with political differences, in the end it was seen as the right thing to do, and with people working together, Wolves was saved.'

Club and council have since worked very closely over recent times, including back in 2010, when some strong and sometimes lively discussions ended with Wolves being granted a 999-year lease on Molineux, offering the stability for the initial stage of redevelopment which followed.

From time to time the association can become strained, like all long-term relationships, and the most recent came back in December 2025, when then executive chairman of Wolves, Jeff Shi, took part in a lengthy radio interview with BBC WM.

Among the many subjects covered, Shi laid criticism at the door of the council, suggesting the club needed more support to push through developments associated with the area around the stadium.

'I want more support, I haven't seen that yet,' Shi said. 'I want more support from the council to have an understanding about the whole plan for that area because the stadium is at the core of the city so we can do a lot, we can do football matches, we can do events, we do theme parks or nightlife.

'By ourselves we are trying to make something happen. If you want a more perfect plan for the whole Molineux, I feel the next step, we should have different parties to work with us and the council should be the core leader.'

Those words predictably drew a response from the local authority, particularly as there had been plans put together to develop a Molineux Quarter Masterplan, and other potential initiatives, which the club had not followed through.

Councillor Simkins hit back with a strong defence, albeit tempered by insisting that partnership working was still very much on the table with the authority ready and waiting to work on plans with the club.

For owners Fosun, however, the die had been cast.

A week after the interview, Shi stepped down from his role, to be replaced, initially on an interim basis and then permanently five months later, by – no relation – Nathan Shi.

Looking back now, with plenty of time having elapsed since the brief flashpoint, Councillor Simkins reiterates that it was important to stand up for the council.

'We had tried for years to work with Jeff and the Wolves board on those plans, as we always will, as we always want what's best for the city and the club,' he says.

'Maybe it was a throwaway comment, I'm not sure, but so many people from the council had worked so hard on the project, and I felt what had been said was both inaccurate and an injustice.

'People from many organisations had been working very hard and I felt it was important that they were treated fairly because they had put their heart and soul into it.

'It was really important for me to push back on that, even if that prompted a further pushback from the club, because the time, effort and hard work that had gone into the plans was going to benefit the club and the city.

'I would say now the relationship with Nathan and his team at the club is excellent, and we are working together to try and push open doors.

'What is pleasing is that we can have a bit of a disagreement like we did, but still move forward, because those disagreements can happen and, ultimately, we all want what is best for the club and the city.

'There is so much potential not just on the football side but in other areas such as hospitality and entertainment, and that's what we want for the club and city moving forward.'

Alongside the relationship with the club, the City of Wolverhampton Council has, for many years, enjoyed a strong connection with Wolves Foundation, the club's official charity.

The Foundation officially began life as a charity as Wolves Community Trust in 2008 but, prior to that, was already very much the club's charitable arm, including some strong influence from the late Baroness Rachael Heyhoe Flint OBE DL.

Heyhoe Flint, also a key figure to positively impact the relationship between club and local authority, continued to play a part prior to her death in 2017, as the charity stepped up its operations, which have continued to increase in the years since.

Now boasting a workforce of over 60 employees and delivering over 40 unique projects for people aged from birth to in their nineties, Wolves Foundation's sphere of influence in the city is widespread, including groups for toddlers, delivery in schools, disability sport, mental health groups, youth engagement, college and university courses, and groups for the elderly to help combat dementia and loneliness. And that's just a brief snapshot.

The Foundation's place at the heart of the city and community is now paramount, and so too, the strong relationship with the local authority.

Will Clowes is the director of Wolves Foundation, having first arrived at the charity as a general manager in 2002.

'As the club's official charity, in recent years we have continued to grow and expand our influence to now becoming one of the key stakeholders in delivering a range of different projects across the city,' he said. 'Never before have we delivered so many varied initiatives, for people of all ages and abilities, under our overriding motivation of creating opportunities and changing lives.

'We are hugely grateful to all the partnerships and funders which help us deliver this invaluable work, and our relationship with key stakeholders across the city, including the local authority, is crucial.

'It's a close connection which means, when necessary, we can adapt our delivery to respond to local needs and objectives, and continue to represent the club actively and positively in the community.

'As one key example of that connection, when we developed our five-year strategy for the years 2025 to 2030, we worked closely with the council to align ourselves with their own strategy and plans for the future.

'In a sense, this is the Foundation's contract to the city, and we share the same objectives and commitments that shape our work and how we support the people of Wolverhampton.'

The bond between city and club is one which has remained prevalent throughout history.

Out of Darkness Cometh Light – the city's unique crest is once again adorning the team's kit during the 150th anniversary season, just as it has done on different occasions throughout history.

It was worn for the first time in the 1921 FA Cup Final, as Wolves were beaten by Tottenham, but only for the first half, as in the second, the team changed kit.

Then again in the 1939 FA Cup Final defeat to Portsmouth, before finally tasting Wembley success in 1960, against Blackburn.

The crest had also appeared on the shirts during the 1947/48 season, and was back again, under Goodyear's sponsorship between 1993 and 1996.

'I had to sign the contract to sign off the club being given permission to use the crest for the 2026/27 season, and that was a special moment,' says Councillor Simkins, who is also particularly pleased to see the women's set-up flourishing as well, going professional for the first time after promotion to WSL2.

'It's still not all that long ago that football was a sport which was mainly for men who had worked during the week – "hard collar" as they say – and you didn't see women at games.

'So how brilliant that women are now just as enthusiastic about football as men, if not more, and that we have a women's team at Wolves that is so amazing.

'We've worked with Wolves on hosting the England women's team on several occasions, which is great, and we are very much looking forward to seeing how the Wolves team continue to develop in the coming years.'

The memories from both go all the way back to their schooldays. The mayor recalls attending Pool Hayes at the same time as the father of Mark Davies, and feeling that pride when the talented young midfielder progressed through the academy to the first team.

Councillor Simkins also has memories of inadvertently getting his mate Peter Davies in trouble, when carelessly revealing to school headmaster Mr Palmer that he was away from school to queue up for his ticket for the 1980 League Cup Final!

Or of heading into the centre for the game after watching *Saint & Greavsie*, sporting all the fashions of the time such as Farah trousers, Pringle jumpers and linen shoes, popping into Beatties pre-match for a generous splash of free tester after shave!

Mixing with contemporaries from not just Bilston, but Low Hill and Ashmore Park, proper community in action, and going further back his grandad was at school with goalkeeping legend Bert Williams.

The mayor has similar memories of people and experiences. Of the dramatic fall from grace down the divisions and the Wolves fan falling through the roof at Scarborough, and being at the Hawthorns for Iwan Roberts' hat-trick and the 4-2 local derby win in 1996.

Not to mention the joyous atmosphere always brought to Wolves games by Punjabi Wolves.

'I think that sport is so important, and a really big part of my year in office, because it's such a way to grow and develop, with the discipline involved and the feeling of being successful,' he says.

'Wolves is obviously at the forefront of all of that, as a club which brings us all together with a sense of pride and the togetherness and camaraderie.

'It's a special club in a special city.'

The city's motto, Out of Darkness Cometh Light, is perfect for a proud but sometimes troubled city which has had its ups and downs, but whose people are strong, stoic, and always ready to show strength and bounce back from adversity.

The same goes for the football club, which has also matched some ridiculously incredible highs with truly unbearable lows.

But as the motto states, there is always a reason to be positive. And, for both club and city, to have hope and optimism for a bright and golden future.

Chapter 20

A Fosun Future?

THE SHANGHAI skyline is one of the most recognisable cityscapes in the modern world. The Oriental Pearl Tower, Shanghai World Financial Centre, Shanghai Stock Exchange, Jin Mao Tower and Bank of China Tower form an imposing and unique collection of buildings on the Lujiazui peninsula towering over the Huangpu River. The busy waterway flows through the centre of the city, with cargo, commuter and tourist boats flowing in each direction almost 24 hours a day.

On the opposite bank to the financial hub is a waterfront promenade flanking the historical central Shanghai region. Locals and tourists gather here each evening to wander up and down the promenade taking photographs of the impressively lit buildings of Lujiazui illuminating the skyline. Here, too, is Fosun International's S2 building in a newer business district. Its stunning sixth-floor rooftop terrace overlooks the river and city skyline. One night, in July 2019, this terrace was converted into a fashion show. Chinese pop stars performed in front of Wolves players, staff and ownership, along with local celebrities and the business community. The rap artist Simba and the rock band Miserable Faith, both with huge Chinese followings, headlined the evening's music performances.

The guests enjoyed a drinks reception before sitting down in front of a raised stage, lit by LEDs with the Wolves logo running through it. Above the stage, a huge pair of neon wolf eyes looked down as catwalk models strode past wearing Wolves-branded clothing designed by Christelle Kocher, founder and creative director of the Parisian fashion label Koché.

No other scene quite encapsulated the Fosun revolution that took the club from the middle ranks of Championship football and into the higher echelons of the Premier League and European competition, along with elevating the club's name on a global scale. One hundred and fifty years of Wolves culminating in a decade – and counting – of ownership from the Chinese investment conglomerate.

That pre-season tour came after chairman Jeff Shi successfully lobbied the Premier League to ensure Wolves was one of four clubs invited to participate in the Premier League Asia Trophy – alongside Manchester City, Newcastle United and West Ham United – in Shanghai and Nanjing. It was strategically important for Fosun to have Wolves there in the owners' home city. Over the course of the week-long tour, a slick and well-organised marketing campaign took place, with corporate partners hosting events with Wolves. Later that month, Nuno Espirito Santo's side returned home to embark on a Europa League campaign that would take them all the way to the quarter-finals.

The ambition and upward trajectory was short-lived, though. A culmination of the unprecedented effects of the Covid-19 pandemic, a strategic attempt to maximise player profits and some misguided decision-making within the football hierarchy put Wolves on a path that would lead to relegation back to the Championship within seven years of the tour.

Shi exited Molineux through the back door in the wake of fans' protests along the Waterloo Road ahead of a Premier League fixture against Manchester United, in December 2025, followed by a calamitous interview on local radio which rendered his position untenable. As Wolves embark on their 150th year, the Wolves of Fosun's early tenure feels a million miles away.

Understanding the business model that brought Fosun to Wolves' door is an important part of assessing the landscape for the present and future. How much has changed since Fosun acquired the club in 2016? Does the same model exist today and, if not, what does the future hold for Wolves?

In 2015, an internal Fosun presentation revealed that, in their eyes, the only profitable part of the football industry was the trading and representation of players. That year, the conglomerate acquired a 15 per cent stake in Jorge Mendes' Gestifute agency. Early in 2016, Mendes travelled to Shanghai and, alongside Fosun chairman Guo Guangchang, announced the launch of an agency to expand football in China with the aim of developing players' careers and attracting interest from abroad, primarily Europe where the transfer fees paid were highest.

In August 2016, just a month after the acquisition of Wolves, an analyst working for Fosun privately emailed the agent Luis Correia at Gestifute. 'Our goal is to build a complete system in the global football world with you, with different levels of clubs and training facilities,' the message read. 'I believe together we can establish our strong presence in every major league.'

Clearly, Wolves was a key vehicle in this concept and the success of the club would be integral to the implementation of Fosun's and Gestifute's plans.

'Our goal is crystal clear,' Shi announced, on taking over as chairman from the outgoing Steve Morgan. 'We will do our very best to help take Wolves back to the Premier League as soon as possible and to stay there. We believe the club and the fans belong at the top of English football and getting there is our first and top priority.'

That promise materialised in impressive fashion as, with huge financial backing and Gestifute's considerable weight in the transfer market, Nuno was allowed to build a side fit for the upper reaches of the Premier League.

Wolves captured the heart of Fosun's chairman. Guo would host events in Shanghai with friends and business partners to watch live screenings of Wolves games. On that tour to China, he laid on an exclusive dinner for the first team squad at the famous Yu Garden, where he gave a heartfelt speech to the players and staff, expressing his delight at having the club as part of the Fosun family.

'It's all about the trust and the friendship,' Nuno said during the trip. 'I met the ownership, I think we share the same view. If you compare the idea of Fosun with Wolves, it's more or less the same. It's a building process. Even for me and my coaching staff, I always thought that was the right moment to come here. We had other options, we were managing Champions League clubs. We came to the Championship because we wanted to develop an idea; let's try to achieve something that we believe can be a success.'

Wolves had also now visibly become an important cog in this wider strategic operation. In Portugal, four years before Nuno, Gestifute and Fosun set about transforming Wolves, Diogo Jota scored 39 goals in 37 games from midfield while playing for both Gondomar's under-17s and under-19s. That earned him a move to Pacos de Ferreira and while there Gestifute acquired a 40 per cent stake in the player for €35,000. In March 2016, Spanish giants Atletico Madrid bought Jota for €6.4m. A year later Wolves agreed to pay £10m. And, in September 2020, Liverpool took him from Molineux for a fee of £45m. It was the perfect illustration of player development and transfer fee acquisition.

At no stage prior to the global pandemic did Fosun deviate from their plan to develop players alongside strengthening the team to establish Wolves in the higher reaches of the Premier League. But after the 2019/20 season reached a delayed conclusion and the following campaign was played behind closed doors, both the Chinese conglomerate and Wolves emerged to a different environment.

With businesses spanning tourism, healthcare, finance, mining and insurance, Fosun's outlook was mixed. The conglomerate played a key role in the development of a vaccine across China and elsewhere in the Far East. Demand for healthcare offset declines in tourism and other consumer-related activity. But the pandemic brought with it a new global caution. The strategy shifted from growth and investment to selling assets, managing debt and focusing on core assets.

Back in Wolverhampton, Nuno's relationship with Shi had broken down and he left in sad circumstances, with only 4,500 allowed into Molineux for the final game of the 2020/21 season to say their goodbyes to the most transformative manager the club had seen for several generations.

The assured and astute moves in the transfer market had gone too. Vast sums had been shelled out on Nelson Semedo and Fabio Silva ahead of the second pandemic-affected season but incoming manager Bruno Lage was given virtually nothing to spend a year later, with only new goalkeeper Jose Sa making any impact on the team, replacing Rui Patricio.

Had Gestifute's scouting network run dry or were Wolves no longer a priority for Mendes, who was starting to establish a firmer footing in English football? Lage guided Wolves to a tenth-place finish but did not last until Christmas the following year when more of Nuno's team departed over the summer without being replaced by the necessary calibre of player.

There was real concern amongst the fanbase about the direction of travel under Fosun when initial attempts to persuade Julen Lopetegui to become head coach failed. Whereas the Spaniard's head was turned by another job back in the summer of 2016, when his country came calling, on this occasion he wanted to spend more time with his elderly and ill father.

There were still seven games remaining until the break for the autumn 2022 World Cup in Qatar and the lack of a credible Plan B was threatening to derail the season. Steve Davis and James Collins had stepped up from their academy roles to take temporary charge while the deliberating continued. One-time interim manager Rob Edwards had an informal meeting with the recruitment team about taking the job, Chelsea first team assistant coach Anthony Barry was also approached, former Lyon and Ajax head coach Peter Bosz was a realistic contender and even Nuno was spoken to about the possibility of returning to the club.

It was Michael Beale, Queens Park Rangers' head coach, who eventually agreed to take charge only to change his mind after he visited the west London club's training ground to say his final goodbyes to the QPR staff.

A hastily drafted press statement was released, confirming Davis and Collins would continue in their interim roles until 2023. But after a chastening 4-0 defeat to Leicester City, with Wolves hurtling into a relegation fight, Shi made one more attempt to persuade Lopetegui to take the post, and this time he accepted.

January 2023 was the last time Wolves fans saw the sort of ambition that characterised Fosun's early years. Sporting director Matt Hobbs declared the 'project is back on' as Matheus Cunha, Joao Gomes, Mario Lemina, Pablo Sarabia and Craig Dawson were ushered in to stop the rot on the pitch.

Less than six months later the project was emphatically off again. The ownership in Shanghai wanted to recoup as much as £100m from the summer transfer window and Wolves were forced into a fire sale while Lopetegui watched on in despair. Dirty laundry was washed in public as the head coach gave interviews without club approval, laying bare his frustrations, before forcing his exit a week before the start of the 2023/24 season.

The pattern since has not been dissimilar. Like Lage and Lopetegui, Gary O'Neil and Vitor Pereira made a great early impression only to falter when it became clear the squad was short in key areas. The ownership would point to the reinvestment of transfer funds during the summer of 2025, but that just showed up the failures elsewhere within the hierarchy as a botched transfer window saw Semedo, Cunha and Rayan Ait-Nouri depart, leaving Wolves with one of the poorest squads in the Premier League. Relegation was inevitable. Eight successive seasons of Premier League football had come to an end.

Supporters hope that the events of 8 December 2025 will prove to be a line in the sand, but there is also a genuine fear that the scenes ahead of that game at home to Manchester United will be repeated. The fans' protests along Waterloo Road were the culmination of a collaborative effort – a fans' alliance – between several supporters' groups and individuals with established social media and digital platforms. That they gained such widespread support amongst the fanbase spoke volumes for the way the club had been allowed to decline on the pitch.

'This originally started when they released ticket pricing [in May 2024] and they put prices up for disabled fans and kids – we got them to backtrack on that,' Keiran Newey, founder of the Old Gold Pack, which creates flags and tifo displays at Molineux, explains. 'The last time we saw protests was during Steve Morgan's time. Fosun had relatively good success from the start so they hadn't seen the rough side of Wolverhampton. They can deal with a few boos and chants but seeing fans along the Waterloo Road and banners inside the ground, with real anger towards them, it felt like it needed somebody to activate that. We wanted it to be done in the right way. It was a process of uniting fans and getting everyone together.'

'A lot of people said it wouldn't make any difference but within a couple of weeks Jeff Shi was gone,' adds Ryan Leister, host of *The Wolves Report* podcast. 'Everyone's biggest aim from the protest was that we needed change. It proved fans do have a voice and if you do things properly and make noise then you can have change. We partially got what we wanted.'

The increase in season-ticket prices was perhaps the catalyst, with Shi announcing that Wolves were benchmarking against similar clubs in the Premier League. Yet, that argument was undermined when investment in the team did not match others. Many fans believed Fosun had taken their eye off the ball. Shi's real passion lay in the development of an eSports team under the Wolves brand which, while relatively successful in the Far East, did not draw in any significant new funds to the football club. Wolves Records was launched in September 2021, as a joint venture between the club and Warner Music UK's Alternative Distribution Alliance, making it the first UK football club to launch its own record label. Local grime artist Reepa was the headline signing, but the project failed, leaving many of the artists in limbo.

'I ain't got a clue if it still exists or what happened there tbh, an exciting idea initially but shocking execution,' Reepa wrote on social media in February, 2025. 'I was there as the first artist and ended up being the last artist, what exactly happened I'll never know.'

By the time of the protests there were also concerns about the structure of ownership. Wolves had become part of Fosun Sports Group, a subsidiary of Fosun, which was established in 2021 as a global sports and gaming entity. It owned a stake in Sudu, who became kit manufacturers for the club in July 2024. Supporters became worried that the Wolves brand was being used to grow Fosun Sports Group rather than the club itself.

Nathan Shi was installed as the new chairman and a public relations drive ensued, with the club keen to reassure fans that they were totally committed to the success of the team on the pitch. Huge reductions in ticket prices were announced ahead of the 2026/27 season. A fans' forum towards the end of the previous campaign involving Nathan Shi, head coach Rob Edwards and technical director Matt Jackson drew praise from some quarters, as the trio faced some direct questioning.

But, as if to highlight the scepticism that existed where transparency was concerned, there was a surprise managerial change at the end of the season. Just days after Edwards had appeared in a club promotional video to announce the signing of Raul Jimenez he was replaced – while on holiday – by Cesar Peixoto, a client of Gestifute. Did this herald a return to the strategy that was so thrillingly executed in 2017/18, or had Guo simply gone back to a tried and trusted confidant?

'We need transparency,' Leister continues. 'One of the things that the fans' alliance said when we met the chairman was, "Tell us the truth, we can take bad news. But if you don't tell us the truth and something comes out further down the line, it distances yourself more. Deliver on your words." I would say that the foundations for the bridges are being put back in place but those bridges are far from being mended.'

'Wolves fans are clever enough to realise when they're being sold a dream,' Newey adds. 'I'm not saying that has happened, but there is a lot more they can do. Jimenez returning is unreal and Kieran Trippier is a great signing, but it is about everything else that comes along with it and there's an awful lot for the club to do to win back all the fans. There are green shoots, they've sold out of season tickets which is a positive, but I think the club are aware that the fans are up and ready to go again if we need to. It feels like we've been used, to some extent, to grow other businesses and that the football has been put on the back burner.'

In part, the attempt to grow Wolves in areas away from football was a decision made when Fosun realised that the club had limited potential for growth within the local fanbase. Taken in isolation, these were admirable aims. But exacerbated by the ceiling that exists at the top of the Premier League and the acknowledgement that under the current regulations clubs the size of Wolves cannot sustain a place at the top of the table, the ownership's ambitions changed.

So, what happened to the initial strategy of player development and trading? Deviating from that plan and failing to invest in the sort of elite scouting and data systems that have allowed smaller clubs like Brentford and Brighton to thrive may have played its part. Relationships have changed, too, and while it appears Gestifute are now fully on board with Wolves again, that has not always been the case.

As Wolves enters its 150th year there is uncertainty about what the future looks like under Fosun. This has been an ownership that has delivered some of the greatest times in living memory for so many supporters, but it is an ownership whose motives have been questioned and where an opaque line of command exists between Wolverhampton and Shanghai.

Heading into the 2026/27 season after another period of change, it was difficult to predict if Wolves would struggle upon returning to the Championship, or have the firepower and capability to blaze a trail at the top of the table. Above all, the safeguarding of the club for future prosperity must be the priority as the club passes this historic milestone.

Chapter 21

Wolves Through the Generations

In this chapter we, the authors, wanted to explore a devotion to Wolves through generations and how the club has meant different things to us at various stages of our lives. We hope some of the transcript that follows will resonate with supporters. Every fan has their own story of how they came to support Wolves. It often traces their formative years through to adulthood. It is a deeply personal relationship and each one is unique.

We first got to know each other during Mick McCarthy's tenure at Wolves when both our jobs – head of media at the club and football reporter at Sky Sports, respectively – brought frequent meetings. Much of our conversation took place at the Sir Jack Hayward Training Ground, while organising filming and scheduling players' media appearances. It felt fitting for this book, which has tapped heavily into the locations that have come to symbolise the Wolves story, that we went back to the club's Compton Park training base towards the end of the 2025/26 season to sit down for a coffee and a chat about the club that has played such an integral part in our lives …

JP: So how did Wolves enter your life Paul, what were the earliest memories?

PB: I think it was my grandad. He used to take me and my cousin Simon up to reserve games. It would either be Saturday afternoons when the first team were playing away or sometimes Wednesday afternoons in the school holidays. I'd have been about four or five years old. They played in the Central League and the games were at Molineux. We'd walk around the whole ground outside before the game. I wasn't massively interested in the football at the start, but I do remember they used to put the half-time scores from the first team games on that scoreboard with the big letters.

My mom and dad used to watch Wolves, so we went together in the Waterloo Road Stand, the old wooden one. All the family used to go, and I would sit on one of my parent's laps, so we didn't have to pay for the ticket. I remember one day, as I was getting older, the turnstile operator said we couldn't keep doing that! So, when I got my first season ticket we moved into the family enclosure and I used to sit on the wall at the front. There was a load of redgra around the perimeter which I remember, because your shoes would get absolutely filthy.

Watching the game so close in front of you was great. We'd run down to where the tunnel was at half-time to see the players coming and going. The crowds when I was growing up weren't massive, because it would have been early eighties as the decline started. Some of the early first team games I clearly remember were the FA Cup ties in 1981, Wrexham and Middlesbrough at home.

What about you? Remind me of how you ended up following Wolves again?

JP: It was from my dad. We grew up in Liverpool. He'd emigrated from Dublin with his mum, uncle and aunt when he was nine years old in the mid-1950s and they'd initially settled in Hornsey, London. So, Spurs were the local team and he went to watch them one day and it just happened to be Wolves who they were playing. He loved the name, the gold kit, and of course they were a great team then.

Later he moved to Liverpool to attend university and met my mum, who was local. My earliest memories of Wolves are him going off to watch them every now and then with friends. I vividly remember him coming back from the 1981 FA Cup semi-final with a massive A4 match programme. I think it was the centenary year of the cup so it was this big glossy thing and that was my earliest tangible Wolves memory.

January 1983, Tranmere Rovers away in the third round of the FA Cup, that was my first game. I was nine years old. What sticks out most colourfully from that was the 'football special'. We got a stopper train from Liverpool to a station called Rock Ferry, which is not far from Prenton Park, and it wasn't busy. But at the same time, this football special pulled in from Wolverhampton, and it just disgorged fans. The noise, the colour, it was wonderment, 'This is what going to the match is!'

We sat in the main stand with the home fans. Kenny Hibbitt scored and the only other two things I really remember was the mudbath of a pitch and a bloke behind me swearing a lot. I think that was the first time I'd ever heard swearing in front of my dad.

PB: That was similar for me with my dad, he didn't swear at home. I think we were at an away game, it might have been Port Vale, and there was a huge surge on the terrace and there was a lot of swearing, from everyone! Interesting how things like that stick in the memory.

JP: Not being from Wolverhampton, we used to go to away games at first, but I didn't get to Molineux until '87 in the Fourth

Division. I remember seeing the floodlights from a long way away, they were so tall. And walking up the South Bank when we got in was pretty impressive, but the ground was only two sides open. I never got to see it any earlier than that.

It felt like a choice – choosing Wolves. When I was really little I vaguely remember being given a red t-shirt, with a number 7 sewn on for Kenny Dalglish. Everyone was Liverpool. But I asked my dad to take me to Wolves. I remember it being a conscious decision to ask my dad, whereas I guess with a lot of fans it's not a choosing, they're almost raised as Wolves fans.

PB: Yes, for me it probably was that, like most fans. I wish I could accurately remember my first game but I was younger than you when I went so it's not so clear. My grandad was a Methodist minister and had travelled around everywhere, and then eventually settled in Wolverhampton. But my mum was born in Huddersfield, and my dad was born in Stoke, and they met at college. So, none of them were Wolverhampton born and bred. That was my sister and me, who are from here. But because my grandad and parents were football fans and they ended up watching Wolves, by that point when I came along, we were all Wolves fans.

JP: Tell me about that time you were a mascot? I've seen the photograph, it's such a cool photo!

PB: Yeah, I remember being massively excited about that and I think they were the days when you could just write in to the club and ask. So, whether I wrote in or my mom and dad did, I'm not sure, but I remember getting that news that I was going to be a mascot and it was just massive! It was the 82/83 Second Division promotion season, although the crowds weren't huge.

I was told I was going to do it with Steve, who is Geoff Palmer's son, and was a similar age. But then, in the week, Geoff got injured and didn't play, so Steve didn't do it. It's a sketchy memory, but I remember turning up with my dad and going through the players' tunnel, which I had never seen inside before at that age. Then going in the dressing room and meeting the players, I was obviously excited and nervous at the same time. It was Kenny Hibbitt who was captain and I was with him for the walkout. A member of staff, who looked after the mascots, told me that when I ran out on to the pitch, I had to make sure to run quick. So, that was just in my head. I just remember, as soon as we got out of the tunnel, I had to leg it!

Then in the warm-up I remember being on the pitch with the midfielder Gordon Smith and we'd just be passing it to each other. I was only seven or eight so I couldn't have kicked it very far! We drew 1-1 in the game, it was against Cambridge, and Mel Eves scored. But, yeah, just that experience of kicking the ball around at Molineux at that age.

JP: You probably saw Molineux closer to how it was in the golden age then, three of the four stands would have been there in the fifties?

PB: Yes, the old Molineux Street Stand had gone but the North Bank was still open. The atmosphere for those FA Cup games against Wrexham and Middlesbrough was massive. Those crowds were a lot bigger than they were getting in the league at the time. But at that age you don't really compute the good and bad times. I'd have been sat on the enclosure wall in 83/84, which was a horrific season, but I don't remember feeling disappointed in anything. I just remember feeling it was great to be watching, because there was no context at that age. I think the ups and the downs started to come in later, probably when Bully arrived.

JP: Do you think that makes the Bully era more special to us as kids than the older fans at the time? Because all those fans had seen a lot better, and we hadn't?

PB: I reckon so. I was similar to you, probably coming into teenage years then, and starting to go to the match on your own for the first time, or with your mates. That was a special atmosphere and you could just resonate with those players, couldn't you? Winning every week, I think, whatever level of football you're watching, if you're winning every week, it just feels special.

JP: Bully was a hero, a true terrace hero. It's only as you get older and you look at so many clubs, the biggest clubs in the world, who have tons of success, but they haven't really got that icon that we had. Look at Manchester City, there's just lots of great players. Whereas, for all that we didn't win anything, I'll always be grateful for having Bully. And it felt like he belonged to me, and I guess there's tens of thousands of other fans who feel exactly the same, that he belonged to them, just because of what he gave us; that connection. I felt that particularly going to the away games, by then. All the songs were about Bully.

PB: Definitely. I think you're right. John Richards was probably his predecessor, and I only saw a bit of John at the end of his career, and he won two League Cups so he did have that success. But I think the Bully story is unique, as you say, for that coming through the divisions. And I get what you mean about the away games. You just felt really proud, didn't you? And especially as he was someone just so well-known at that point because of the goals he was scoring. When you saw him run out, yeah, it just felt like part of you, didn't it?

JP: It did, and I guess by the late eighties, well, we'd become a small club, essentially. Everyone had heard of Wolves but they weren't in the national coverage any more. And it felt like Bully did put us back. Particularly on the school playground in Liverpool. It gave me talking points that, finally, my mates could put a name to. They knew I went off to watch Wolves, but they had no idea about anyone who played for them, until Bully. Particularly by the time Italia 90 came around.

I remember watching Wolves on Ceefax, too, in midweeks on school nights when I'd never be able to get down to games. It was an absolute joy. Watching the page turn over when we were in Divisions Four and Three and just seeing 'Bull 86' or whatever minute it was when he inevitably scored. They were good times.

PB: I think for all the brilliant stuff that modern technology brings, Ceefax was unbelievable! Watching those football scores and seeing the page flicking over, that was just part of childhood. Especially seeing Bully's name on there! So, were you still not able to get down to Molineux regularly in that time?

JP: No. There were two other teachers who were Wolves fans at the school my dad taught at, which was strange really as it was in Liverpool. I used to get a lift down with them, but midweeks were rare. I remember coming down for the Sherpa Van Trophy semi-final against Notts County once. They'd pick me up at a bus stop just before the start of the M62 in Liverpool, and we'd drive down.

Mike Watkins, who became a great family friend, and another teacher called Richard Preston. We used to go to Mike's parents' house, have a bit of dinner, go to the match, then drive straight back to Liverpool. That was quite a treat, with school the next day. So that didn't happen all the time.

It was only when I went to uni when I had some disposable income – albeit borrowed – that I got a season ticket for the 1994/95 season. I must have gone to virtually every game. And it ended in absolute despair at Bolton, but I really enjoyed that season going home and away.

You know, it felt a bit more tribal, you weren't a kid anymore.

PB: Yeah, I'd probably say for a ten-year spell in my 20s, going to a lot of away games with my mates, it was tribal. Stopping off for a few beers. We went with Hatherton Wolves a few times, which was a different and enjoyable experience. Other times someone would drive. But you're spot on, I think especially for all those years in the Championship, you still watched the football and enjoyed it, but the day out became almost as important – being with all the other Wolves fans. You started to feel disappointments by then, too, year after year not getting up and the Bolton play-offs.

Following Wolves was almost part of your routine, being part of something bigger. Every Saturday. I'd probably go to 80 per cent of the away games. You felt, not that you were ever going to get involved in any trouble, but you just felt part of that Wolves tribe.

JP: I remember going to Port Vale away once, walking up the main street in Burslem, and hearing the away fans before you could see them, just singing, 'Ooh Bully, Bully' and it felt like we'd arrived in town.

PB: I'm sure every club's fans say it, but you just always think your fans are the best. The most special, the loudest, the most tribal, but yeah, all of that. Bumping into people, fans you didn't know but you just recognised, that sort of thing. I think the age we were as well, that plays a part in it, doesn't it? I imagine there are fans now that have grown up with Nuno's team, and nothing will ever top that, but I think for me, nothing will top that Bully team because I was a teenager, football was one of the only releases I had away from school and stuff. It was pure joy.

JP: I do wonder what it must have been like to have had that first sense of economic freedom at the time that Nuno's side were playing in Europe. That ship had sailed for me by then, I was mortgaged up, bringing up a family. But imagine doing that in

Europe, that must have been something else. I got a little taste of it when I went out for the Espanyol game and spent the day down Las Ramblas drinking with mates, but some of the fans must have been everywhere in Europe.

PB: The world has changed, as well, hasn't it? You went to an away match back in the day and your parents may not even know the score until you got home if they hadn't put the radio on. There was no making phone calls and keeping in touch with family. You'd leave the house at eight in the morning and come back at ten o'clock at night. No internet, no mobiles, no 24/7 sports channels. Just living in the moment.

So, when did you start working?

JP: I did a bit of media work while I was still at uni and then got more later. The first time I ever covered Wolves was at Grimsby for a radio station called Viking FM. I was supposed to be doing it from a Grimsby angle. It was the opening day of the 96/97 season when Bully scored three.

PB: I was at that game as a fan, but didn't cover Wolves until much later. Were you in the stadium, reporting on the game?

JP: Yes, and of course with each Bully goal I just kept sounding more excited. I think I might have been ticked off by the producer for not giving it enough of a Grimsby angle, but when your hero's getting a hat-trick, what are you supposed to do? I'm not sure they gave me any more games after that. What about you, when did you first work on a Wolves game?

PB: I'd done about five or six years as a journalist for local papers and ended up at the *Birmingham Mail*. Ian Willars, who was a bit of a legend of the Midlands reporting scene, retired in 2002. I was covering Walsall and I think they knew I was a Wolves fan, so they moved me on to Wolves. And I think my first game properly covering Wolves was Swansea City away in the League Cup, and you were at that one, weren't you?

JP: Yeah, that was the first live match I covered for Sky, Wolves just scraped through that night.

PB: Some game to start that was! Very lively. I remember being in the press box and Bill Hatton and Robbie Dennison were commentating for The Wolf. They were getting a bit excited and the locals were really not happy. They had to move them somewhere else in the end. Crowd control! But that was the 2002/03 season, my first as a Wolves reporter, and it ended in promotion.

JP: Yes, the play-offs, of course! What a brilliant season. So, you did them home and away? Did it feel like anything had changed in terms of you being a fan, then doing it professionally?

PB: I think it does change a little bit, doesn't it? I think it's just natural. Probably less so as a journalist. I think it changed more when I went on to work for the club. But those first couple of years, the relationship that the players and management had with the media was really difficult. They'd just had that huge failure the previous season when Albion overhauled them and from a local newspaper point of view, there was a lot of tension. I'd come into this, and I think I struggled. I was still quite naive, in terms of journalism, so it was difficult from a work point of view.

There were some big characters that didn't really want to stop and speak most of the time, because of the legacy of the previous season. But like anything, gradually you kind of try and win them over, don't you? They begin to trust you. There were exceptions at the start like Matt Murray and George Ndah, who were amazing. And then over time I started to get on better with all the players. Paul Ince in particular was incredible to deal with. Given everything he had achieved in the game, and all the media scrutiny, he was still so helpful and giving of his time. Did you find any issues in those early days?

JP: I only really started covering them regularly when I moved to *Soccer Saturday*, just doing phone reports and then the gantry camera stuff talking to Jeff Stelling in the studio. They had that one season in the Premier League in 2003/04, and it was just exciting to be able to cover them in a work capacity. I guess it slightly peeled back the veneer of any romanticism attached to the place. They'd be down at Newbridge Tennis Club after training and we'd be trying to grab a word with a footballer who wasn't massively keen on being interviewed, like you said.

The lows probably didn't feel as disappointing by then, but I never lost the joy of the highs. I was able to go to Cardiff with my dad. So seeing us finally getting to the Premier League, that was just one of the great days.

PB: I was working at Cardiff, and as much as I struggled a bit that first season, I think that was obviously an exception. A part of me wished I was with my mates who I'd travelled to games for 15, 20 years with, but a part of me was like, 'This is a historic day, and you get to report on it, you get to interview players afterwards.' You can't be in two places at once, can you? I travelled down with a couple of mates, actually, and then they went off to the pubs. My family was there as well, we were all just in different parts of the stadium.

JP: You must have still had that sense of shared experience, that's one of the most important parts of being a fan, be it with your family or your mates.

PB: Absolutely. We all travelled back together and shared stories from the day. I don't know what you think, but it felt the most surreal day, because you expected to lose. All that play-off misery, you're building up to the day and thinking, 'Sheffield United are tough, it's Warnock. There's not a chance.' Then at half-time you're thinking, 'This doesn't happen to Wolves!' In the press room, a lot of Wolves fans in the media were in there completely numb with silence, really. I don't know what it was like in the stands?

JP: My dad always feared the worst when it came to football. And I do remember him saying, 'Surely, we can't mess this up from here?' I just remember at half-time thinking it was done, we were celebrating and lots of people around me were. There was that early penalty in the second half, but I don't have any recollection of feeling that it was letting them back in. After Matt Murray saved it, the rest of the game felt like a victory lap.

PB: We had some massive characters by then. Ince, Irwin, Butler, Kennedy, Cameron. Even younger ones like Joleon Lescott, massive personalities and characters that once they clicked that season, it took a while, but once they clicked they were unstoppable.

JP: You'd give anything to have a team like that in the Championship again, it was a great team for the Championship. So, when did you move to the club to work in the media department?

PB: It was in 2008 and, again, my first year was a promotion. Maybe I should move somewhere else again now we're back in the Championship! Mick McCarthy was already there. John Hendley – Fozzy – and Lorraine Hennessey, who was moving on, were really helpful in settling me in. I'd kind of got to know Mick and those first team players over a couple of years. So when Lorraine moved on, and I went for the job moving from journalism into PR almost, it was a bit different, but I felt I would be able to do the job.

I was over the moon to be inside the club but I think that's when it does change, and the job peels back a lot more. You see a lot more behind the scenes. There was a really good group of players and staff, but you also see how they're affected by fan criticism as well. Do you know what I mean? I don't know, it probably is guilt, I mean we've all shouted stuff as fans. And then, when you actually see how it affects players, I remembered some of the stuff I'd shouted from the terraces in the past, or articles I'd written, letters I'd sent to the paper. I'd have probably stopped and thought about it, knowing the people, the human beings behind it.

When they won promotion in that 08/09 season, I was happy as a fan, but I think more happy for these people that I'd worked with every day. I'd watched Mick go through it, watched the players, so to see them achieve all that, those pitch invasions at the end of the season, you're almost more happy for them that they've done it. What were you like by then?

JP: Similar to you, I'd been in the industry a while and had become removed from what it was like to be a supporter. I wasn't investing money and time in a way that I had previously done. I was getting to cover the club and doing lots of positive things around that, and giving the club lots of coverage. But the days of investing so much time and money in Wolves were behind me.

It's really interesting listening to you saying how made up you were for the players rather than your own supporter-self. Because they were such a different group from the 02/03 team. They had to prove themselves in a way that the others didn't. That 08/09 promotion probably had a human story impact on me because of the players' own journeys. And when we got together to put on that Mick McCarthy night at The Halls this year, you could see how much they treasured that part of their life.

PB: Definitely. And when it all went pear-shaped a few years later, a lot of those players ended up leaving, in not great circumstances. When you think of Kites getting stick for moving on, and he's explained his reasons, when you think of Wayne Hennessey, whose story I don't think was told completely accurately, Matt Jarvis went through it a bit over his transfer away. Karl Henry was put in the bomb squad after everything he'd done. And even though that decision about the bomb squad proved right in the end, I remember being in the club and really feeling for Karl, Stephen Ward, Kevin Foley and all those who had given their all for the club. It didn't feel like a great way for them to be treated, but you look back now and you understand why it was done. It probably needed a clean break. Maybe those players should have been treated differently, but it was a means to an end, I guess. And it seems to happen a lot more often in football now.

You mention that reunion night, what's nice is that Kites, Jarvo and Karl have gone full circle and they're now looked back on with a lot more fondness than how it ended.

JP: Did you find a lot of conflicting emotions in your role working for the club, in that you were seeing the club make decisions that as a fan you thought weren't right?

PB: Absolutely. A lot of the time, and you've probably seen this in your job as well, you end up being caught between a lot of conflicting interests. You can be handling a story or writing a press release where you've got the chairman, chief executive, manager and players all saying very different things. And I think it's quite a difficult job to then bring all that together when there are some big personalities and egos, and it can be a really tense environment. Especially in crisis management when big things are happening.

But I think because that group was so good, you do build up that trust where they listen to you. They take your opinion into consideration. So I would have to say, 'This is how the fans are going to receive this news, this is how the media are, so this is what I'd advise.'

But many times they took different decisions, and that's understandable, because as managers and chief executives you're not there to be popular. You obviously want to be popular, but sometimes you have to take decisions which aren't. The bomb squad is a really good example of that because people like Karl and Wardy, who I got quite close to working every day with them, you feel their pain a little bit. But I have to say, working with all the managers I did, it was always such a privilege. And then the people at the top – Steve Morgan, Jez Moxey, Richard Skirrow. I know Jez gets a lot of stick and has turned into a bit of a pantomime villain but speak to most people who worked for him and you will get nothing but positive responses. He was hard and demanding, but very fair. And would recognise when people were working equally hard.

There were tensions though sometimes. That's natural. Have you had a time when you've upset press officers or players or anyone at the club?

JP: Not when we did those features for Sky when I first met you, but when I started writing about the club in the local paper at weekends there were a couple of times when Jeff Shi took umbrage, to the point where I thought, 'Why? What's your point?' I ended up contacting him directly and we met up a handful of times, and we sort of thrashed it out, but it was about finding a balance. I was never writing critique pieces from the perspective of a fan, but there was obviously a fan in me.

You've got to stand your ground. I'd been in the industry for such a long time, so there was a bit of experience in judgement there. I'd not agreed to his point of view at all, and he certainly hadn't agreed to mine. 'Let's just see how things go' tended to be how we usually left it.

It's strange, he's the villain now, because a lot of things did go badly wrong on his watch, but he was quite an approachable character, and more accessible than previous chairmen. Ultimately, the major problem was that he never really got what the club was about, and never got that concept of being a fan. I guess that goes to the whole point of why we ended up being involved as supporters, because of that legacy being handed down by family. And, going forward, whoever runs the club has to understand this generational thing, otherwise there's no point being in it. The club must be treasured for future generations.

PB: Having been at the club when it was a lot smaller in how it operated, numbers of staff, I think the huge challenge for Wolves now – like any club that has grown and become huge – is recreating what we had in that Mick McCarthy era where everyone pulled together. Trying to recreate that in a huge monster of a football club, where the priorities have understandably changed, where there is more global investment because they were in the Premier League for a more sustained period of time with so many more markets and opportunities, is tricky.

Do you lose that personal touch a bit? I think that's almost natural. With the reset Wolves are going to have to go through now they are out of the Premier League, then regenerating that atmosphere is key. The 2013/14 League One season, for me, working at the club, was unbelievable. Kenny Jackett was so easy to deal with, so low maintenance. There were a lot of young players, others like Kevin McDonald who was just hilarious. Sam Ricketts was a brilliant captain at the time. Dicko, Afobe, Sako. Just magic.

I rarely got jealous about no longer watching Wolves as a fan, but going to some of those games that League One season, seeing the packed away ends, probably took me back to my childhood and I found myself sitting in the press box looking over to the away end thinking, 'I wish I was there.'

That whole season, after the absolute horror show of the two seasons before, the way Kenny and the players turned that around – with some clever decisions from Steve Morgan, Jez Moxey and Kevin Thelwell – felt like a big reset. I'll always remember that season fondly. Is it possible to recreate a feeling around the club like that? I guess Nuno did it to a certain extent in those two or three years when everyone was together again. So much of the atmosphere inside and outside of a club is dictated by results.

JP: Nuno got that buy-in from players and fans. It was funny, because that was probably when I did most of my work at Wolves – for both Sky and writing a newspaper column. We made three documentaries for Sky and got quite close to that squad. It never felt as if Nuno had got the buy-in from everyone at the club, though. It felt as if he had created an incredibly tight-knit squad and backroom staff. I've never seen a bond like that before or since. And he had this connection with the fanbase which was similar, it just felt so strong.

But watching him at work you never felt like you knew him, he came across as an intensely private man. But that whole squad and coaching staff seemed to sense it was a moment. Conor Coady very quickly grasped that it was a moment. And I think the fans, who had been starved of success for so long, spotted that this was like nothing else before.

PB: That resonates a bit. I had six months working under Nuno and, I'm sure he'd accept this, he was difficult away from the football. He's an intense character. He was difficult from a media perspective. I remember talking to someone high up at the club at the time, explaining to them that our department was finding it difficult. And he said, 'It's not just you, it's the whole club.'

And that's because all Nuno was interested in was coaching the players, being on the training ground, the planning around it, that was where he came alive and he didn't give a monkeys about the media. He didn't care about trying to sell tickets. Or commercial operations. He didn't really care about sorting hotels and travel. And that explains almost the genius of him. The football, the players, that was his entire focus and it's why it worked so well. And everyone else at the club just had to put up with that. And of course, when the football was as incredible as it was, quite rightly everyone else put up with it. His job was on the pitch.

JP: I suppose there's something quite pure about that, isn't there? Football at its purest. A winning football team. Nothing else matters. Just him, his staff and the players. And for the supporters, nothing else mattered. No one was complaining about the state of the stadium. It's when you're losing that the stand is falling apart and the ticket prices are too high. Win and that fades away.

I thought those days of getting involved emotionally had gone, because by the time Nuno came around I had a family of my own with my own kids who don't follow Wolves, but it took me back to childhood. I got so carried away with Nuno's side winning football matches, I almost fell in love with Wolves for a second time. It was incredibly special.

What about your work for Wolves Foundation now, which is separate from the club? Does that feel a more natural fit for you, after all your years as a fan but no longer having to deal with the distractions that come with professional football?

PB: Yes I think you're right, it almost feels like the Foundation is more like the football club of 20 years ago, isn't it? That's not to say the link with the club isn't great. Because it is. You still get those moments where you go on visits with Foundation and club staff, player visits, and that's when you see the magic of what we have been talking about. If they go to a school or a Foundation activity you can see the players are properly invested in that.

But with the way football has gone now, the commercial activities are so important as well. That's what brings the money in. And adds to the demands. In a way it's kind of nice not to have to worry about that side too much! So it is a nice role now, a nice fit. The Foundation are doing the work of the club in the community, aren't they? And it's a good partnership that works well.

JP: Those player visits you speak about remind me of George Elokobi. We covered one of your Christmas community visits for Sky when Mick was in charge. I went to a local hospice to interview George but my cameraman didn't turn up, so we couldn't do the interview. But another Sky crew had gone to New Cross Hospital to meet another group of players there, so George just said, 'Why don't we go there when I'm done here?' So, he met the residents at the hospice and then drove me to New Cross, did another tour of the wards there and then did the interview. What a guy!

PB: I'll add two more examples of that. When the Covid pandemic happened, Karl rang me. He's a Wolverhampton lad, born at New Cross, and he wanted to do something to help New Cross and the Royal Wolverhampton Trust. To cut a long story short, he ended up mobilising all the former players and former staff to donate and they raised around £50,000 for a new building at the Royal. And that, to me, was a legacy of Karl in the community. It was also a legacy of all those guys from Mick's time who wanted to do that. They loved their time at Wolves, and those feelings have endured.

And then the other one was in the League One season, which was led by Danny Batth and Carl Ikeme. There was a young girl who needed an operation. She needed thousands of pounds for this operation and she had started this appeal. All the players made a donation and they raised the money for her to have this operation. I remember the day the family were invited to training, I think they just thought they were coming to watch, and then the players produced this big cheque. You saw the emotion of the parents. And again, that was just another example of footballers caring.

JP: Brilliant. Always great to hear. So let's bring it around to where we started. Do you still get to go to Wolves with your family, are your parents still involved?

PB: Yeah, they still come when they can, health permitting. My two lads have had season-tickets for a long time now. They've grown up now. They've loved it until the last couple of years. It's still a massive part of our lives. My sister comes with her family. It's still very much a huge topic of conversation. I think when you get older, you don't feel so high and low about it as much. I mean, Wolves getting relegated now is obviously really dreadful, disappointing news but 30 years ago, it would have been all I'd been thinking about, whereas now you're a bit more worldly wise and it's the cycle of being a Wolves fan, isn't it? It was never going to stay as it was under Nuno forever. And now you're just hoping that things pick up again. What's it like for you? Your kids probably aren't into it as much, not being local.

JP: Yeah, my eldest boy loves football, and loves going to watch games but he's a Manchester City fan. I've taken him to the odd Wolves game and he enjoys it. My dad's no longer here and my mum and sisters are Liverpool fans so it's not got that lineage any more, although one of my much younger nephews appears to have taken a shine to Wolves so who knows! But I'm grateful I got to Wembley with my dad, it was the last game we watched together.

PB: The Watford semi-final?

JP: Yes, and this might sound bizarre because of the heartache at the end, but I actually enjoyed the day. I'd never been to Wembley to watch Wolves with him before – I'd been on holiday all those years ago for the Sherpa Van Trophy Final. And by the time of the Watford game he wasn't coming to Wolves much, anyway. We went along in the Wolves end and the fans were incredible, singing all the way up to the stadium and on the concourses. We went 2-0 up and it felt like the best thing ever, and I remember as it got towards the end we were both thinking the same thing: 'This is it. We've done it. Wolves are going to be in the FA Cup Final.' And then it all went pear-shaped.

But I did come away thinking at least I got to go to Wembley and watch Wolves with my dad. And also a little bit of me thought, 'Well, why should this semi-final be any different?' Following Wolves has just been one long series of heartaches. Burnden Park in 1995 was brutal and we watched that together on that horrible terrace. That was probably the worst. Maybe after all those years it just felt like another way of losing a semi-final. But, it was also great that my dad and I were still going and watching them after all that time had passed.

PB: You're spot on, because I went with my dad to the Sherpa Van, so obviously I got to enjoy that one, and then for Watford I was with my wife and two boys but they were quite young. When it went to 2-0, I was wondering how we were going to afford tickets for the final – typically pessimistic Wolves fan!!! – but then when Watford got their third, my youngest, Liam, wanted to leave. My wife had to take him to go and wait for the coach because he just couldn't handle it. And I was thinking, 'Blimey, we've been through this loads of times,' so I stayed with my other son Jack and saw it out.

I know what you mean, though, Bolton just stung beyond anything, just the injustice of it with McGinlay. That picture of Bully at the end, it was his last chance really, wasn't it? You couldn't get more classic Wolves than those two legs. Absolutely hammering them at home. It should have been three or four up going into the second leg, and then you go to the second leg, play alright, but end up with the injustice of the bloke who should have been sent off scoring their winner. If you ever wanted to describe the journey of Wolves in two games of football, that was it.

JP: We're a similar age so it's interesting sharing these experiences with you, and what our favourite and not-so-favourite eras have been. All fans will have their own peers they can share different eras with. I often think, when walking up to a Wolves game, that there will be at least one fan here today who is experiencing Wolves for the first time. Their story starts here, at their first game. Or maybe it's their last match, and it might be the end, but they'll have their own story. That's the beauty of it, no era is better or worse for each fan, it's just different depending on where they are in their life journey.

PB: We're biased, but it does feel like Wolves have had a rough trot compared to a lot of other clubs, like Manchester City or Liverpool. And yet, fans just keep coming back. You know, the nights you've hosted for Wolves Foundation with all those different eras, the fans will always come back. Even in this difficult, horrific season, the home games against Aston Villa, Liverpool and Arsenal, the atmosphere is there, special, and it's literally just waiting to go again.

Fans will always forgive. I remember the first game of the Kenny Jackett era in League One, Preston away. Kenny had done some brilliant things in that summer, but working at the club and witnessing us being pummelled by that double relegation before he came in, you're not sure, and you get to that first game wondering what the fans are going to be like. How's this going to pan out? So, to get that roar before kick-off, with 5,000 of them in that away end at Deepdale, if you wanted to describe the loyalty of Wolves fans that was it.

You can keep knocking them down, but they'll keep coming back time after time. That was such an amazing moment. Bizarrely, Rob Edwards was working for the local radio that day and I looked at him in the press box after that roar from our fans and his mouth was wide open. He was like, 'Wow.' They'd forgiven, they were moving on, and obviously we had that great season. Hopefully Wolves will be able to turn it around this time.

JP: It's hard to know what will happen now, because it has felt a particularly bad time of late. But the club always finds a way of carrying on. Even in the Bhattis era when the supporters were not coming in their droves, they came back.

PB: Absolutely. And it becomes part of the history, doesn't it? The Bhattis, as bad as they were, have become part of the legacy of the club.

JP: I guess it's a difficult time when we are bringing this book out now for 150 years of history. It feels a tough time to make any judgements or pronouncements about what the future might hold, because it does feel at the point where it could go either way. It wouldn't surprise me if they found themselves in the Premier League again soon but, equally, it wouldn't surprise me if the administrator was called in!

PB: That's just one of the beauties of following Wolves, as we have done for so many years. It's not a club that's always going to be in the Premier League and the top six and winning stuff. When it does happen it just feels that more magical, even if, for us, it's only a League One title or a Championship title or a European quarter-final. Or for the older fans the two League Cups, or the even older ones the glory days of the fifties. It just feels a bit more special, because it doesn't happen very often. That's Wolves.